Race, Gender, and Image Repair Theory

Race, Gender, and Image Repair Theory

How Digital Media Change the Landscape

Mia Moody-Ramirez
and Hazel James Cole

LEXINGTON BOOKS

Lanham • Boulder • New York • London

Published by Lexington Books
An imprint of The Rowman & Littlefield Publishing Group, Inc.
4501 Forbes Boulevard, Suite 200, Lanham, Maryland 20706
www.rowman.com

6 Tinworth Street, London SE11 5AL, United Kingdom

British Library Cataloguing in Publication Information Available

Library of Congress Cataloging-in-Publication Data Available

ISBN 978-1-4985-6861-6 (cloth : alk. paper)
ISBN 978-1-4985-6862-3 (electronic)

♾™ The paper used in this publication meets the minimum requirements of American National Standard for Information Sciences—Permanence of Paper for Printed Library Materials, ANSI/NISO Z39.48-1992.

Printed in the United States of America

Contents

Acknowledgments

We use this opportunity to express our gratitude to everyone who supported us throughout the process of writing *Race, Gender, and Image Repair Theory: How Digital Media Change the Landscape*. First, we thank our family members, mentors, colleagues and friends who have been supportive of our goals throughout our academic careers. We appreciate the kindness extended during the entire research and writing process for this book as well as other endeavors.

In particular, we acknowledge Augustine Ramirez, Nelda and Jerry Moody, Todd Howard, WaylandMoody, Tish Moody, AshleyKelsey, Michael Kelsey, Heidi Hall, Tim Hall and Bill Hall. We also acknowledge Mrs. Hosley Mae Lynch Bratcher, Cecelia James Webb, Kimberly Cole Souder, Sterling Lynch Cole, Melissa Medley, Dr. Cheryl Jenkins, Dr. Camilla Gant, Viloice Posey, Monica Turner, Dr. Pete Smith and Dr. Jerlen Y. Canada. Your support over the years and on this project has been steadfast and important, both personally and professionally.

We would like to thank the former students and colleagues who contributed to the research in this book. In particular, we thank Macarena Hernandez, Endia Turney, Liz Fassih, Mayra Monroy and Tina Libhart. We thank Baylor Journalism, PR and New Media Graduate Student Andrew Church for providing the vision for our book's cover.

We also thank our students who over the years have consistently encouraged us to take on new endeavors and to persevere in this research project. The contents of this book have been in the works for many years. Your encouragement helped us realize the true value of such a text.

We thank the anonymous reviewers, who offered feedback, and the editors at Lexington Books (an imprint of Rowman & Littlefield), who offered us the opportunity to publish this important text. Your input and resources have been invaluable. In particular, we thank Lexington acquiring editor Nicolette Amstutz for the painstaking feedback and work she undertook in helping us complete this project.

Finally, we thank the institutions to whom we have dedicated our careers, Baylor University and the University of West Georgia. We are beyond grateful for your support and encouragement!

Part I

OVERVIEW OF THEORIES

Introduction

Using a Critical Race Theory (CRT) lens, *Race, Gender, and Image Repair Theory: How Digital Media Change the Landscape* explores themes that are relevant to the sociopolitical landscape of 21st-century America, including race and gender representation, social media and traditional media framing and image restoration management. Early chapters provide a comprehensive discussion of Critical Race Theory (CRT) and Image Restoration Theory (IRT) to establish a baseline for a conversation on celebrity image restoration tactics. Subsequent chapters explore noteworthy cases.

In addition to pivotal moments in history, such as presidential elections and social movements, we analyze cases in which public figures shared hate speech and racist rants both in person and online—often creating the need for image repair tactics. The first four chapters in this text explore hate speech and the image repair strategies used to address them. These chapters illustrate that context and intent make a big difference in how people perceive free speech.

Recent trends illustrate how social media messages can alter public opinion at a much faster rate than traditional media because of the ease with which the information is shared. In the tradition of McLuhan's the "medium is the message" communication via social media challenges traditional communication theories. While previous media studies hold immense value and offer a strong foundation for research, innovations have made it important to replicate their objectives in today's media climate.

The Internet makes information more easily accessible to a large number of people and gathers information from a wider array of sources than any instrument of information and communication in history. Consequently, media dynamics have changed considerably. For instance, Black Twitter created an online culture of African American inctuals and trendsetter that offered a platform to share many issues that historically have remained concealed from the mainstream radar (Williams, 2015). During this era, many African Americans shifted to online platforms such as YouTube, Twitter and Instagram, where they shared memes, videos and varied assortments of social media content.

In another example, the #MeToo movement initiated a worldwide effort in 2017 to campaign against sexual harassment and assault in the workplace. During this avalanche of accusations, dozens of well-known public figures were fired from their jobs. However, the person who floated to the top in the midst of the #MeToo movement was Harvey Weinstein, after *The New York Times* and *The New Yorker* published articles detailing the Hollywood producer's inappropriate sexual behavior. We highlight #MeToo and Weinstein's image repair tactics.

With these new media dynamics in mind, the intent of *Race, Gender, and Image Repair Theory: How Digital Media Changes the Landscape* is twofold: first, it delves into cases involving race and gender; secondly, it analyzes the influence of media platform on the success or failure of each case's image repair tactics. Specifically, the text looks at the high-profile cases of Donald Sterling, Justin Bieber, Harvey Weinstein, Bill Cosby, Yahoo Finance, Hulk Hogan, Reggie Bush, Chris Brown, Kanye West, Rachel Dolezal, Monica Lewinsky, Hillary Clinton and Barack Obama.

For each case, we address three key questions: What image restoration tactics did the individual use following his or her crisis or scandal? How did media outlets and audiences respond to these tactics? What are the implications of each case for IRT and CRT?

Creswell (2004) suggested the use of a case-study format when a researcher seeks to provide an in-depth understanding of the cases or a comparison of several cases. A case-study design allows researchers to target one issue, using multiple case studies to illustrate his or her hypothesis. Although case studies have drawn criticism for their descriptive nature (Coombs & Holladay, 2008; Coombs & Schmidt, 2000), Len-Rios (2010) asserts that they are an important research aid, as they can help researchers synthesize multiple data sources derived from real-world crisis situations. Furthermore, she adds, "Data triangulation in case studies, if well-conceived, increases reliability when different sources point to the same conclusion." She adds that findings obtained from studying crises in their contexts may help raise the external validity of such cases.

The case studies in this text are important for numerous reasons. First, media provide historical content that researchers may use to analyze trends in the reporting of gender, race and culture. CRT has affirmed popular culture represents women and people of color in narrowly defined stereotypical roles that are long lasting, dichotomous and degrading. While media have made inroads in improving representations of women and people of color, stereotyping is still a prominent part of cultural narratives.

Citizen awareness of image restoration strategies used in crisis management increased after the ABC television show, *Scandal*, debuted in 2012. The show featuring Kerry Washington as a "fixer" is loosely based on Judy Smith's life. In real life, Smith, a one-time special assistant to former U.S. president George Bush, Sr., has represented numerous public figures, including Michael Vick, Steve Harvey, Monica Lewinsky and Paula Deen (News ABC, 2017). The popularity of IRT continues as individuals realize the importance of maintaining a positive image.

TEXTUAL ANALYSIS AND IMAGE RESTORATION THEORY

The textual analysis approach provides an ideal tool for to explore the cases in this book. The method seeks to get beneath the surface of a topic and help researchers outline culture as a narrative in which texts consciously or unconsciously link themselves to larger stories at play in the society. Textual analysis of cultural studies often looks at how cultural meanings convey specific ideologies of gender, race, class, sexuality and other ideological dimensions.

To provide uniformity across case studies, we analyzed each case in two phases that combined both CRT and IRT strategies. First, we used qualitative content analysis to study each person's social media, personal statements and interviews. Secondly, to judge the success or failure of each image repair campaign, we looked at public opinion polls and media coverage of each case. Combining these two steps provided a comprehensive look at: (1) context of each case study, (2) representations of gender and race, (3) image repair strategies, (4) audience reception based on public opinion polls and media content.

WHAT MAKES THIS TEXT UNIQUE

Several noteworthy books explore Benoit's IRT in various circumstances, illustrating the value of case studies in new contexts. In general, similar books fall into one of three categories: theory application, media studies and case studies of a particular group such as sports, politics and entertainment. *Accounts, Excuses, and Apologies, Second Edition: Image Repair Theory and Research* by Benoit (2014) includes a literature review on IRT studies and new case studies from sports, international politics and third-party image repair. The text describes image-repair strategies that may be used to help defuse threats, such as denial and apology. The text also reviews various image repair cases, and extends prior research on the topic to include work on persuasion or attitude change. Similarly, *Putting Image Repair to the Test: Quantitative Applications of Image Restoration Theory* by Blaney (2015) examines content analytic, attitudinal, and behavioral claims to advance current assertions made about image repair discourse, its effects and the surrounding discourse.

Offering a look at image repair and sports, *Repairing the Athlete's Image: Studies in Sports Image Restoration*, edited by Blaney and Smith (2012), includes case studies and conceptual frameworks about athletes and their organizations as they attempt to mitigate the effects of malfeasance. The scholars present case studies of athletes, sports and public relations scenarios with prescriptive advice for those attempting to repair athletic reputations. Conversely, in *The Clinton Scandals and the Politics of Image Restoration*, Blaney and Benoit (2001) analyze five cases that plagued former president Bill Clinton's presidency. The book concludes Clinton employed denial of the accusation in response to the Whitewater scandal and the Lewinsky scandal and provides six definitions of the president: a father figure, visionary, head of government, policy maker, architect of national identity and role model. It concludes Clinton used a combination of evading responsibility and reducing the offensiveness of the accusation.

These books offer an overview of IRT and explore various case studies that have emerged in the 21st century. This text differs from previous books by focusing specifically on CRT, IRT and the representations of gender and race using timely and thoughtful case studies. Similar to other books on this subject, students of crisis communication and rhetoric will benefit from reading this text. It is also relevant to students in social media programs, public relations, journalism, political science and sociology programs.

In particular, we emphasize cases occurring between 2005 and 2018, the years leading up to former president Barack Obama's presidency, his eight years in office, and the election of his successor President Donald Trump. During this period, Americans experienced many firsts: the election of the first African American president of the United States, the legalization of gay marriage in many states and the near election of the first female U.S. president in 2016. To some Americans, the election of President Barack Obama signaled the beginning of a "post-racial" society in which racism no longer existed. To others, the prevalence of racism became more prevalent. Many U.S. citizens, hate groups and blatant racists used Obama's election as a reason to spread hatred.

Eight years after Obama began his first stint as president, former secretary of state Hillary Rodham Clinton made history as the first viable female contender to compete for the title of U.S. president. Although the former senator led a successful campaign and had good numbers at the polls, Trump ultimately won the bid for the 45th U.S. Presidency. Clinton's loss (despite winning the popular vote) coupled with Trump's stance on issues regarding women, immigrants, people of color and members of the LGBTQ+ community fostered unrest among many groups.

Following President Trump's election, activists organized protests in several major cities across the United States, including Austin, New York, Boston, DC, Philadelphia, Chicago, Portland and Oakland. Various forms of protest included a Women's March on Washington, a Day Without Women and the sharing of social media content, particularly memes of President Obama and Biden discussing their last days in office and Trump's pending leadership (Dates & Moody, 2018).

Also, prominent during the period under analysis was the #BlackLivesMatter Movement, which emerged in 2012 to help spotlight the prevalence of police brutality in their interactions with African Americans (Dates & Moody, 2018). The movement, founded by Patrisse Cullors, Opal Tometi and Alicia Garza, launched after neighborhood watch coordinator George Zimmerman shot and killed Trayvon Martin, 17, in 2012. However, the undertaking did not firmly take root until 2014, following the shooting of 19-year-old African American Michael Brown. Years of frustration and anger came to a head after a grand jury voted not to indict Officer Darren Wilson—one of the numerous policemen who had shot and killed unarmed black men that year. The #BlackLivesMatter movement became a prevalent topic on mainstream and social media platforms (Moody & Cole, 2018).

OVERVIEW OF CHAPTERS

Race, Gender, and Image Repair Theory: How Digital Media Changes the Landscape is divided into five parts, which are subdivided into 14 chapters. Each chapter offers historical context and themes of IRT and CRT. The depth of each chapter varies, as many of the cases are still under litigation—including Bill Cosby and Harvey Weinstein. Also worth noting is some of the cases included in this text are not as in-depth as they were handled swiftly without much media coverage. Nonetheless, all cases we chose to include are significant, as they provide examples of the importance of being proactive in handling image-damaging social media scandals. Many chapters in this text contain similar case studies in their literature review sections. This repetition is intentional, as chapters may be assigned as separate readings.

PART I

Part I explores the theories relevant to the studies in this text and highlights a few notable case studies. Chapter 1 introduces Critical Race and Image Repair theories and offers an overview of this text. Chapter 2 offers a closer look at IRT, CRT and the methods used to explore the case studies in this book. Chapter 3 offers an overview of IRT, the gatekeeper effect and Web-related case studies.

PART II

Part II delves into outbursts and offensive language with an emphasis on prominent race-related case studies of the 21st century. In particular, it explores the broad range of cases that deal with hate speech, stereotypes and negative representations of people of color. It offers an in-depth look at cases that include the use of the N-word.

In chapter 4, we explore an IRT case study that examines Donald Sterling's racist rant after his mistress, V. Stiviano, posted a photo on Instagram of herself with Lakers star Magic Johnson. The Clippers owner asked her not to publicly associate with African Americans. Following this revelation, Sterling used numerous image repair tactics such as *mortification, minimization, celebrity endorsements* and *bolstering* with varying degrees of success. The chapter concludes Sterling's tactics were not effective because of his age, previous race-related incidents, profession and delayed apology.

In chapter 5, we continue to explore image repair and race in a similar case in which two videos surfaced featuring Bieber using the N-word. Both videos originated when the celebrity was 14 or 15 years old. One highlighted him telling the racist joke, "Why are black people afraid of chainsaws?" to which his friend responded, "Don't even say it." Bieber's response to the joke was, "Run n****r, n****r, n****r, n****r!" The other video featured him singing "One Less Lonely Girl," replacing "girl" with the N-word. Bieber immediately apologized and was successful in his use of image repair tactics primarily because of his profession as a singer, his youth and the age of his target audience.

Chapter 6 examines the N-word, social media and image repair (Stein, 2010). Specifically, it looks at by Yahoo Finance's apology and Black Twitter's response. This chapter breaks new ground, as it is one of the first to analyze how Black Twitter's "clap back" culture may be used as an image repair tactic. Unlike other image repair cases in which celebrities used remorse and mortification, Yahoo Finance primarily took a back seat in its own image restoration process and others took control—using social media. In addition, this chapter illustrates how social media have become a necessary platform for dissent, discussion and breaking news. "Black Twitter," in particular, offers an outlet for black people to express their ideas and opinions publicly in the 21st century.

Continuing this vein, chapter 7 focuses on the image restoration of Hulk Hogan, who experienced a debilitating blow to his career in 2015 after a video of him using the N-word was released. Hogan's statements, which were included in a sex tape, include candid moments during which Hogan discusses his daughter's relationship with a "black billionaire": Hogan later apologized for his rant and won a settlement from Gawker, but it was too late to undo the damage the statement had done to his image. He was scrubbed from WWE's website and erased from the WWE Hall of Fame (Trotter, 2015). The WWE terminated Hogan's employment, including his role on WWE's "Tough Enough" (Manfred, 2015). These severed ties and the public's perception of Hogan created the need for the superstar to repair his image.

PART III

With the #MeToo movement as an impetus, part III turns to case studies emphasizing sexual assault, harassment and violence. Using a feminist lens, the two chapters in this section highlight the heavily covered cases of Bill Cosby and Harvey Weinstein. The section offers history and context on the Me Too movement, feminism and media coverage of the two cases.

Chapter 8 examines the intersection of race, sexual assault in an analysis of the image restoration tactics Bill Cosby used following his 2014 sexual assault allegation scandal. The allegations began in 2000, but many were settled out of court. It was not until November of 2014 that the sexual assault claims received widespread media coverage. Because of the numerous and widespread accusations, Cosby's upcoming NBC show was pulled, his Netflix special canceled and his various titles revoked (O'Connell, 2015). Originally, Cosby remained strategically silent, and then he used humor, followed by attack of accusers.

Continuing the topic of sexual assault, chapter 9 includes an in-depth examination of sexual assault, the #MeToo movement and online media response. Specifically, this case study uses a feminist lens to analyze Weinstein's use of personal statements to repair his image and the media's response to his image restoration tactics. It also emphasizes sex scandals among celebrities and examines the ethical considerations for companies and individuals handling sexual harassment cases. Sexual assault and feminist theory are important concepts to consider in this analysis of Weinstein, #MeToo and his use of image restoration tactics.

PART IV

Part IV continues this vein of research with an exploration of gender representations, stereotypes, crises and image repair. Using a feminist lens, it highlights the prominent cases of Monica Lewinsky and Rachel Dolezal.

Chapter 10 examines the image repair tactics Rachel Dolezal used following the 2015 revelation that she was passing for black. This textual analysis adds a new perspective to IRT literature by analyzing Dolezal's response to the crisis, citizen response through memes and how traditional media outlets framed the case. Demonstrating the dual nature of the Web, on one hand Dolezal used statements released on TV shows, online publications and social media to explain and minimize her actions. Viewers also used the Web to respond to the case. In many instances, comments supported Dolezal in her decision to "become black." Other media responses were not as positive.

Using a feminist lens, chapter 11 explores Monica Lewinsky's use of a TED Talks speech to counter narratives of shaming that emerged in the late 1980s and remained for several decades. The Lewinsky-Clinton scandal occurred before social media and before the term "cyber bullying" existed, but the case has implications today as the same narratives that plagued Lewinsky and endured in the 1990s are much more prevalent. Findings indicate the speech was well received, as audience feedback was favorable on Twitter and the TED site that highlighted a video of her talk and a transcript. The former intern used her TED Talk to discuss timely topics such as Internet shaming, suicide and bullying. While Lewinsky opted not to use *mortification*, she *reduced the offensiveness* of the affair by using humor and building on the narrative that she was young and did not know any better.

PART V

Rounding out this text, part V emphasizes politics and image repair. In particularly, these three chapters highlight the image repair tactics of President Barack Obama and former Senator Hillary Clinton. It explores how their personas changed throughout the heavily covered 2008 presidential race.

Beginning with chapter 12, we explore the dynamics of gender, race politics and the image repair. The chapter's textual analysis examines how CNN and FOX framed the coverage of senators Hillary Clinton and Barack Obama in the 2007–2008 presidential primaries.

Findings indicate gender was more salient than race in how journalists framed candidates in their coverage of the two candidates. Journalists and sources emphasized patriarchal representations of Clinton, choosing to focus on gender-related issues such as attire, hairstyle and mannerisms. Although race-related frames were prevalent in the coverage of Obama, they were not as prominent in his campaign coverage.

Chapter 13 continues the emphasis on politics with an analysis of the image repair tactics of Hillary Clinton during the 2016 presidential race. Social media and citizen journalism played a key factor in how the media covered the election. This chapter analyzes U.S. citizen framing of the candidate and how she responded in image repair tactics. Citizens raised many questions that were, in turn, addressed by the mainstream media.

Chapter 14 offers a conclusion for the book and a look at suggestions for future research. Text limitations and ideas for future research are offered to encourage continued research on image repair, social media, gender and race-related issues.

IMPORTANCE OF BOOK

This text is important for several reasons. First, the growing usage of the Internet as a source of information has spurred a growing interest in the medium as a tool for image repair. While traditionally communication has been top-down giving greater influence to elites, the Web opens up the possibility of horizontal communication without gatekeepers. Wright and Hinson (2008) note, "The potential impact of blogs on public relations and corporate communications is phenomenal" (p. 4).

Secondly, most IRT studies use rhetorical criticism, or case studies, so generalizations are difficult to make. The cases in this book provide a good opportunity for the exploration of IRT within the realm of a relatively new platform—social media. As Lau and Pomper (2002, p. 63) state, "We should encourage researchers to continue studying campaigns in a multitude of different settings and with a variety of different methods." Existing media theories are the most efficient way to account for trends.

Thirdly, this text adds a critical lens to IRT to help conceptualize and contextualize stereotypical behaviors of the individuals in our case studies. Media provide historical content that researchers may use to analyze trends in representations of gender and race. Representations of race and gender are noteworthy because overall, careless and insensitive portrayals of groups might promote stereotypes and resentments (Carlin & Winfrey, 2009; Heldman, Carroll & Olson, 2005; Ross, 2002).

Finally, the case studies in this text will help PR practitioners develop solutions and measurable objectives that make a difference in addressing shortcomings related to image repair following race and gender-related crises.

Study findings may prove useful for social media and celebrity crisis/scandal management and provide insight into the best strategies for improving a scarred public image in today's rapidly changing media climate.

Ongoing analyses of IRT, race and gender in varying settings may help audiences become more aware of the dynamics at play in such cases. Public relations specialists may become more knowledgeable and better able to help clients navigate and avoid such cases. The exploration of the various types of racially charged cases is important, as they illustrate the importance of image restoration using cases that explore gender and race.

Chapter 1

Image Repair Theory
General Terminology

The literature used in *Race, Gender, and Image Repair Theory: How Digital Media Changes the Landscape* is primarily divided into three streams of research: IRT, gender and race representation; media platform; and usage.[1] In beginning the discussion on image repair, scholars generally define image as the perceptions of a communicative entity shared by an audience (Benoit, 1995).

A solidly constructed image must contain elements that will enhance an organization or individual's ability to project a perception of power, character, trust, leadership and name recognition (Benoit, 1995). Because of this relationship, image repair has become an important part of conflict management (Wilcox & Cameron, 2006).

Benoit emphasizes the importance of image to an organization or individual. The scholar adds that while image repair efforts may differ between individuals and companies, the basic options for image repair tactics are the same. "The key to understanding image repair strategies is to consider the nature of attacks or complaints that prompt such responses" (Benoit, 1997, p. 2). Benoit adds that an attack has two components: (1) the accused is held responsible for an action and (2) that act is considered offensive. Both of these components must exist for accusations to be considered an attack.

Benoit further points out two important ways to explore image restoration: rhetorical criticism and case studies. Rhetorical critics take a speech-oriented view of image restoration specifically to human communication patterns by examining "entire speeches or discussions, rather than by looking at single image management statements" (Elsbach, 1997, p. 584). Benoit's research also focuses on case studies and public records that "describe both the image restoration discourse and audience reactions to that discourse" (Elsbach,

1997, p. 584). Together, Benoit's combination of rhetorical criticism and case studies focuses more on the content and processes of image management, rather than a more psychological approach.

Typically, a crisis is understood to be an extraordinary disruption of standard operations that threatened the safety, reputation and success of an organization or individual. Crisis management has become increasingly common today in the field of public relations because of the negative impact an issue can have on a person or company if not addressed. Every public figure needs to have a crisis management plan, but it is especially important for athletes and celebrities to implement one. Conversely, a scandal is defined as a situation or event that is thought to be shocking and immoral and that everyone knows about.

Drawing on the works of Rosenfield (1968) and Ware and Linkugel (1973), Benoit (1995) developed a taxonomy of defensive accounts that organizations and individuals may employ in a time of crisis. Rosenfield's theory of apologetic discourse is a four-part process in image restoration speeches and includes brief controversy, attack on the opponent, concentration of data in middle of the speech and recycling of arguments.

By its very human nature, a public figure's image is subject to change based on how he or she presents him or herself to the public. Celebrities, politicians and athletes are notorious for making mistakes in the public eye—often affecting their image negatively. So, how might one restore a tarnished image? Benoit's study (1997) clearly outlines his image repair theory, tactics and ideas. First of all, Benoit states, "perceptions are more important than reality." If the public perceives an action as being offensive or troublesome, that will be enough to tarnish an individual's image—despite the truth about the situation.

Benoit (1995) asserts that individuals and organizations tend to use one, or a combination, of five strategies when confronted with an embarrassing or damaging situation to repair a tarnished image. They are: (1) *denial of the accusation,* (2) *evading responsibility of the act,* (3) *reducing the offensiveness of the accusation,* (4) *offering corrective actions* and (5) *mortification or apologizing* (Table 1.1).

Denial is one of the most common approaches to image restoration. When engaging in denial, an organization or person usually *denies* that a crisis occurred (*simple denial*). Benoit's (1995) definition of the term makes allowances for instances in which an organization or person shifts the blame (scapegoating) and thus denies its implication in an unpleasant event. The second tactic, *evading of responsibility,* refers to instances in which an organization or person resorts to the excuse that the action was induced by a third party and the organization only responded to an external provocation.

Table 1.1 Image Restoration Strategies

Image Restoration Tactic	Description of Image Restoration Tactic
Denial	Simple denial—did not perform the act
	Shifting the blame—act performed by another
Evading of Responsibility	Provocation—responded to act or action of another
	Defeasibility—lack of information or ability
	Accident—act was unintentional mishap
	Good Intentions—meant well in doing the act
Reducing Offensiveness of Event	Bolstering—stress good traits
	Minimization—act not very serious
	Differentiation—act is less offensive than it appears
	Transcendence—act is negative, but other vital considerations at stake
	Attack accuser—reduce credibility of accuser
	Compensation—reimburse victims and affected persons
Corrective Action	Plan in place to solve and prevent action from reoccurring
Mortification	Take responsibility and apologize for action

Benoit (1995).

Defeasibility, is another tactic, in which the organization states it lacked the ability or the information to avert the crisis. The use of *good intentions* is the idea the initial intent was honorable, favorable and so on, but the situation turned into a crisis.

Additionally, individuals can make use of strategies that aim *at reducing the offensiveness* of an event with strategies such as bolstering, emphasizing the good, *minimization* and asserting the magnitude of the crisis is not what the media describes. Another tactic to *reduce the offensiveness* is differentiation during which the individual differentiates himself/herself from who/what caused the crisis; *transcendence*, placing the crisis in a broader context to diffuse it and be able to appeal to higher values; *attack the accuser*; and compensation, the individual helps the victims of the crisis, thus showing sympathy and proving itself to be responsible.

These strategies have the potential to succeed to an extent; however, studies indicate the usage of a proactive strategy is more effective in generating positive media coverage (Brazeal, 2008). After an offensive act is committed, the public is more lenient toward those who take responsibility and seem genuine in apologies than toward those who shirk responsibility or direct it elsewhere. *Mortification* is often the most effective strategy. However, to gain forgiveness, a person needs to extend a sincere apology (Bachman, 2006). The elements of a sincere apology are admission of responsibility, expression of remorse, a promise of forbearance and an offer of repair.

Failure to include these in an apology can significantly damage the effectiveness of image restoration.

After introducing these different categories, Benoit offered suggestions for effective image restoration discourse. He suggests that, first, the individual must perform persuasive discourse (Benoit, 1997). Then, if the individual is at fault, he or she must admit this immediately. This is crucial to successful image repair. Benoit adds that it is possible to shift blame successfully, but it is very rare. There are more successful approaches. Benoit asserts the same thing about *minimization*; it is possible, but the tactic can easily backlash and hurt the individual's image even more. He encourages the use of *corrective action* and *mortification*. He mentions that many people employ multiple tactics at once during their image restoration campaign and that this can be a very successful approach (Benoit, 1997).

For example, Hugh Grant, who paparazzi spotted with a prostitute in the 1990s, discovered using several approaches improved his image (Benoit, 1997; Grossberger, 1995). Grant used *mortification, bolstering, denial* and *attacking one's accuser* as consistent defenses to this incident and past risqué events on each guest appearance (Benoit, 1997).

Grant was scheduled to appear on five talk shows, *The Tonight Show, Larry King Live, The Today Show, Live with Regis and Kathie Lee* and *The Late Show*, to publicize the release of his new movie, *Nine Months*. He strategically used these appearances to simultaneously restore his reputation. He said on *Larry King Live*, "I realize it would be absurd to pretend it hasn't happened" (Benoit, 1997). Grant kept it simple, and, most importantly, admitted to his mistake when he said, "I think you know in life what's a good thing to do and what's a bad thing, and I did a bad thing. And there you have it" (Benoit, 1997). Though his statement was basic, it fulfilled public interest enough to forgive him for his actions as he returned to his previous status in people's minds.

In another case study, Benoit (2011) analyzed the 2010 incident in which NPR senior news analyst Juan Williams appeared on the Fox Network show *The O'Reilly Factor* and said that when he saw people on an airplane dressed in Muslim garments he became "worried" and "nervous." Two days later Williams was fired by NPR for expressing these sentiments in public. Williams then released a statement in which he attacked his former employer: "Yesterday NPR fired me for telling the truth."

In handling the case, CEO Vivian Schiller utilized *mortification* and *corrective action* to respond to one accusation (the manner in which Williams was fired) and *transcendence, bolstering* and *attack accuser* for the accusation that NPR was wrong to fire Williams. Her defense may have helped with her intended audiences (NPR employees and member stations) but is unlikely to have appealed to many others.

Schiller's image repair discourse in this controversy had two parts: a brief statement about Williams made during a speech and then a memo that she disseminated. In a speech at the Atlanta Press Club on October 21, Schiller indicated that Williams' remarks were inappropriate (essentially denying that it was wrong to fire him). With the proliferation of new media, effectiveness of medium use has become a common topic. Benoit (2011) concluded this discourse may have helped repair NPR's image with the intended audiences: NPR employees and member stations. However, NPR's image generally had been damaged by the firing of Williams and this image repair effort was not particularly well designed for other audiences.

Grebe's (2011) analysis of the AWB corporate scandal highlights post-crisis responses and how organizations may successfully recover from the damage of a scandal. The study argues that although AWB initially misman-aged its response, the corporation was ultimately able to rebuild trust two years after its crisis because it undertook genuine reform and successfully changed its culture, systems, structure and governance. While this case study highlights a corporation rather than an individual, it offers a detailed look at the difference between scandal and crisis.

In another example, Oles (2010) concluded Oprah Winfrey succeeded in repairing her image in by beginning with *denial* and then moving to *reducing offensiveness*. Her image was not only repaired, but also regenerated, as she emerged from the crisis more influential and powerful. Winfrey's crisis occurred in 1996 when on an episode of *The Oprah Winfrey Show* she dis-cussed "Mad Cow Disease" and said, "It has just stopped me cold from eating another hamburger!" (Oles, 2010). Because of this remark and her influence over the public, cattle futures plummeted and Winfrey was sued for libel by the Texas Beef Group in Amarillo, Texas. Winfrey chose a state of *denial* when in the sense that she denied she did something wrong. She could not deny what she said, because it aired on television nationwide. But she denied that she had malicious intentions.

This case became an issue in court when she was sued for libel. Before the trial, the public, specifically in Amarillo, expressed negative sentiments toward Winfrey (Oles, 2010). The final image repair strategy is to admit *responsibility*, express regret for the action and then ask for forgiveness (Benoit, 1995). Winfrey did not have the option to admit responsibility for the cattle futures crash because that would mean she accepted the blame; accepting blame would have limited her legal options (Oles, 2010). However, she said the right things to gain her positive public image back, and, most importantly, she did certain things that helped her more than just talking. During the four-week trial she moved her show to Amarillo. The local taping of the show allowed her to capitalize on her status as a television celebrity, which swayed local public opinion in her favor.

NOTE

1. Benoit changed the name of image restoration theory to image repair because he thought the former might imply that persuasive defense ought to be able to completely restore the image. According to Benoit, although it is possible that image repair might be completely successful, fully dissipating all bad feelings, a persuasive defense often only partially succeeds, repairing the damaged image.

Chapter 2

Critical Race Theory and Image Repair Studies

Critical Race Theory (CRT) emerged in the 1970s and 1980s as an outgrowth of the civil rights tradition and the Critical Legal Studies movement that advanced an understanding of law as deeply connected to lived experiences and social power. CRT examines how messages portray underlying ideologies that reflect social relations of domination based on a pervasive yet unobtrusive racial hierarchy (Crenshaw, 1988). The theory is more important than ever as race relations continue to wane in the United States.

A primary goal of CRT is to recenter inquiry and experience from a marginalized perspective. CRT is also concerned with consciousness-raising, emancipation and self-determinism. Another goal of applied CRT is to deconstruct social, historical and political understandings to lay the path "for moral commitment to inclusion and shared decision-making" (Deetz, 2005, p. 91). As such, CRT points to aspects of society and culture that should be challenged and transformed, and thus attempts to inform and inspire change. Social actions must follow the identification of weaknesses in the social structure (Deetz, 2005).

CRT's main tenets are that "racism is a common, everyday lived experience for people of color" and "individuals and their specific roles in society are socially constructed based on a system of power relations that favors the majority" (Crenshaw, 1988; Delgado & Stefancic, 2012; Ladson-Billings, 1998). Parker and Lynn (2002) characterize CRT as incorporating three goals: (1) to present storytelling and narratives as valid approaches through which to examine race and racism in law and society; (2) to argue for the eradication of racial subjugation while simultaneously recognizing that race is a social construct; (3) to draw important relationships between race and other axes of domination.

CRT allows researchers to examine race by acknowledging the inherent privilege of "whiteness" and analyzing race from a perspective that recognizes privilege. A literature review exploring these topics provides a framework for understanding the present text.

IMAGE REPAIR AND RACE-RELATED CASE STUDIES

Image tarnishing cases have increased in recent years with the popularity of the use of social media platforms to share information. In response, race-related IRT case studies have also increased. Using a critical race lens, Center (2009) analyzed image restoration tactics used following the 2001 death of unarmed Timothy Thomas in the Midwestern U.S. city, Cincinnati, Ohio. Thomas was the 15th African American shot and killed by police officers in the previous six years. When the community was not given a specific answer, race riots ensued, followed by a boycott of businesses in the downtown area.

To address the racial issues that surrounded the riot, Center (2009) incorporated CRT, which aims to expose the racially marginalized voice; analyzing this voice gives key critical insights into the success of Cincinnati's image restoration tactics. The author concluded Cincinnati unsuccessfully used reducing offensiveness in its image restoration tactics. Attempts by the leadership of Cincinnati's refused to genuinely engage of the marginalized voices that cried out for justice and healing. In the end, the city lost valuable tax dollars because of its inefficient handling of the case—and primarily not paying proper attention to the voices of the marginalized citizens of Cincinnati.

In another example, Brinson and Benoit (1999) analyzed Texaco's use of image restoration tactics after a secret tape of an executive meeting surfaced and the company was accused of racism. The most damaging comments on the tape involved the executives' references to African American employees as "black jelly beans" who were "glued to the bottom of the jar." The tape also revealed insensitivity toward two holidays: "I'm still having trouble with Hanukkah. Now we have Kwanzaa" (Brinson & Benoit, 1999).

The media widely disseminated these allegations of racism at Texaco, and Bijur wasted no time in initiating a response to this threat. On the same day that the article appeared in *The New York Times*, Bijur issued a news release (Brinson & Benoit, 1999), mailed a letter to employees and delivered a video address to employees. On the following day, Bijur made a live appearance on ABC's Nightline. Two days after the story broke, he released another statement regarding "allegations of employee misconduct," which was followed in four days by a statement after a meeting with African American leaders (Brinson & Benoit, 1999).

In the end, Texaco settled the racial discrimination lawsuit by taking swift and relatively effective action. The company used *bolstering, corrective action, mortification,* as well as a new form of *shifting the blame,* separation (Brinson & Benoit, 1999). Separation seeks to place the blame on a small part of the organization that can be separated from the remaining (and good) part of the organization; separation requires three conditions for successful use. After only a few weeks, the allegations of racism, which had occupied newspaper headlines and television news across the country, disappeared. Boycotts were called off.

Following this analysis, Coombs and Schmidt (2000) employed an empirical study to look at the same Texaco messages. Claims about the effectiveness of various image restoration strategies used in Texaco's efforts to combat a racism incident were tested. The study analyzed the use of image restoration strategies Texaco employed: (1) *bolstering,* reminding people of Texaco's policies against discrimination and noting the actions where outrageous; (2) *corrective action,* indicating an investigation of the allegations and policies designed to prevent a recurrence of the problem; (3) *shifting blame,* identifying the problem employees as bad apples who are not representative of Texaco as a whole; (4) *mortification,* admitting guilt and apologizing for the racist comments; and (5) *separation,* a combination of bolstering, shifting blame and corrective action that the analysts argued was a new form of image restoration strategy.

Empirical tests of the Texaco image repair case did not support some of the major conclusions drawn in the Brinson and Benoit (1999) case study. Respondents seemed to view all five strategies as positive steps by the organization. However, there were no significant differences between the scenarios. Even when no specific corrective actions are listed, respondents believed the organization was working to prevent a repeat of the crisis.

These study results by Coombs and Schmidt (2000) suggest that many conclusions drawn from image restoration case studies should be taken only as tentative. The researcher recommends a more rigorous application of image restoration theory to unpack its utility for crisis management and public relations.

Other cases illustrate the different strategies public figures use following a crisis. As mentioned in chapter 1, *mortification* is noted as the most effective tactic for image repair. This rule transfers to race-related cases. For instance, actor Mel Gibson succeeded in repairing his image using *mortification* in 2006, after he was arrested for speeding and driving under the influence and with an open container. Gibson delivered a stream of choice words leading up to a climatic tirade of anti-Semitic racial slurs including "Jews are responsible for all the wars in the world," before going on to ask if any of his arresting officers were Jewish and referring to the one female as "sugar t*ts" (O'Connor, 2010).

Gibson released two apologies through his publicist and took full responsibility in an interview with Diane Sawyer. He showed a great deal of remorse for his actions, meeting all his court-appointed legal requirements to satisfy his charges as well as reaching out to Jewish leaders to guide him in his salvation. Gibson also took measures for corrective action by addressing his addiction to alcohol. In response, Gibson acquired a great deal of sympathy after his supporters continued to see backlash in the media. Robert Downey Jr., a good friend of Gibson, chose Gibson to present his award at the 25th American "Cinematheque" Awards Show. While on stage, Downey, who has also experienced his share of hardship and addiction, chose to make part of his acceptance speech about Gibson (Flows, 2012):

> I humbly ask that you join me, unless you are completely without sin, and in which case you picked the wrong industry, in forgiving my friend of his trespasses and offering him the same clean slate that you have me and allowing him to continue his great and ongoing contribution to our collective art without shame.

In another example, Michael Richards, who played "Kramer" on the TV show *Seinfeld*, found his career in shambles after going on a racist rant at a comedy club. In November of 2006, Richards performed at the Laugh Factory where two African American males in the audience made comments about Richards not being funny to which Richards replied with many racist and hateful comments including:

> Fifty years ago we'd have you upside down with a f***ing fork up your ass." They're going to arrest me for calling a black man a ni*ger." And "You can talk, you can talk, you're brave now motherf**ker. Throw his ass out. He's a n*gger! He's a n*gger! He's a n*gger! A n*gger, look, there's a n*gger!

The entire rant was captured on a cellphone video camera belonging to a member of the audience that went viral on the web. In the video, many other people in the audience were seen leaving their seats in disgust (Paul, 2006). In response, Richards made a public apology to two civil rights leaders, the Reverend Al Sharpton and Jesse Jackson. Gloria Allred, an American civil rights lawyer, complained that Richards "has not apologized to his victims directly, face to face, man to man." His publicist, Howard Rubenstein, said Richards was not considering any demand for payment, and while he would like to apologize personally to the two men he targeted in his rant, he is unable to locate them.

Don Imus provides another example. The radio personality used a variety of tactics to repair his image following an incident on April 4, 2007, during which the radio personality discussed Rutgers University women's basketball team, a contender in the NCAA Basketball Finals. Imus characterized the women's basketball team players as "rough girls" and commented on their physical appearance (Associated Press, 2007).

The name-calling continued with Imus describing the team of eight African American and two white players as "nappy-headed hos." At first, MSNBC executives made the argument that Don Imus was using his First Amendment rights when he insulted the women's basketball team. They challenged viewers to consider his comments as a by-product of freedom of speech. However, after heated criticism from the public, on April 11, 2007, Steve Capus of NBC News announced that MSNBC would no longer simulcast Imus' morning show. Capus said he made this decision based on the general reaction of the public, anger from the show's sponsors and out of consideration of the high-profiled African American personalities working for the NBC Corporation.

MSNBC issued a news release stating their plans for discontinuing the simulcast broadcast of Imus' show. The release also dispelled rumors that this decision was made after major corporate sponsors pulled their advertisements from the broadcast. It featured a comment from Bruce Gordon, former head of the NAACP and director of CBS Corp., who stated that Imus crossed the line and violated the African American community.

Don Imus tried to repair his image by using *differentiation* (Kramer, 2014). Kramer (2013) concluded utilizing this particular strategy with a sensitive social issue like racism was not the best option. In other words, trying to lessen such an offensive by explanation does not redeem the offender effectively. Those affected are not concerned with what Imus was trying to convey or express, because it was not received that way initially.

In another example, American actor Charlie Sheen and his now ex-wife, former fashion model Denise Richards, appeared in tabloids concerning a series of dramatic events throughout their marriage. The couple became known for publicly displaying their personal lives to the public but things started to get nasty following their divorce and custody battle. In June of 2008, many voice recordings of an angry Sheen were leaked. The voicemails were three years old and included racial slurs, cursing and lots of bitterness (Francese, 2008). Sheen released an apology the following day saying that he should not have used such language and extended a personal apology to one of his close friends Tony Todd, an African American, who was the best man at his wedding. However, Sheen did not apologize to his ex-wife. Instead, he pointed out that she had not shown up at the custodial meeting they had scheduled for that day.

These cases illustrate the importance of a skillful, proactive use of image restoration tactics in race-related cases. The immediate use of sincere mortification helped many of these celebrities and politicians successfully repair their image. Conversely, those who postponed their apology or tried to cover up their indiscretions were not as successful. This chapter provides an introduction to CRT and image restoration. Subsequent chapters of this book will analyze race-related case studies in greater detail.

Chapter 3

Image Repair Theory and the Web

Broadening the application of Benoit's image repair theory, this text looks at how celebrities presented themselves through user-generated content (UGC) such as personal blogs, Twitter and Facebook and so on. The Web allows citizens to disseminate messages and UGC instantaneously; therefore, gate-keeper/audience dynamics have changed, which warrants further study, particularly from a critical theory perspective. Throughout this text, we add to the literature an examination of blog posts, personal statements and social media content disseminated by individuals after a crisis. It has long been understood and accepted that traditional media function as the primary gate-keeper in disseminating news to the public (White, 1950). However, with the rise of UGC and social media sites such as Facebook, Instagram and Twitter, a varied group of gatekeepers emerge as numerous as those individuals who use the medium.

Race, Gender, and Image Repair Theory: How Digital Media Change the Landscape is significant in today's rapidly changing media climate in which consumers often gather news and information from blogs, YouTube, consumer Web sites, twitter and so on. Today's gatekeepers and opinion leaders often are bloggers and citizen journalists on social media who lead the dialogue in breaking news situations.

Media function simultaneously as both modern agenda setters (Entman, 1992) and orthodox gatekeepers of traditional mores and values. The concept of gatekeeping is historically connected to the effects of mass communication. Digital media is reshaping the concept by transforming a mass audience into smaller and atomized audiences. Gatekeeping remains an important concept for research about digital networks, particularly when networks rely on intermedia sources such as blogs and tweets. In this text, we examine social media, personal statements and posts coupled with a textual analysis of print articles in mainstream media to offer insight into how the two are used for image repair in the 21st century.

Landmark studies indicate the gatekeeper process is highly biased and based on a person's own set of experiences, attitudes and expectations. For example, in the study, *White News: Why Local News Programs Don't Cover People of Color*, Heider (2000) observed two newsrooms, one in Honolulu, Hawaii, and one in Albuquerque, New Mexico, and found that even in areas where people of color account for the majority of the population, those persons in charge of the news programming did not reflect the makeup of the population covered. The researcher's subsequent findings clarified that although people of color sat in news meetings in both newsrooms, their positions did not include leadership authority.

Whereas gatekeeping in traditional media was performed by individual editors, in digital networks individuals filter ideas and information (Bastos, Raimundo & Travitzki, 2013). However, when digital networks became popular, it became possible to communicate with millions of users at little or no cost. What was once an internal decision-making process carried out by the media is currently a decentralized process of following up on a story (Bastos et al., 2013).

The Internet presents a flood of content too massive for any small group or organization to control. This massive surge of data has forever changed the nature of gatekeeping. Today, anyone with a computer can encounter a universe of unregulated content and information. Who are today's gatekeepers— anyone with access to a computer can choose the type of news they receive.

Reading the news has become a new type of social experience. People share links, articles and videos on their Facebook walls or Twitter accounts as a form of cultural currency. Social media users take part in an ongoing process of evaluating and sharing what they think is important to other social media users. It is increasingly difficult for individuals to control their image or information as social media sites allow for the proliferation of personal data.

SOCIAL MEDIA AND PEOPLE OF COLOR

Anderson and Hitlin (2016) found that researchers and activists credit social media—in particular, Black Twitter—with giving racially focused issues to greater national attention. Two of the most used hashtags around social causes in Twitter history focus on race and criminal justice: #Ferguson and #BlackLivesMatter.

In addition, black social media users (68%) are roughly twice as likely as whites (35%) to say that at least some of the posts they see on social networking sites are about race or race relations (Anderson & Hitlin, 2016). A 2016 analysis found that over a 15-month period (from January 1, 2015, through

March 31, 2016) there were about 995 million tweets about race—or, on average, 2.1 million tweets per day on the subject. In contrast, about 500 million tweets were posted on Twitter each day in 2015—meaning that tweets mentioning race made up about 0.04 percent of all tweets posted.

Throughout the early 21st century, Black Twitter was used to share African American culture and to address race-related issues (Dates & Moody, 2018). Twitter's power to provide individuals with a platform to speak back is part of its attraction. Black Twitter is often noted for encouraging a clapback culture or giving people a platform to respond to others in a humorous yet stern manner (Dates & Moody-Ramirez, 2018). A clapback is deemed by most as a targeted, often viciously acute comeback intended to place someone in much-needed check (What's a Clapback? n.d.).

Barksdale (2015) adds that Black Twitter usually ignites when someone tweets something inappropriate or something happens that indirectly or directly impacts the African American community. In 2015, Black Twitter users called out cultural appropriations, celebrated moments of black excellence and showed solidarity against racial injustice (Barksdale, 2015). Barksdale's list of popular Black Twitter hashtags included: #StayMadAbby, #OscarsSoWhite, #GrowingUpBlack, #SayHerName and #PattiPie.

The popularity of #NiggerNavy provides an example of how social media users used Twitter to call out social injustices (Dates & Moody-Ramirez, 2018). Black Twitter was ablaze in January 2017 when Yahoo Finance misspelled bigger with an "n," in a Twitter link to a story on president-elect Donald Trump's plans to enlarge America's navy. The tweet containing a racial slur gained more than 1,000 retweets before being deleted, almost one hour after it was shared (Mezzofiore, 2017). Yahoo Finance published an apology shortly after, saying it was a "mistake." It was too late. "Black twitter" turned #NiggerNavy into a joke and fond memory for many Twitter users.

> Imma let you finish. But the #NiggerNavy tweets were the best tweets of all time.—@KamauWaset

> #NiggerNavy is yet another reason I love #BlackTwitter.—@TwistedViper215

> #niggernavy needs to be cataloged at the Smithsonian. Black Twitter, that was your finest night.—@AmericanDreamin

IMAGE REPAIR THEORY AND SOCIAL MEDIA STUDIES

Scholars have theorized beyond Benoit's original categories of image restoration. The intersection of public relations, participatory culture and community engagement has also been explored. Researchers, however, have found that social media use during a crisis can create new image management issues and that social media use can be less effective in repairing an image when it replicates strategies used via traditional media (Liu & Kim, 2011).

Facebook, Twitter, YouTube and blogs allow users to share opinion-based information that can potentially be regarded as truth (Rasmussen, 2015). Twitter is a unique social media platform that allows users to share posts that are up to 140 (now 280) characters long. Kent and Taylor (2010) concluded that social media sites, such as Twitter and blogs, might be very invaluable in modern PR strategies.

Twitter now has 241 million monthly active users and it has increasingly become a major source of information for journalists ("Topic," 2017). Instead of tracking down a team's publicist or calling an athlete's agent for leads, journalists may now simply sign onto Twitter. If something catches their eye, they do a little follow-up (usually online), maybe check the source, and then write an article, blog post or television spot, and so on. This information is gleaned entirely from the 280 characters they read on Twitter.

Not only does the Internet offer an unlimited number of outlets for fans to find information about their favorite celebrities, it also offers the first platform from which they can present themselves directly to the public, eliminating traditional media gatekeepers. One concern with self-publishing is celebrities might disseminate information with little or no regard for its impact. While control over self-presentation can be empowering, it can be very problematic in a time of crisis. Celebrities are not always able to express themselves in ways that actually help them repair a tarnished image.

Hambrick and Sanderson (2013) explored how Lance Armstrong used image repair across both traditional and social media. They observed that while Armstrong used similar strategies on both platforms, he failed to engage fans on social media after admitting to using performance-enhancing drugs. In analyzing the Lance Armstrong case, Hambrick et al. (2013) established two additional categories of image repair "conforming" and "retrospective regret" (Hutchins & Tindall, 2016).

In a case involving the N-word, Len-Rios et al. (2015) used a multi-method approach to examine the use of social media in Paula Deen's image repair campaign in the wake of the *National Enquirer*'s revelation that she admitted to using the "N-word" during a lawsuit deposition. The researchers looked at the effectiveness of tweeted message strategies in a race-related crisis via Twitter. Study findings indicated her image repair strategies were unsuccessful because her apology did not center on the allegations, and she was contradictory in her bolstering, minimization and mortification strategies.

In their research on the Planned Parenthood crisis, Rasmussen (2015) concluded while social media was a catalyst to creating the crisis, it was also a valuable tool to help manage it. The crisis occurred on February 1, 2011, when the nonprofit pro-life organization, Live Action, released an undercover video footage to show Planned Parenthood clinic staff disregarding the reporting laws and aiding sex traffickers. The videos posted on the Live Action blog and YouTube channel quickly garnered more than one million views and placed Planned Parenthood at the forefront of national news.

Planned Parenthood acted quickly to take advantage of the anger that erupted on Facebook and Twitter. The organization was able to respond immediately to the controversy partly because it had been building its advocacy strategy, including the use of social media. They added that issues management in online environments allows practitioners an opportunity to address concerns before significant damage can be done. The crisis was twofold; the organization managed a funding crisis that threatened its ability to function while dealing with damage to its image. The organization strategically focused on the impact defunding would have on the public, which allowed it to simultaneously engage in image repair and manage its funding crisis. It is not necessarily the Internet advancements or the emergence of social media that has impacted the basic functions of practitioners; instead, it is the interplay of advancements that are more significant to the practice (Rasmussen, 2015).

Social media played a role in the handling of the well-publicized divorce case of Jon and Kate Gosselin. The Gosselins rose to fame when Kate gave birth to sextuplets in 2004 after already birthing twins just three years earlier. Because of the public's interest in their family, Discovery Health decided to make their life into a reality show. In 2009, Jon and Kate divorced, which led to a variety of image crises. Moody (2011) concluded Jon and Kate handled their case with varying degrees of success. The two were wildly different in the ways they reacted to the accusations and stories coming out about them.

Kate did not use social media in the beginning phases of her divorce and its aftermath. She primarily stuck to traditional media, which did not help her much at all because she was sending conflicting messages to the public. However, when she began to utilize social media and began blogging, she connected with the public more effectively through personal stories and photographs. Jon, on the other hand, went straight to social media. Unfortunately, instead of using his Twitter to express remorse and hurt for the downfall of his family, he used them to place blame on others while also keeping himself in traditional media, but not with interviews and articles, like Kate, but with irresponsible behavior. Eventually, Jon realized that when he focused on family and his children on social media, the public was much more receptive to forgiving him. From this case study, one can note how taking responsibility on social media can have a positive impact on image repair. When one continues to interact with fans and the public through Twitter or blogs, and is honest about their feelings in a responsible and respectable way, the media and public are much less harsh.

These studies foreshadow the promise that social media offer for celebrities who use them to repair their image. However, it is important for scholars to continue to research the topic. As the various types of social media continue to transform as well as how celebrities use them, it is imperative for scholars to continue to study their effectiveness.

Part II

OUTBURSTS AND OFFENSIVE LANGUAGE

Chapter 4

Hate Speech and Crisis Management

A Case Study of Donald Sterling's
Use of Racist Rhetoric

On April 25, 2014, entertainment media TMZ Sports posted on the Internet an exclusive story featuring the audio tape of Sterling's racist rant with his mistress, V. Stiviano, after she posted a picture on Instagram posing with Magic Johnson. In the recording, Sterling stated, "The world will think certain things if you're seen with black people, so you should not be seen with them in public, and under no circumstances should you bring them to Clippers games" (Wagner, 2014, n.d.). TMZ reported having the audiotape of the conversation between Sterling and his girlfriend, who is according to TMZ Sports, "Black and Mexican," which led to an immediate crisis for Sterling. This incident provided the ideal case to explore race and image repair from a critical race perspective as Sterling immediately began to repair his image once the news broke.

In public relations terms, a crisis is defined as a "major occurrence with a potentially negative outcome affecting the organization, company, or industry." Studies in the past have looked at theories pertaining to crises and how media frames a tragedy based on frames similar to a previous crisis (Cho & Gower, 2006). In 1946, W. Lippman wrote "The only feeling that anyone can have about an event he does not experience is the feeling aroused by his mental image of that event." Media provides a feeling for the publics that are not experiencing the crisis first hand. Frames cause publics to create their own opinions of the events and the people and organizations involved. Exploring the frames of a crisis is important during any type of crisis. During a crisis, media sources communicate their findings to the world and among reports on what is happening, certain language and viewpoints eventually find their way to the surface. The usability of such language can be products of the past. These reflect theories of media framing.

For this case study, the crisis is set within the boundaries of public relations and the management of "serious" events that have national media and cultural implications (Coombs, 1999; Fearn-Banks, 2011; Friedman, 2002; Seeger, Selnow & Ulmer, 1998). Communications scholar Benoit (1995) articulates image or reputation as "extremely vital to us" and "we feel compelled to offer explanations, defenses, justifications, rationalizations, apologies, or excuses for our behavior" (p. 2). Further, Benoit's Theory of Image Restoration suggests that a threatened reputation means, "reprehensible act must have been committed" (p. 72).

The literature indicates that individuals take different approaches with the sole purpose of presenting a positive image: denial, evading responsibility, reducing offensiveness, corrective action and mortification. All of these strategies have the potential to succeed, to an extent; however, studies show that the usage of a proactive strategy is more effective in generating positive media coverage (Brazeal, 2008).

CRT examines how messages portray underlying ideologies that reflect social relations of domination based on a pervasive yet unobtrusive racial hierarchy (Crenshaw, 1991). CRT's main tenets are that "racism is a common, everyday lived experience for people of color" and "individuals and their specific roles in society are socially constructed based on a system of power relations that favors the majority" (Delgado & Stefancic, 2012). CRT is relevant in this case because the N-word is still the most offensive curse word based on a public opinion poll conducted by Harris Interactive. The N-word was voted offensive by 85% of participants in the poll.

The literature suggests hate speech is dangerous and entails a person with more power acting against a person or group with less power (Cunningham, Ferreira & Fink, 2009; Greene, 1995). Cunningham, Ferreira and Fink (2009) in their study of reactions to racial prejudice found that the effects of prejudicial statements were amplified when the commenter was a "prototypical perpetrator" specifically Caucasian or male (p. 59) and could provoke swift responses.

Drawing on Marti, Bobier and Baron's (2000) prototype/accessibility model, Cunningham et al. found that racist comments were deemed "more offensive than were gendered comments" and the "effects were qualified by the characteristics of the person making the comment" (i.e., Whites, men) were perceived as "particularly offensive" (p. 69).

IMAGE REPAIR AND OFFENSIVE LANGUAGE

Image repair strategies used by persons who use offensive language vary. Rush Limbaugh waited too late after calling a law student a "slut" because of her encouragement of mandated birth control before Congress. He continued his rant for two days during which he initially applied three defensive strategies—denial, good intentions and attacking the accuser (Bentley, 2012). However, Limbaugh's strategies did not work and his show started losing sponsors. In response, Limbaugh switched strategies and began to show mortification. In the end, his apology proved ineffective because of timing.

In another example, Kauffmann (2011) found that British comedian James Gervais tarnished his image in 2011 during the 2011 Golden Globes Awards ceremony when he targeted many celebrities in attendance and people in the television audience with harsh, mean-spirited jokes about the awards, guests and nominees.

Four days after the show, Gervais responded to the backlash by appearing on *Piers Morgan Tonight* to defend his performance and to repair his image (Kauffman, 2011). He apologized twice: the first time stating he hoped no one was truly offended, and the second time, he stated that he was sorry that they were offended but not sorry for anything that he said. His response left his audience puzzled and questioning his sincerity. Ultimately, Kauffmann (2011) concluded Gervais failed to adapt to his audience and failed to repair his image.

One of the more intriguing cases involving race featured George Allen, a Republican candidate from Virginia who was running for reelection in 2006, ruined his chances to succeed in politics after he was involved in three race-related incidents. Allen gave a stump speech in rural Virginia. During the speech, he referred to a Webb campaign volunteer as "macaca" twice, and welcomed him to America. The volunteer, an Indian college student, was born in Virginia and was employed by Webb to videotape Allen's campaign tour. The incident became the No. 1 downloaded video on YouTube, and ignited massive blog and media criticism. Afterward, Webb gained 10 percentage points in the public opinion polls (Liu, 2007).

Liu (2008) concluded Allen ineffectively used the mortification strategy in response to using the racial slur, because he waited four days—to implement the strategy rather than apologizing right away. The longtime lapse between the incident and the apology not only gave the media time to depict Allen negatively, it also placed doubt in everyone's mind as to the sincerity of the apology (Liu, 2008).

In another incident, on September 18, 2006, during a televised debate, a reporter asked Allen if he was Jewish. Allen angrily responded that he was raised a Christian. The next day, he released a statement revealing his recently discovered Jewish ancestry. To smooth over this crisis, he attempted to shift the blame by stating he did not know about his Jewish heritage when he forcibly denied his Jewish descent. He also blamed Webb for questioning his heritage. This strategy was ineffective as a simple denial tactic. He would have been more effective to blame the interviewer and the Webb campaign.

Allen's third incident occurred on September 25, 2006, when the website www.salon.com stated that two of Allen's former University of Virginia football teammates had accused Allen of using the N-word. The politician used denial effectively when confronted with the N-word allegations. He shifted the blame to the accusers, and this worked well because the allegations turned out to be false (Liu, 2008).

These cases illustrate the importance immediate mortification after using hurtful language. Being open and honest to the public early in their scandals helped many of these individuals successfully repair their image. Conversely, those who waited until later to apologize or who lied and tried to cover up their indiscretions were not as successful. All of these factors will likewise play a role in the image repair tactics of Sterling.

Using Benoit's Image Repair Theory, this case analyzes how Sterling responded to the crisis via his own personal statements and social media content. Finally, it looks at how audiences and the media responded to this case. The literature is lacking articles that focus on social media representations of the recent phenomena of race and culture.

Based on a review of the literature, the following research questions guided this analysis: (1) What image repair tactics did Donald Sterling use following his racially charged incidents? (2) How did media outlets and audiences respond? (3) What are the implications of this case study for IRT and critical race studies?

TEXTS EXAMINED

Using a critical race lens, this IRT analysis looked at multiple texts to assess the image repair strategies of Donald Sterling following a highly publicized racially charged incident during which he used hate speech. Specifically, we looked at his personal statements, social media accounts, news reports and public opinion reports surrounding the events to assess his image repair tactics.

Online sources are of interest because they were heavily used to help spread the word about race-related topics and the two incidents in general. We gathered the texts used in our analysis by searching for Sterling's name on the Google search engine from November 2013 to May 5, 2014. The texts were read closely using a textual analysis. Media outlets included in sample: Sterling's interview with CNN reporter Anderson Cooper and his interview with RadarOnline, *USA Today*. The analysis also looked at Sterling's statement titled, "Why I am fighting the NBA?" and his personal statement of apology released on TMZ. Public opinion polls analyzed were conducted by the following sources: MSNBC, Billboard.com. *Washington Post*/ABC News poll and E-Poll Market Research.

DONALD STERLING'S IMAGE REPAIR TACTICS

We began our analysis with *denial*, which involves shifting the blame or simply denying the offense. Sterling initially used the *simple denial* tactic by stating he is "not a racist" on CNN's Anderson Cooper. He made this claim nearly two weeks after the NBA Commissioner fined him $2.5 million, banned him from the NBA games and urged league owners to force him to sell his team. Sterling relied on the mainstream press as a channel to tell his story. This tactic expanded his reach to key stakeholders and other supporters who might favor his pejorative rhetoric and First Amendment stance. Table 4.1 explores his image repair tactics in detail.

Sterling and the Clippers' organization issued this statement to TMZ in response to the recording. "We have heard the tape on TMZ. We do not know if it is legitimate or it has been altered. We do know that the woman on the tape—who we believe released it to TMZ—is the defendant in a lawsuit brought by the Sterling family, alleging that she embezzled more than $1.8 million, who told Mr. Sterling that she would 'get even.' Mr. Sterling is emphatic that what is reflected on that recording is not consistent with, nor does it reflect his views, beliefs or feelings," they added. "It is the antithesis of who he is, what he believes and how he has lived his life" (Goyette, 2014).

Evading Responsibility

In addition to *denial*, Sterling *evaded responsibility* by claiming he was "set up" by Stiviano. He stated, "When I listen to that tape, I don't even know how I can say word [*sic*] like that . . . I don't know why the girl had me say those things" (Anderson, 2014). Perhaps a more effective *evading responsibility* strategy was Sterling's use of the jealous lover frame in his image repair tactics. CNN reported Sterling reportedly said "jealousy" was the reason for his comments by stating that "I'm jealous that she's with other black guys" (Hanna, 2014).

Sterling also used *evading responsibility* by attacking his accusers or in this case, the NBA. Sterling, who received a lifetime ban and a $2.5 million fine from NBA commissioner Adam Silver after the audio recording became public, called the NBA "a band of hypocrites and bullies" and referred to the league as "despicable monsters" (Golliver, 2014).

Table 4.1 Donald Sterling's Image Restoration Tactics

Strategy	Supporting Sub-Strategy	Donald Sterling's Actions Identified
Denial	1. Simple denial	1. Initially denied making racist remarks saying he is not "racist."
	2. Shifting the blame	2a. Sterling's estranged wife and news reports suggest "dementia" as a health-related problem.
		2b. Sterling's s examination compromised due to alcohol consumption and friendship with the physician as a conflict of interest.
		2c. Sterling says "jealousy" behind racist comments.
Evasion of responsibility	3. Provocation/Attack the accuser	3a. Asserted his girlfriend, V. Stiviano, set him up.
		3b. Sterling made threats to doctors, according to news reports.
	4. Defeasibility	4a. Sterling says he did not expect private conversation to become public.
	5. (New) Age reference	4b. Sterling was emotionally paralyzed; he blamed slow response to make public apology on "being emotionally distraught."
		Sterling and third parties blamed his racist rant on his age. Reports surfaced that he might have Alzheimer's.
		4c. Donald Sterling called the NBA "a band of hypocrites and bullies" in angry statement.
		4d. "Adam Silver is content with focusing his energy on violating my rights, attempting to take my property."
		5. Sterling's estranged wife, Shelly, referenced him as "80-year-old" suffering from "onset of dementia."
Reduce Offensiveness	6. Transcendence	6. Sterling asserted his ownership of a mainly African American team makes him not a "racist."
	7. Minimization	7. Fined $2.5 million and banned from NBA for life. Sterling called for meeting with new owner of the L.A. Clippers.
	8. Bolstering	
Mortification	9. Mortification	9a. Sterling offered an apology, but said he was "entitled to one mistake." His apology inferred that his comments were not hurtful; it was how people interpreted that made them hurtful.
		9b. He described how he was "brought up in America and educated to believe that every citizen has a right to privacy and right to freedom of speech. As a lawyer and citizen, I am shocked (but not surprised) that the NBA wants to take away those fundamental rights." (Golliver, 2014).
Endorsement		

Source: Benoit typology (in Wilcox & Cameron, 2012, p. 267).

Reduce Offensiveness

Sterling used transcendence and *minimization* to *reduce offensiveness.* In a CNN interview, Sterling claimed that Stiviano tried to trap him by getting him to say the things that he said about Black people. She allegedly deceived him and kept pressing him. In addition, Sterling stated that what he said was not meant to be offensive. He claimed he was not saying anything against African Americans or Hispanics but against Stiviano hanging out with other men altogether (Estrada, 2014).

Sterling stated that he is "entitled to one mistake," alluding to his hate speech and documented racists acts toward minorities as isolated incidents, uncharacteristic of him as a business mogul and team owner for over 30 years (Anderson, 2014). However, conflicting reports of unfair housing practices to minorities and women would emerge, which contradicted his "one mistake" comment.

Mortification

Mortification is the final step of image repair. Referring to the literature, in order for mortification to succeed as an image repair tactic, it must be sincere and immediate. Sterling did not immediately release an official written statement. However, he apologized during an interview with CNN reporter Anderson Cooper two weeks following the NBA Commissioner's ban, multi-million dollar fine and possible sale of the team. Sterling also stated on RadarOnline, "I know I'm wrong, what I said was wrong. But I never thought a private conversation would go anywhere out to the public" (Hanna, 2014). Scott (2014) included this assertion from Sterling in his article, "I can't explain some of the stupid, foolish, uneducated words that I uttered" (May 12, 2014).

Sterling's official apology came after the NBA banned him and announced that they might force him to sell the Clippers. On June 10, 2014, he released a statement titled, "Why I am fighting the NBA? The NBA wants to take away our privacy rights and freedom of speech." While Sterling stated he was sorry he hurt so many people by what he said, he never actually apologized for his comments.

His apology inferred that his comments were not hurtful; it was how people interpreted that made them hurtful. In it, he described how he was "brought up in America and educated to believe that every citizen has a right to privacy and right to freedom of speech. As a lawyer and citizen, 'I am shocked (but not surprised) that the NBA wants to take away those fundamental rights (Golliver, 2014).'" He continued:

> I feel that every American has to protect those rights and that the NBA should not be allowed to take away those rights. I have apologized for my mistakes. My

apology is sincere. I want every American to know that I will not give up fighting for those rights. I also feel that the leadership of the NBA is incompetent, inexperienced and angry. It is clear that they took this opportunity to settle the personal grievances they have harbored against me for years.

Sterling's statement also alleged that the NBA has a history of discriminatory practices, which he supported with allegations of numerous lawsuits filed by NBA employees claiming gender-based discrimination. He ended his description of the NBA's discriminatory practices with the statement, "If the NBA is sincere about their approach, Adam Silver needs to publicly examine the NBA's own conduct and the conduct of each and every Owner." He continued (Golliver, 2014):

> For now, it seems Adam Silver is content with focusing his energy on violating my rights, attempting to take my property, and signing autographs for TMZ. Maybe once the dust settles, he will have some time to focus on the NBA's own transgressions. The NBA continues to thrive and exact its reign of terror in large part from the money it receives from the Fans. The NBA is a band of hypocrites and bullies. They will not stop until someone stands up.

He ended the statement with, "We have to fight for the rights of all Americans. We have to fight these despicable monsters. THIS IS THE REASON I WILL NOT SELL MY TEAM." In a CNN interview, Sterling stated. "I'm apologizing and I'm asking for forgiveness. Am I entitled to one mistake? After 35 years. I mean, I love my league, I love my partners . . . . It's a terrible mistake, and I'll never do it again" (Estrada, 2014).

Age as a Blame-Shifting Technique

Sterling is of the generation where the use of the N-word was not as commonplace unless it was used in a derogatory manner to demean African Americans. Because of these factors, Sterling resorted to using his age in his image repair tactics. Sterling's estranged wife, Shelly, reported to ABC's Barbara Walters that she believed her 80-year-old husband was suffering from the "onset of dementia." She thought this could be an explanation for his erratic behavior and mentioned her plans to "eventually" divorce him (Anderson, 2014).

According to *Forbes*, "The numerous press reports told us that two doctors had diagnosed him with dementia. . . . Many who saw him on TV or read about him from any news source might have wondered if he really did have dementia or if that allegation was just part of the fight over billions of dollars" (Rosenblatt, 2014). Sterling's image was used as part of the *evasion of responsibility* strategy and *blame shifting* to divert attention to "other" characteristics such as age to that could make his racial utterances acceptable among key audiences/supporters.

MEDIA AND AUDIENCE RESPONSE

The news media and the Internet play a critical role in reporting crises, incidents and news accounts, as journalists and news reports are legitimate sources of information for stakeholders and mass audiences. In today's digital age, the offender can quickly communicate a response using multimedia platforms such as the Internet, and social media to reach both a broad audience and targeted publics/stakeholders.

Anger toward Sterling spread rapidly through media platforms across the nation within a few hours after the news broke regarding Sterling's statements. Kontera, a company that measures Internet content and social media impressions for brand marketers, reported "200,000 tweets" about the announcement, with the most tweets being about the $2.5 million fine and "lifetime ban."

In response to this negative coverage, L.A. Clippers, head coach and senior vice president of Basketball Operations Doc Rivers, issued an official statement on behalf of the organization:

> I would like to reiterate how disappointed I am in the comments attributed to [Donald Sterling] and I can even begin to tell you how upset I am and our players are . . . from our fans' standpoint, I want to say that they have been amazing . . . we need unbelievable support right now from other people and I'm hoping we get that. (NBA, April 28, 2014)

Other individuals added to the social media outrage to vent their anger, disappointment and discontent with Sterling. CBS Sports reported that former NBA great and Bobcats owner Michael Jordan said, "As an owner, I'm obviously disgusted that a fellow team owner could hold such sickening and offensive views. . . . As a former player, I'm completely outraged. There is no room in the NBA—or anywhere else—for the kind of racism and hatred that Mr. Sterling allegedly expressed" (Bontemps, 2014).

CONCLUSIONS AND IMPLICATIONS

This study analyzed the use of image repair strategies by Sterling following his use of race-based hate speech in 2014. Findings provide important practical implications for public relations, crisis management and image repair scholars and public relations professionals as it has implications for celebrities, business owners and high-profile individuals who may need to use similar strategies to repair an image following a hate speech crisis.

This analysis revealed Sterling used four image repair strategies after negative publicity surfaced regarding his racist commentary: (1) *denial*, (2) *evade responsibility*, (3) *reduce offensiveness* and (4) *mortification*. Sterling's image repair tactics were not successful, primarily because he did not apologize right away and because he had a history of discriminating against black people in his low-income housing area inhabited by mostly minorities.

During this controversy, Sterling played the victim card to no avail, stating that he was jealous, and he did not know that he was being recorded using the hate-filled language that described African Americans and Hispanics in a pejorative manner. Society envisioned Sterling as a wealthy mogul who looked down on members of minority groups, although he employed many of them on his basketball team.

Chapter 5

Free Speech versus Hate Speech

An Image Restoration Case Study of Justin Bieber's use of the N-Word

In 2014, two videos surfaced featuring Bieber using the N-word. Both videos originated when the celebrity was a teenager. One featured him asking, "Why are black people afraid of chainsaws?" to which his friend responded, "Don't even say it." Bieber's response to the joke was, "Run n****r, n****r, n****r, n****r!" The other video featured him singing, "One Less Lonely Girl," replacing "girl" with the N-word. The video surfaced the first week in June of 2014 (Ross, 2014).

The literature suggests that hate speech is dangerous and entails a person with more power acting against a person or group with less power (Cunningham, Ferreira & Fink, 2009; Greene, 1995). Greene (1995) posits that the 1960s Civil Rights Movement graphically portrayed the violence associated with racial epithets, which "helped us to understand the relationship between hate speech and the question of equality both emotionally and intellectually" (p. 32). Scholars consider hate speech any communication that disparages a person or a group based on some characteristic such as race or sexual orientation (Levy & Karst, 2000, p. 1277).

Bieber used the N-word in a parody of one of his songs in which he directly attacked a racially oppressed group—African Americans. In the end, Beiber's use of the N-word created the need to repair his image. Bieber's incident provides the perfect case to explore race and image repair from a CRT perspective.

In another case involving the N-word, Len-Rios et al. (2015) used a multi-method approach to examine the use of social media in Paula Deen's image repair campaign in the wake of the *National Enquirer*'s revelation that she admitted to using the "N-word" during a lawsuit deposition. The researchers looked at the effectiveness of tweeted message strategies in a race-related crisis via Twitter. Study findings indicate her image repair strategies were unsuccessful because her apology did not center on the allegations, and she was contradictory in her bolstering, minimization and mortification strategies.

Similarly, Compton (2011) studied David Letterman's crisis management campaign following the joke he made aimed at Palin's older daughter that the audience perceived was aimed her younger daughter. The audience of the show believed the joke was too harsh for such a young girl who was not even involved in the media much. After making a first ineffective attempt to fix the problem, Letterman tried again and apologized to the Palin family directly. He admitted that he made a mistake and "promised to do better" (Compton, 2011). What made this image repair effort so effective was that Letterman promised to do better in the future. He was upfront, direct and explanatory about his mistake. Of course, humor was what led to the crisis, but it was also what helped remedy the situation in the end. Letterman came across likeable and apologetic, ultimately leading to a successful image repair.

European fashion icon John Galliano experienced an image-tarnishing crisis after a video of him expressing anti-Semitic beliefs and proclaiming, "I love Hitler," was obtained by British tabloid *The Sun* and released online, where it quickly spread across the Web in December of 2010. The video was allegedly taken of him during a dinner party after Galliano had consumed excessive amounts of alcohol. At one point, Galliano said to two Jewish Italian women in attendance, "People like you would be dead today. Your mothers, your forefathers would be f**ing gassed and dead," a hate-filled statement clearly referencing the Holocaust (Goldwert, 2011).

As a result, Galliano was fired from his position as the creative director of Christian Dior, a prominent brand in the fashion world from which Galliano earned much of his success. Galliano was fined by the court $16,500 dollars and a symbolic $1 dollar to his three victims as the judges ruled that he had "sufficient awareness of his act despite his addiction and his fragile state." The designer, who was intoxicated at the time of the incident, denied that he was in any way a racist and suffered from a triple addiction to alcohol, sleeping pills and Valium (Addley, 2013). He also gave many heartfelt apologies both to his victims specifically and to the public in general including one to *Women's Wear Daily* in which Galliano said:

> I am an alcoholic. I have been in recovery for the past two years. Several years prior to my sobriety, I descended into the madness of the disease. I said and did things that hurt others, especially members of the Jewish community. I have

expressed my sorrow privately and publicly for the pain that I caused, and I continue to do so. I remain committed to making amends to those I have hurt.

Galliano took time out of his career to focus on his health and sobriety. He has since been able to redeem his career because while his morals and ethics as an individual are questionable his talent and skill are not.

These cases illustrate the dimensions of image repair and racist rants. A person's age, circumstances and handling of the scandal have an impact on his or her successful image repair. These cases are helpful in building a case study about Bieber because many of these celebrities, athletes and public figures faced crises that parallel to that of the musician.

Building on this review of the literature, this three-pronged case study uses a critical race lens to analyze the racially charged comments made by Bieber. Specifically, it analyzes how the singer responded to the crisis via his personal statements and social media content. Additionally, it looks at how audiences and the media responded to Bieber's image repair tactics. The literature is lacking articles that focus on social media representations of the recent phenomena of race and culture.

Based on a review of the literature, the following research questions guided this analysis: What image repair tactics did Justin Bieber use following his racially charged incidents? How did media outlets and audiences respond? What are the implications of this case study for IRT and critical race studies?

TEXTS ANALYZED

Using a critical race lens, this IRT analysis looked at multiple texts to assess the image repair strategies of Justin Bieber following highly publicized racially charged incidents during which he used hate speech. Specifically, we looked at the celebrity's personal statements, social media accounts, news reports and public opinion reports surrounding the events to assess their image repair tactics.

Online sources are of interest because they were heavily used to help spread the word about Bieber. We gathered the texts used in our analysis by searching for Bieber's names on the Google search engine from November 2013 to May 5, 2014. The texts were read closely using a textual analysis. Texts analyzed included Bieber's personal statement of apology released on TMZ and his personal statement of apology released on his Twitter account and in *The Sun*. Public opinion polls were conducted by the following sources: MSNBC, Billboard.com, *Washington Post*/ABC News poll and E-Poll Market Research.

BACKGROUND

Born on March 1, 1994, Bieber, a Canadian native, immediately discovered his passion for music. The young Bieber excelled in hockey, soccer and chess, keeping his musical ambitions to himself. Participating in a local singing competition at the age of 12, Bieber took second place in the contest (Bartolomeo, 2010). His mother shared his video on YouTube in an effort to show his family and friends who missed his performances. Bieber and his mother soon discovered these videos attracted a larger audience than just family. Searching for another artist, Scooter Braun accidentally clicked on one of Bieber's homemade videos. The Atlanta-based music executive remembers feeling like "my gut was going crazy, so I tracked him down" ("Justin Bieber: Biography," 1981).

After sharing recording demos and more YouTube videos, Bieber sparked the attention of both Usher and Justin Timberlake. Usher ultimately won, signing the young star to Island Def Jam records. Usher recalls, "His voice was so magical and his personality was so keen, sometimes he's like a little brother or son to me" ("Justin Bieber: Biography," 1981). With Usher as his original "swagger coach," Justin's image transformed from the YouTube star to a world-renowned heartthrob ("Justin Bieber: Biography," 1981).

JUSTIN BIEBER'S IMAGE REPAIR TACTICS

While he waited five years to release the two videos that featured him using the "N-word," he never denied using the term. He owned up to his mistake. Bieber used many image repair tactics to repair his image. Most prominently, Bieber used *bolstering* and social media as a way of self-promotion, to depict himself as a family man and to share positive quotes. On June 3, for example, he tweeted: "Be kind and loving. It is a great way to live." The next day, he tweeted: "Family time." He also congratulated 2014 graduates and helped other artists promote movies and music.

Actor Kevin Hart thanked him for promoting his movie. Justin Bieber continued to demonstrate bolstering on June 18 when he posted information about participating in a Bible study with Judah Smith on his Twitter and Instagram accounts (Table 5.1).

Liu (2008) introduced endorsements as a newer image repair strategy in his analysis of Senator George Allen's image repair tactics following his use of the N-word. Bieber's also used third-party endorsements in his image repair tactics. Bieber has many friends and associates, such as Usher, who

Table 5.1 Justin Bieber's Image Restoration Tactics

Strategy	Supporting Sub-Strategy	Just Bieber's Actions Identified
Denial	1. Simple denial 2. Shifting the blame	1. While Bieber did not release the two videos of him using the "N-word" until five years later, he never denied using the term.
Evasion of responsibility	3. Provocation/attack the accuser 4. Defeasibility 5. Age reference	5. Bieber blamed his use of the racist term on his age. He was 14 or 15 when he made both videos.
Reduce Offensiveness	6. Transcendence 7. Minimization 8. Bolstering	6. Bieber stated he was parodying a parody of his song. 7. Bieber claimed he did not know the harm that using the word caused. 8. Justin Bieber, on June 18, 2014, posted information about participating in a Bible study with Judah Smith http://instagram.com/p/paUCURAvk4/
Mortification	9. Mortification	9. Bieber apologized immediately via statements in TMZ and *The Sun*.
Endorsement		10. TMZ, Usher and Will Smith and various other celebrities spoke on Bieber's behalf

are African American and who came to his defense after the release of the tape. Usher offered this statement in support of Bieber (O'Kelly, 2014):

> At my core, I am a person that supports growth and understands without judgment, that growth often comes as a result of pain and continues effort. As I have watched Justin Bieber navigate difficult waters as a young man, I can tell you that he hasn't always chosen the path of his greatest potential, but he is unequivocally not a racist.

Similarly, Bieber's roommate, Lil Za, showed his support on Instagram. On June 4, he posted, "This guy right here changed my life and others in many ways. A true brother and friend, you're appreciated and loved by all of us and millions of fans" (Ross, 2014). Worth noting is other celebrities responded negatively to Bieber's footage. Killer Mike stated, "Bieber you think you are Black, but you are really Yacoubian." Amanda Seales commented "GET HIM OUTTA HERE" (Tardio, 2014).

Bieber is a millennial who experimented with in-group language that is part of the vocabulary widely used by some African Americans in the hip-hop music industry. Bieber characterized himself as too young to know any better.

Mortification

While it took years for his video-taped racist jokes to surface, his apology was immediate upon the release of the video. TMZ released this statement ("Justin Bieber—I'm Sorry For My Racist Joke," 2014):

> Thanks to friends and family I learned from my mistakes and grew up and apologized for those wrongs. Now that these mistakes from the past have become public I need to apologize again to all those I have offended . . . Ignorance has no place in our society and I hope the sharing of my faults can prevent others from making the same mistake in the future. I thought long and hard about what I wanted to say but telling the truth is always what is right. Five years ago I made a reckless and immature mistake and I'm grateful to those close to me who helped me learn those lessons as a young man. Once again....I'm sorry.

In Bieber's statement, he spoke of learning from his mistakes four times. The repetition of the word "mistake" indicates he does not plan to use the N-word publicly again. He apologizes twice in the statement and says he is "sorry" once, which is an indication he is apologetic for making use of the N-word. He states that ignorance and youth are not an excuse for using hate speech directed at underrepresented groups.

Likewise, following the release of his second video using the N-word, Bieber issued this apology on his Twitter account and in *The Sun*, which leaked the video:

> Facing my mistakes from years ago has been one of the hardest things I've ever dealt with. But, I feel now that I need to take responsibility for those mistakes and not let them linger. Once again, I am sorry for all those I have let down and offended. I just hope that the next kid that age who doesn't understand the power of these words does not make the same mistake I once made years ago. At the end of the day I just need to step up and own what I did.

As with his other statement, the word "mistake" is mentioned three times in this statement. He spoke of making mistakes and taking responsibility for those mistakes. He reiterates that he is sorry for using this type of language and emphasizes that he was young when he made this statement.

Media and Audience Response

The news media and the Internet play a critical role in reporting crises, incidents and news accounts, as journalists and news reports are legitimate sources of information for stakeholders and mass audiences.

Media response was mixed for Bieber. For instance, Mitchell (2014) reported that on June 4 Bieber had posted a photo on Instagram of Bible verses that definitely showed his pain and regret over the leaked videos. He took full responsibility for what he said, but did not "understand the power of certain words and how they can hurt" when he was younger. Justin is definitely going to need to issue another apology in the wake of the recent video leak (Mitchell, 2014). Likewise, TMZ focused on the idea that Bieber made the videos when he was young and was very sorry.

However, other sources were not as positive in their framing of the incident. Bieber's use of the endorsement strategy was not well received by Morris O'Kelly, host of *The Mo'Kelly Show* and author of *The Mo'Kelly Report* stated that Usher used the classic tool of the straw man tactic in an attempt to protect Justin Bieber, his investment (O'Kelly, 2014). He described a straw man as a "flawed argumentation technique based on the misrepresentation of the issue. It is answering a question not asked and/or making a claim not in contention." O'Kelly added (2014):

> In today's world it is convention to label people as "racists," categorizing people with respect to behavior. All-too-often, people misalign any "racially offensive behavior" with being a "racist." From Paula Deen to Donald Sterling and now Justin Bieber, the straw man argument revolves around debunking whether (insert celebrity name) is a "racist." When you fall into the trap, you've already missed the point.

In a tongue-in-cheek column, *People South Africa* stated, "Justin Bieber is reportedly crying frequently due to the backlash over his use of a racial slur. The 20-year-old pop star caused widespread outrage this week after footage of him using the N-word in two videos was made public" ("Justin Bieber 'crying a lot,'" 2014).

Public opinion polls indicated people did not find Bieber's apology sincere. For example, an MSNBC reporter asked, "Do you accept Justin Bieber's apology for using the N-word?" Of those individuals who took the poll, 236 responded yes; 167 responded he should do more to address the issue; and 441 responded No ("Do you accept Justin Bieber's apology for using the N-word as a teenager?," 2014). In another survey, Bieber ranked fifth in a ranking of the most hated men in America (Table 5.2).

A poll on Billboard.com had similar results. In response to the question, "Was Justin Bieber's racist joke understandable or unforgivable?" 81.56 percent chose "Unforgivable! This is the last straw. I'm done rooting for Justin Bieber." Of those individuals who responded, 13.79 percent chose "Understandable! That video is from years ago, and Justin has already apologized for his past mistakes," while 4.65 percent chose "I'm still angry about the incident, but Justin apologized, and that's all he can do" (Lipshutz, 2014).

Table 5.2   Rankings of the Most Hated Men in America

Rank	Name	%
1	Donald Sterling	92
2	Bernie Madoff	90
3	O. J. Simpson	88
4	Conrad Murray	88
5	Justin Bieber	86
6	Phil Spector	83
7	Aaron Hernandez	81
8	Michael Lohan	76
9	Eliot Spitzer	73
10	John Goselin	71

E-Poll Market Research.

Conclusions and Implications

This study analyzed the use of image repair strategies by Justin Bieber, revealing that Bieber actively used three image repair tactics (1) *mortification,* (2) *defeasibility* and (3) *minimizing action.* Findings provide important practical implications for public relations, crisis management and image repair scholars and public relations professionals as it has implications for celebrities, business owners and high-profile individuals who may need to use similar strategies to repair an image following a hate speech crisis.

Bieber's case involved the use of satire—singling out and targeting a person's race as the basis of mockery operates within a context of victim shaming and blaming. In such situations, one must observe the perpetrator's intention of using humor to explicitly acknowledge a prejudice or hatred toward a marginalized group. In this instance, Bieber spoofed one of his songs and inserted the N-word. The spoof highlighted undesirable qualities of the minority group in question. This form of hate speech created the need for image repair for Bieber.

Secondly, Bieber's profession and peer group made a difference in how people perceived his transgressions. Bieber is a celebrity whose fans are in the teen to mid-20 range. Bieber continued to make headlines throughout 2014 because of run-ins with law enforcement officials; however, his image was repaired with his target audience.

Bieber's reputation has survived numerous allegations, including going to brothels, a DUI, and smoking marijuana. And while the media is not always forgiving in its coverage of Bieber, his fans continued to support him. Bieber has more than 73 million followers on Twitter and 73.6 million followers on Facebook. He is one of the few celebrities to ever have earned a Klout score of 100 (Wong, 2010).

Chapter 6

What Happens on Twitter
stays on Twitter

Black Twitter, "#NiggerNavy" and the
Image Repair Tactics of Yahoo Finance

In continuance with our theme of image repair following corporate or individual use of the N-word, this chapter briefly explores how the ever-increasing presence of social media has significantly changed the ways in which the public receives and responds to race-related messages. Social media platforms allow individuals to participate actively in crisis communication and to become opinion generators. Because of this change, preparation for the possibility of image repair has become essential for almost anyone in the spotlight. The necessity of image repair strategies has become more important today as polls indicate 81 percent of the world's population has a social media profile. The increased use of social media has a direct correlation with the speed of release for traditional media outlets and social media platforms (Statistica, 2017).

With more than 336 million monthly active users worldwide as of 2018, Twitter is one of the more noteworthy social networks in the world (Statistica, 2018). The social networking site has become an important tool for marketers and celebrities to connect with their respective audiences in real time.

For the African American experience in social media—Twitter offers a "cultural identity consisting of Black Twitter users from around the world on the Twitter social network focused on issues of interest to the black community, particularly in the United States" (Brock, 2012). African Americans' presence and engagement in social media interaction has taken the Twitter platform to another level of interaction and message meaning. A *Washington Post* article provides insight on the subtleties of Black Twitter (McDonald, 2014, n.p.):

Understanding the ethos of Black Twitter can be a high bar to clear if you've never socialized significantly with black people. You may not understand that

51

when someone says, "*sips tea*" they don't mean it literally. It's shorthand for conveying a low, barely perceptible drone of contempt, similar to the back-handed compliments and clever passive-aggression that comprise shade. Plenty of cultures have shade, even if it's not identified as such. When a Southerner wraps a well-concealed insult with a treacly "Bless your heart," she is being shady. There are levels. (n.p.)

McDonald (2014) reported that a 2013 Pew Research Center study found African Americans use Twitter at higher rates than other ethnic groups:

Those large numbers mean that a community has evolved online to reflect one that has long existed offline. The difference is now it's out in the open for any-one to observe. (n.p.)

During the 21st century, many African Americans shifted to Twitter to share memes, videos and other social media content, addressing social and cultural issues. Black Twitter offered an online platform for African Americans to share content on race-related issues that may have otherwise gone unnoticed (Williams, 2015).

Black Twitter heated up on January 5, 2017, after Yahoo Finance mis-spelled "bigger," using the N-word, in a tweet about president-elect Donald Trump's plans to enlarge America's Navy (Figure 6.1). Despite Yahoo Finance's speedy correction and apology for the error, Black Twitter users shared the tweet containing the N-word more than 2,000 times. A variety of memes mocked the incident. Memes often provide an outlet for public conversations on topics such as gender, race and culture. In this prominent example, memes offered a high-profile response to the incident that fostered interest and support in racial equality for African Americans.

Social media platforms, in general, have become a powerful way to dis-seminate messages about the circumstances of a crisis to a wide range of audiences (Hutchins & Tindall, 2016). Social media simultaneously change the way organizations disseminate and receive information and respond to stakeholders. Social media content has the potential to hurt or repair one's image, depending on how individuals use it.

Previous studies on social media and image repair have analyzed the use of social media to repair the reputations of individuals and corporations (i.e., Lancaster & Boyd, 2015; Moody, 2011; Rasmussen, 2015). Meme-related studies have highlighted the influence of memes in different contexts, particu-larly their power to change public opinion and to promote social movements (Harlow, 2013; Hristova, 2014; Sci & Dare, 2014). Memes have been studied from various other perspectives including definition of the term and the role memetic texts have played in political debate, protests and online conversa-tions (i.e., Dawkins, 2006; Shifman, 2013, Spitzberg, 2014).

Yahoo Finance ✅
@YahooFinance

Trump wants a much nigger navy: Here's how much it'll cost yhoo.it/2iVAieO

10:01 PM · 05 Jan 17

Figure 6.1 Yahoo Finance Tweet Featuring the Word "Nigger" Instead of "Bigger."

However, absent from the literature are studies that examine IRT, race-related memes and the image repair of corporations. As such, this study fills a void in the literature with an examination of social media and image repair (Stein, 2010). Specifically, it looks at Yahoo Finance's apology and Black Twitter's response following the company's accidental use of the N-word. As society adopts new media, Benoit (2014), recommends they investigate image repair in new settings.

While short lived, Yahoo Finance's crisis merits scholarly attention for several reasons. This study breaks new ground, as it is one of the first to analyze how Black Twitter's "clapback" culture may be used as an image repair tactic. Unlike other image repair cases in which celebrities used remorse and mortification, Yahoo Finance primarily took a back seat in its own image restoration process and others took control—using social media.

Secondly, this brief study illustrates how social media have become a necessary platform for dissent, discussion and breaking news. "Black Twitter," in particular, offers an outlet for black people to express their ideas and opinions publicly in the 21st century (Williams, 2015). For instance, using

#blacklivesmatter, Black Twitter users informed the world what was happening regarding the murders of black men and women—popularizing the cases of Michael Brown, Eric Garner and many other Blacks. In essence, "Black Twitter" created an online culture of black intellectuals, trendsetters and talking heads giving voice to many of the issues that 20 years earlier would have remained far away from the mainstream radar (Williams, 2015).

Black Twitter offers the means for individuals to respond to a negative situation in a relaxed environment. As mass media continue to transform the need to study group interactions in new media environments increases in importance. Scholars must continue to test all mass media theories, and existing media theories are the most efficient way to account for trends.

THEORETICAL FRAMEWORK: MEDIUM THEORY

As mentioned in chapter 3, medium theory uses a variety of approaches to examine how the means of expression of human communication impact the meanings of human communications. Meyrowitz (1985) coined the term in his book *No Sense of Place*, to describe the incorporation of history and culture in studying media. One reason for the general reassessment of medium theory among critical theorists and others concerned with issues of political power may be that the fear of top-down control over information and thought is not as good a fit for the era of the personal computer, Internet, mobile phone and other new technologies.

Marshall McLuhan is perhaps the best-known medium theorist. McLuhan explored how each medium offers a unique environment for audiences to share and experience messages. The scholar investigated and described the differences between the digital media and printed media, even before World Wide Web and email system formed the network society.

It is worth noting that medium type plays a tremendous role in the ways in which individuals share messages (McLuhan, 1964). In the 20th century, radio, tape recordings, records, TV shows and movies were used to disseminate messages. In the 21st century, social media changed how such content was delivered. The rapid communication of how social media makes information travel presents the use of the theory of image repair by Benoit even more challenging than ever before.

Medium type is important in IRT, as social media creates an incredible impact on perception of information, especially for how it travels from channel to channel. Converged media creates the possibility of a complex network of media in which several kinds of technology are involved. As a result, users have a high capacity to produce and receive content as cable and satellite delivery have helped to eliminate restrictions of cost, distance and capacity.

There are various implications for the importance of social media in image repair. First, the formative use of celebrities engaging with audiences on social media creates a means of authenticity and emotional attachment that may not occur with traditional media (Kowalczyk, 2016). In today's highly connected world, the ability to ruin a person's or company's reputation can begin with one simple social media post. One of the risks of social media includes the share of materials aligned with the user's views, which can be seen as positively or negatively to the audience. This influence of social media can be seen in the lives of celebrities. Kowalczyk (2016) concluded that social media has changed communication, specifically in regards to famous individuals. Followers want to know about the personal lives of celebrities—and activism is a key part of that.

BLACK TWITTER AND THE "CLAPBACK" CULTURE

Twitter, which turned 11 years old in 2017, changed how people communicated and was especially significant for black users. The segment of the population, collectively known as Black Twitter, used the platform to "clap back" (giving appropriate, sharp-tongued answers to negative messages from others) at social injustices and to drive visibility to discussions about black life and culture, led by those who knew it best: black people (Dates & Moody, 2018; Workneh, 2016). Popular "clapback" hashtags included: #Oscarssowhite, #blackgirlmagic., #StayMadAbby, #NiggerNavy, #ThanksgivingClapback and #YouOKSis.

Particularly relevant in this study are memes, which often include pictures juxtaposed with text that are replicated until the pictures transcend the importance of the original posting and its underlying work (Shifman, 2013). The Internet provides a participatory platform to display memes that allows anyone to contribute to dialogue on a particular topic (Mina, 2014). Online memes spread fast, mutate significantly and remain active for a period of time (Hristova, 2014).

As such, Black Twitter memes have taken on some heavy-hitting issues, including "Stay Mad Abby," which highlighted Abigail Fisher, whose case against affirmative action was argued in front of the U.S. Supreme Court after Fisher was rejected from the University of Texas at Austin in 2008. She claimed that it was because she was white. In another example, Black Twitter clapped back with #AskRachel questions, which quizzed readers on their true blackness. The questions built on the idea Rachel Dolezal knew a lot about black culture; however, she was not truly black because she could revert to white at any time. #AskRachel quizzes included questions such as the following: What color is potato salad (yellow)? Who did Erykah Badu call on (Tyrone)? How should a child pay for food at McDonald's (McDonald's money)?

More recently, Black Twitter spotlighted the "BBQing While Black" incident during which a woman called police officers on a black family barbecuing in the park. Oakland police arrived; no one was arrested. The 25-minute episode was captured on video, then posted on YouTube, where it was viewed more than two million times. The incident was memed hundreds of times with images featuring a white woman in sunglasses showing up to various locations and events, including Dr. Martin Luther King, Jr.'s monumental speech, a *Soul Train* taping and the Oval Office during Barack Obama's presidency.

One of the few examples of mainstream companies clapping back occurred when Ambien maker Sanofi Aventis responded to Roseanne Barr, who blamed the sedative for the racist tweet she posted that resulted in the cancellation of her show, *Roseanne.* Barr wrote that she was "ambien tweeting" when she compared former Obama adviser Valerie Jarrett to the spawn of "Muslim brotherhood & planet of the apes." Sanofi responded:

> People of all races, religions and nationalities work at Sanofi every day to improve the lives of people around the world. While all pharmaceutical treatments have side effects, racism is not a known side effect of any Sanofi medication.

While Black Twitter responses are not a replacement for traditional image repair tactics such as mortification and corrective action, they provide a platform to help tackle tough issues that might aid in the image restoration process of an individual or a company. This chapter breaks new ground by attempting to document this trend.

IRT AND HATE SPEECH

Given its focus on stereotypes and narratives told from the standpoint of people of color, CRT is useful in a study of this nature. In this case, hate speech is relevant, as Yahoo Finance inadvertently shared the N-word in its Twitter post. Hate speech is defined as any communication that disparages a person or a group based on characteristic such as race or sexual orientation (Levy & Karst, 2000).

Harris, Rowbotham and Stevenson (2009) assert that an inevitable problem in any discussion of hate speech lies in the difficulty of identifying it in different situations. Racial, ethnic or sexual epithets must be judged contextually. Some pejorative terms are okay when used within a community as a means of reclaiming offensive language for themselves, such as women using the term "bitch," Black American use of the N-word or the use of "queer" within the gay community (Harris, Rowbotham & Stevenson, 2009, p. 157).

Individual social networking websites have their own definitions of hate. Google and YouTube ban content that attacks or demeans a group based on race or ethnic origin, religion, disability, gender, age, veteran status and sexual orientation or gender identity. Though sites may include offensive words, content is considered hate speech only if comments or videos target a person simply because of his or her membership in a certain group. YouTube counts on its users to know the guidelines and to flag videos that they believe violate guidelines. It also has a help and safety tool.

As indicated in the Justin Bieber case study in this text, the N-word is thought by many to be the worst racial slur (Anderson & Lepore, 2013). For some individuals, the mention of the N-word conjures up memories of slavery, lynchings and other atrocities against African Americans. Therefore, the question of whether it was hate speech is relevant.

Social Media and Image Repair

Anyone with Internet access can share messages that may challenge practitioner efforts to ensure that goal-oriented and accurate content is disseminated (Rasmussen, 2015). Social media allow for information to be spread greatly and quickly. Through followers and subscriptions, information can flow to a multitude of people in a matter of minutes.

Previous studies indicate individuals and companies have used social media with varying levels of success. Rasmussen's (2015) case study of Planned Parenthood Federation of America provides a look at an attack the organization encountered after video footage appeared to show Planned Parenthood staff disregarding statutory rape and abortion reporting laws and aiding sex traffickers. The footage posted on YouTube quickly went viral, placing Planned Parenthood at the forefront of national news, which sparked debate over government funding the organization. Rasmussen (2015) concluded while social media was a catalyst to causing the crisis; it was also a valuable tool for managing it.

Similarly, Lancaster and Boyd (2015) examined how farmer Gary Conklin responded to allegations of animal abuse by activists who secretly filmed and then released videos via social media. The two concluded Conklin succeeded in repairing his image by using corrective actions. For instance, in addition to removing an employee, he announced he would perform more thorough and careful background checks on potential employees. He began having employee classes and updated employee handbooks to more clearly outline proper handling techniques. He also posted "No Trespassing" signs around the farm's property and required all employees to report any policy violations. Conklin's combination of separation plus corrective action offered a successful formula for demonstrating sincerity and contributed to the organization's legitimacy.

In another study, Moody (2011) concluded that Jon and Kate Gosselin of the popular TLC reality show, *Jon and Kate Plus 8*, handled their case with varying degrees of success. The two were wildly different in the ways they reacted to the accusations and stories coming out about them. Kate did not use social media in the beginning phases of her divorce and its aftermath. She primarily stuck to traditional media, which did not help her much at all because she was sending conflicting messages to the public. However, when she began to utilize social media and began blogging, she was able to connect with the public more effectively through personal stories and photographs. "Blogs can win over publics and improve relationships employing the conversational human voice factor and the responsiveness/customer service factor . . . this may be that establishing and regularly updating a blog gives the impression that an organization is not shying away from discussion of the incident in question" (Sweetser, 2007).

When one can successfully connect to their audience through a blog, they can expect real results in terms of image repair. Jon, on the other hand, went straight to social media. Unfortunately, instead of using his Twitter to express remorse and hurt for the downfall of his family, he used social media to place blame on others while also keeping himself in traditional media, but not with interviews and articles, like Kate, but with irresponsible behavior. Eventually, Jon realized that when he focused on family and his children on social media, the public was much more receptive to his initial feelings. From Moody's case study, we can see how taking responsibility on social media can have a positive impact on image. When one continues to interact with fans and the public through Twitter or blogs, and is honest about their feelings in a responsible and respectable way, the media and public are much less harsh on the way they view you.

Conversely, Tiger Woods' case study provides a different outcome (Bernstein, 2012). Almost a year after he established his Twitter account, Woods finally began to use it in a positive way, following his 2009 affair exposed on Thanksgiving. It was no secret that Woods had fallen from the graces of public; however, with one tweet, "What's up everyone. Finally decided to try out twitter!" he began to etch his way back into mainstream society. Before that tweet, Woods had only tweeted to announce that his Twitter, Facebook and Website had undergone a redesign, but with his new determination to connect with the public gained him over 40,000 followers within three hours (Bernstein, 2012). After the initial tweet, he began to tweet about his children and the fun and rewarding aspects about being a father. It is evident from looking at Woods experience with Twitter that one tweet can change the way the public views you. We can learn that when one is present in social media, the public will listen, no matter the mistakes you've made in the past, they are always willing to see a comeback.

Timeliness can play a huge role in the success of crisis management. Arnold Schwarzenegger won his way into American hearts with his witty comments and infamous one-liners through his several films. When he first began his run for governor, several allegations on him about sexual harassment came forward. Schwarzenegger, in the beginning, denied all claims and evaded the responsibility of his actions, but then decided that he should own up to his mistakes in interviews because the allegations kept coming forward. "I keep saying it now and I said it yesterday, I'm sure that some of it was true. Many of the stories I can't recall," admitted Schwarzenegger (Hernandez et al., 2011).

The governor frequently used his Twitter account to discuss politics and his life in general. However, in the midst of his scandal, Schwarzenegger took a break from posting. There is about a month that the politician was absent from the social media site, not even acknowledging his family crisis. Other members of his family, his son and daughter, voiced their opinions about the topic and made it known that even though the family hit a bump in the road, they will stand by each other and will always love one another, therefore winning favor in the public (Hernandez et al., 2011). Scholars concluded Schwarzenegger stuck to traditional media when he should have also used new media platforms. When responding to a crisis campaign involving race-related issues special consideration must be taken to ensure the appropriate sensitivity and cultural awareness. Len-Rios et al. (2015) discuss Paula Deen's crisis campaign in response to a particular racial scandal the celebrity chef faced in 2013.

Based on a review of the literature, the following questions guided this study: (1) What types of memes emerged following the #Niggernavy crisis? (2) What image restoration tactics Yahoo Financial use following the mistake (3) How did Twitter users respond to these tactics?

TEXTS ANALYZED

Because of the uneasiness affiliated with talking about race, analyses of critical race humor offer a viable alternative that allows individuals to engage in conversations about racial truths and trends. Using a critical race lens, this IRT analysis examined multiple texts to assess the image repair strategies of Yahoo Finance following highly publicized racially charged incidents during which the Twitter account included a post with the N-word. Specifically, the study used a content analysis to analyze Yahoo Finance's image restoration efforts across both traditional media channels and social media platforms.

The sample for analysis included: (1) tweets published immediately follow-ing the #NiggerNavy crisis; (2) Apology tweet posted by Yahoo Finance.

To collect articles, memes and online content on the topic, we used the keywords "nigger navy" and "yahoo finance." Using these keywords, we collected five online articles, Yahoo Finance's response tweet and the top 150 memes shared on Twitter. The rationale for using Google to collect the top memes was they were commonly shared across social media platforms. They also provide a snapshot of what Americans cared about during the inci-dent. This sample proved enlightening for providing an overview for how the Nigger Navy crises evolved in the year following its occurrence and Yahoo Finance, which is a media platform that provides financial news, including stock quotes, press releases and financial reports.

Each meme was read closely using a textual analysis. Through intense interaction with text, one can achieve confidence that his or her analysis makes sense and goes beyond mere opinion. This methodology provided an effective means of analysis for the image repair tactics Yahoo Finance used in response to the 2017 Nigger Navy crisis.

MEDIA COVERAGE OF #NIGGERNAVY

Media response to the incident was scant. Yahoo Finance's crisis was handled solely in an online setting. Reference to the crisis was absent in newspapers and magazines. Two primary online articles emerged that were often quoted by other blogs: Buzzfeed published one article, which chronicled the error and what happened afterwards. Likewise, knowyourmeme.com provided an informative timeline of the incident.

YAHOO FINANCE'S RESPONSE

In reviewing Yahoo Finance's response, it appears the crisis, which origi-nated on social media, was also handled on social media. Mortification was the most prominent IRT strategy Yahoo employed. Yahoo Finance immedi-ately deleted the original tweet containing the N-word and issued another one containing an apology: "We deleted an earlier tweet due to a spelling error. We apologize for the mistake" (Finance, 2017).

As mentioned in previous chapters, mortification is the most effective image restoration tactic. Individuals and corporations that use mortification are generally successful in repairing their image. In this case, it appears Yahoo Finance's apology was accepted. Upon apologizing, most of the responses to the crisis were humorous in nature.

Figure 6.2   Apology Tweet Issued by Yahoo Finance.

Twitter users joked about the accidental tweet in an open social media setting, choosing to make light of the incident rather than to get upset. Buzzfeed traced the initial tweet to one Twitter user, stating the trend appears to have been started by @JeSuisDawn" (Griffin, 2017).

Audience Response

Black Twitter's "clapback" culture has become more common on Black Twitter as African Americans often decide to take care of an issue on their own rather than wait for society to handle it. This trend is illustrated in this case study. Memes featuring pop culture icons, images and narratives, were particularly popular to address the crisis. Twitter users chose to "clapback," rather than get upset about the offensive tweet.

Several themes emerged in the memes following Yahoo Finance's typographical error and apology (Figure 6.2), including stereotypes of black people in general, rationale for the error and images of various celebrities with a caption, and other images to express how funny the error and resulting hashtags were.

Other memes appeared to defend Yahoo Finance. Twitter users emphasized the humor of the error and the tweets that emerged in response. They indicated Nigger Navy was the funniest thing that had ever happened on the platform. Posts included: "#NiggerNavy had me crying real tears, like my stomach was hurting y'all." "Aye highkey #NiggerNavy was one of the funniest modern twitter hashtags since OG twitter in 2012."

Many of the memes shared in response to the error included gifs of various celebrities making faces to demonstrate their disgust. Cartoon characters, singers and actors from popular TV shows and movies included SpongeBob,

Seal and Snoop Dogg. Another tweet contained an image of Bae Bae's kids (from a 1990s movie) and the caption, "collective black confusion."

Memes Twitter users shared in response to the Nigger Navy crisis also emphasized stereotypes of black people—narratives of black people that have been shared for generations—the idea that African Americans are colorful, unreliable and often habitually late. Examples of memes containing stereotypes of black people included "#NiggerNavy gonna be two years late to the war" (Round, 2017). "#NiggerNavy the boat would stay leaning." ("Scrill Murray on Twitter: '#NiggerNavy the boat would stay leaning,'" n.d.).

Other Twitter users offered a rationale for why the error may have occurred, which served to defend Yahoo Finance's apology. Memes in this category, for instance, often pointed out that the letters "B" and "N" are neighbors on the keyboard, and it is common for people to accidentally press the wrong letter or to confuse the two. One such meme featured a cat frantically pounding a keyboard with a tweet that read "Delete delete delete!" (Tatko-Peterson, 2017).

CONCLUSIONS AND IMPLICATIONS

The shift in media platforms has created the necessity to revisit traditional theories to interpret content and audience interactions. To assess the public's reaction to the #NiggerNavy crisis, this brief analysis examined online news articles and blog entries posted to various news outlets.

Worth noting is we expected to find a bigger response from Yahoo Finance. However, we discovered it handled the cases by apologizing and moving on. While Yahoo Finance apologized for the tweet, it issued a tweet containing the N-word, much of its image restoration occurred after Black Twitter users began to share memes addressing the incident. Twitter users used various tactics, including emphasizing that the post was an honest mistake. Other Twitter users took advantage of the opportunity to invoke images of black people and common stereotypes. This demonstrates that user response can generate humor in a situation where a typo caused a stir about racism, and ultimately, the company faced the controversy head on, which was the best strategy when seeking clarity and redemption.

This study indicates humorous tweets offer an effective strategy to repair one's image. Black Twitter users discussed Yahoo Finance's error, used humor to handle it, then moved on. On the anniversary of the crisis, Twitter users continued to frame it as one of the all-time funniest moments on Black Twitter.

This study is important as it provides one of the first examples of social media policing itself. It also illustrates how social media is a two-edged sword—often creating the need to repair a tarnished image while also providing the platform to do so. Study findings have important implications for incidents in which individuals and corporations use the N-word. Because of the mortification stance Yahoo Finance took immediately following the incident, the company managed to keep the crisis confined to the social media platform, Twitter. Yahoo Finance removed the tweet right away and apologized, which limited negative media coverage of the mishap.

As mass media continue to transform, the need to study group interactions in new media environments increases in importance. Scholars must continue to test all mass media theories, and existing media theories are the most efficient way to account for trends.

Worth noting is while the Black Twitter "clapback" culture is not a replacement for true image restoration tactics such as mortification and corrective action, it certainly provides a platform to help tackle tough issues that might aid in the image restoration process. However, this image restoration tactic must be studied in other settings along with audience response to help gauge the effectiveness of the use of the "clapback" method as a legitimate image restoration tactic, worthy of further investigation.

This study provides a springboard for future research focusing on social media, memes and Black Twitter. Study findings will increase in importance as contemporary protest movements continue to use social media to influence, organize and protest various causes, particularly those that include elements of race. Scholars must continue to explore social media and the dynamics of freedom of speech.

Chapter 7

Fighting Words

An Image Restoration Study of Hulk Hogan's Use of the N-word

INTRODUCTION

Terry Bollea, known to many as Hulk Hogan, is a noted pro-wrestler, television producer, entrepreneur and film producer. At the height of his career, he appeared in various movies including *Rocky III, 3 Ninjas: High Noon at Mega Mountain, Suburban Commando,* and *Hogan Knows Best.* In 2015, Hogan lost his superstar status; however, after court documents demonstrated he had made brutally racist statements regarding his daughter's African American boyfriend. Transcripts featuring his remarks were submitted to a Florida court as part of Hogan's lawsuit against the website, Gawker.com. Hogan's statements, which were included in a sex tape, include candid moments during which Hogan discusses his daughter's relationship with a "black billionaire":

> I don't know if Brooke was f*cking the black guy's son. I mean, I don't have double standards. I mean, I am a racist, to a point, f*cking n*ggers. But then when it comes to nice people and sh*t, and whatever. I mean, I'd rather if she was going to f*ck some n*gger, I'd rather have her marry an 8-foot-tall n*gger worth a hundred million dollars! Like a basketball player! I guess we're all a little racist. Fucking n*gger.

Hogan later apologized for his rant and won a settlement from Gawker, but it was too late to undo the damage the statement had done to his image. He was scrubbed from WWE's website and erased from the WWE Hall of Fame (Trotter, 2015). The WWE terminated Hogan's employment, including his role on WWE's "Tough Enough" (Manfred, 2015). These severed ties and the public's perception of Hogan created the need for the superstar to repair his image.

The ex-pro wrestler's lawsuit against Gawker Media was the second attempt to make the media company pay for invading his privacy, but this time for leaking his pejorative comments about African Americans. Hogan had already won a legal victory of $140 million for publishing a short excerpt of a sex tape with his friend Bubba the Love Sponge's wife, Heather Clem, in 2006, and ultimately reached a $31 million settlement with Gawker Media for leaking audio of the N-word rant (McAlone, 2016).

The use of the N-word by mainstream Americans is not a new occurrence. For centuries, the term "nigger" has been used as part of American vernacular to negatively and hatefully define African Americans. "Nigger" is thought by many people to be the worst racial slur (Anderson & Lepore, 2013). It has even been referred to as the "filthiest, dirtiest, nastiest word in the English language" (Kennedy, 2002, p. 23). Black critics note the specific trauma that accompanies the word. The hate speech literature suggests language can have powerfully harmful effects that may be comparable to other negative behaviors such as rape, domestic violence, assault and robbery (O'Dea et al., 2015; Stein, 2010).[1]

For some individuals, the mere mention of "nigger" conjures up memories of slavery, lynchings and bombings (Allan, 2015). However, O'Dea et al.'s 2015 findings suggest that one's reactions to racial slurs depend on the context in which the slur is used and the perceiver's beliefs about the social appropriateness of expressing prejudice. The term has also been used by African Americans, but is considered "in-group" speech with a different meaning than racist speech of others.

For instance, in discussing the N-word in a different context, former U.S. president Barack Obama explained how the N-word is bigger than the word itself. While taping the "WTF with Marc Maron" podcast, the first African American president was asked about the issue of race and the Charleston, South Carolina, church massacre that claimed the lives of Senator Clementa Pinckney and eight other church members.

> Racism, we are not cured of it. And it's not just a matter of it not being polite to say n*gger in public. . . . That's not the measure of whether racism still exists or not. It's not just a matter of overt discrimination. Societies don't, overnight, completely erase everything that happened 200 to 300 years prior.

President Obama's spokesman explained Obama's use of a racial slur was to underscore his point that while the United States has made great progress on race relations, more work needs to be done.

Although using the N-word is considered unacceptable for most, its use by Caucasians is considered to be hate speech due to its prevalent connection to white supremacy and oppression.[2] Thus, Caucasians who use the term and are publicly exposed tend to find themselves apologizing and seeking redemption in the public sphere in contemporary times.

Using critical race theory and Benoit's image repair theory (IRT), this case study explores Hulk Hogan's use of image repair strategies following his 2015 use of the N-word. The goal of this study is threefold: (1) to explore representations of the N-word at different points in history, (2) to study how celebrities and organizations incorporate image repair tactics as part of their image restoration strategies and (3) to examine the intersection of race and image restoration.

Previous literature indicates celebrities employ various tactics for image repair, ranging from issuing statements via multimedia platforms to making appearances on news programs—in an attempt to reach stakeholders and gain favorable news coverage in the court of public opinion. Benoit (1995) posits that persuasive defensive utterances are attempts to "reshape another's beliefs, to change his or her belief that the act in question was wrongful, or to shift his or her attribution of responsibility for that act" (p. 6).

Similarly, Brazeal (2008) suggests that a proactive strategy garners favorable media coverage. Kennedy (2010) posits that admitting guilt is better than denial, and if a person is innocent, they should quickly defend themselves. Benoit's IRT suggests that "human beings engage in recurrent patterns of communicative behavior designed to reduce, redress, or avoid damage to their reputation (or face or image) from perceived wrongdoing" (Burns & Burner, 2000, p. 27). In this case study, there is a relationship between Hulk Hogan's discourse and the intended goal for the discourse relative to multiple audiences.

BENOIT'S TYPOLOGY OF IMAGE REPAIR

Benoit's (1995) IRT provides the ideal theoretical framework to investigate Hulk Hogan's response strategies as a public figure and celebrity. Benoit's typology of image repair identifies five general strategies commonly used to make attempts to either repair or perhaps restore an image: denial, evading responsibility, reducing offensiveness, corrective action and mortification. Within this typology of 5 strategies are 12 subcategories, including: simple denial, shifting the blame, provocation, defeasibility, accident, good intentions, bolstering, minimization, differentiation, transcendence, attack accuser and compensation.

Image repair strategies practiced by persons who use racial slurs and other types of offensive language vary. A review of the literature reveals several prominent studies (Len-Rios et al., 2015; Lui, 2007; Schmittel & Hull, 2015; Stein, 2010). While there have been other IRT studies, they rarely deal with issues of race. Even rarer are studies that examine image restoration and social media platforms. The case studies examined in this chapter provide different perspectives on how to respond in hate speech-related scandals.

Stein (2010), for instance, assessed the appropriateness and effective-ness of apologia to counteract hateful speech with an examination of the Jewish community's response to Mel Gibson's racist comments directed at police officers in Malibu, California. Gibson's tirade included the follow-ing statements: "F*****g Jews. The Jews are responsible for all the wars in the world." Gibson then asked one of the officers, "Are you a Jew?" (Stein, 2010).

Following Mel Gibson's arrest, the fallout from his remarks was wide-spread. Media commentary often compared the controversy surrounding the actor's racial tirade with the accusations of anti-Semitism following Gibson's film *The Passion of the Christ*. Once Gibson's antics became front-page news, the actor felt compelled to issue a series of apologies (Stein, 2010).

Gibson used a variety of apologia strategies in his statement released after the incident, including defeasibility by arguing that he was "out of control" and "inebriated." He also used mortification by taking responsibility and arguing that he was "deeply ashamed" of his actions. Another of Gibson's strategies was differentiation, in which he argued that although he uttered the offensive words, he does not espouse anti-Semitic beliefs. Stein (2010) concluded the Jewish community's response to Gibson's multiple apologies was one of guarded acceptance.

Mortification is often the most effective strategy for any image tarnish-ing incident—particularly for those that include elements of hate speech. For instance, George Allen, a Republican candidate from Virginia who was running for reelection in 2006, ruined his chances to succeed in politics after he failed to apologize right away for race-related comments. On September 25, 2006, the website www.salon.com announced that two of Allen's former University of Virginia football teammates accused Allen of using the N-word. Allen used *denial* effectively when confronted with the N-word allegations. He *shifted the blame* to the accusers, and this tactic worked well because the allegations turned out to be false (Liu, 2007).

He also used *endorsements*—a new tactic introduced by Lui (2007) to indicate to his constituents that he was not racist. The scholar concluded Allen lost the race because he ineffectively used the *mortification* strategy in response to another incident in which he used a racial slur directed at his political opponent's cameraman. Allen waited four days to implement the strategy rather than apologizing right away. The long-time lapse between the incident and the apology not only gave the media time to depict Allen negatively, it also placed doubt in the public's mind as to the sincerity of the apology (Liu, 2007).

Schmittel and Hull (2015) examined the image-repair discourse of Richie Incognito following the Miami Dolphins' bullying scandal in which Incognito's used the N-word during a threatening voicemail to a line mate, Jonathan Martin. Sources familiar with the tapes stated these are terms Incognito used over time and were not isolated incidents, including the use of the racial epithet multiple times. Following the incident, Incognito attempted to salvage his image by utilizing both the social-media platform, Twitter, and through his exclusive one-on-one television interview with Fox Sports 1. Results suggest Incognito used competing image repair strategies on Twitter and traditional media platforms. Via Twitter, Incognito predominantly used strategies of victimization, stonewalling and attacking the accuser, along with a new category—exposing critics (Schmittel & Hull, 2015). On traditional media, he used *shifting blame, good intentions* and *bolstering*. Overall, his strategies were successful.

In another case involving the N-word, Len-Rios, Finneman, Han, Bhandari and Perry (2015) used a multi-method approach to examine the use of social media in Paula Deen's image repair campaign in the wake of the *National Enquirer's* revelation that she admitted to using the "N-word" during a lawsuit deposition. The researchers looked at the effectiveness of tweeted message strategies in a race-related crisis via Twitter. Study findings indicate her image repair strategies were unsuccessful because her apology did not center on the allegations, and she was contradictory in her bolstering, minimization, and mortification strategies.

Building on this review of the literature, this study addresses the following questions: (1) What image repair tactics did Hulk Hogan use following their racially charged incidents? (2) How did media outlets and audiences respond? (3) What are the implications of this case study for IRT and critical race studies?

TEXTS ANALYZED

Using a critical race lens, this IRT analysis examined multiple texts to assess the image repair strategies of Hulk Hogan following highly publicized racially charged incidents during which the two used hate speech. Specifically, we looked at the celebrity's personal statements, social media accounts, news reports and public opinion reports surrounding the events to assess their image repair tactics (Table 7.1).

Online sources are of interest because they were heavily used to help spread the word about race-related topics and the two incidents in general. We gathered the artifacts used in our analysis by searching for Hogan's names on the Google search engine relying on mainstream news and entertainment

Table 7.1   Hulk Hogan's Image Restoration Tactics

Strategy/Tactic	Key Characteristic	Example
Denial		
Simple Denial	Did not do act	
Shift Blame	Another did act	
Evade Responsibility		
Provocation	Act was response to another's offense	
Defeasibility	Lack of information or ability	Hogan claimed to be reared in an environment where the N-word was used frequently; therefore, it was easy to use even if it were wrong.
Accident	Act was a mishap	
Good Intentions	Act was meant well	
Reduce Offensiveness		
Bolster and Transcendence	Stress good traits; act placed in broader context	Hogan claimed to be a better person and used his celebrity to leverage his bad action. Claims to be better than the image portrayed in media after the incident.
		Hogan claimed to use this crisis situation to improve himself. Claimed these comments were revealed as part of the sex tape scandal, which was being litigated as privacy invasion. He claimed to have suicidal thoughts.
Minimize; Differentiation; Attack the Accuser	Act not serious; act not as bad as more offensive acts; attack the person who brought the accusation	Hogan tried to minimize the situation by using his celebrity to claim to not be a racist when he appeared on *Good Morning America*.
		He claimed that "This is not who I am . . . " and "I'm disappointed in myself . . . " using differentiation.
		Hogan attacked the accuser by suing Gawker Media a second time for releasing audio of his N-word rant.
Corrective Action		
Normalcy	The individual can work to return things to the way they were before the incident in question	

(Continued)

Table 7.1   (Continued)

Strategy/Tactic	Key Characteristic	Example
Prevention of repeat offenses	The individual can make assurances of adjustments that will prevent any similar incidents from occurring in the future.	Hogan took ownership of his remarks and claimed to be better because he learned from the experience.
Mortification		
Apology	The person admits responsibility for the actions in question and seeks forgiveness for them	Hogan apologized in *PEOPLE* magazine and appeared on *Good Morning America* to explain his actions. He also appeared on other media programs with similar messages of apology, in some cases seeking audience feedback on YouTube and other social sites.

publications which covered the story in depth. Specifically, *Good Morning America* and *ABC News* were used because Hogan's first televised interview was with Good Morning America. *PEOPLE* magazine and *Us* magazine were used because they followed the follow the story from beginning to trial and after. The texts were read closely using a textual analysis.

HOGAN'S USE OF IMAGE REPAIR TACTICS

By using a slur to target a member of an outgroup, individuals are often asserting an overall negative attitude toward the entire target group, as slurs often imply negative stereotypes or beliefs about the target group or individual beyond simply identifying group membership. For instance, in Hogan's case, calling an individual a "nigger" implies more than simply calling that person "Black."

Because of the negativity association with using the slur, Hogan's crisis did not go away easily or quickly. He had work to do to gain back respect and trust from his stakeholders, target audiences and friends. Hogan cautiously began his image repair tactics when he first spoke out about his use of the N-word with mortification. This effort, which is common among many celebrities and others who find themselves thrust into a personal crisis that has public relations implications.

Mortification

The *National Enquirer* published online the audio transcript of Hogan's offensive racially offensive rant about his daughter's relationship with a black man. Hogan used mortification when he offered an apology.

According to PEOPLE magazine, Hogan said in an exclusive statement to the magazine, "Eight years ago I used offensive language during a conversation. It was unacceptable for me to have used that offensive language; there is no excuse for it; and I apologize for having done it." (Kimble, L., July 24, 2015)

During his first television appearance to discuss the crisis on Good Morning America, Hogan apologized again for his comments. He said:

"Oh, my gosh. Please forgive me. Please forgive me," he said Monday. "I think if you look at the whole picture of who Hulk Hogan is, you can see over all the years that there's not a racist bone in my body." (Khatchatourian, M., August 31, 2015)

Differentiation

Hogan's IRT tactics play out when he used *differentiation* as a response strategy when he would not acknowledge his bigotry and racism after his words were publicized. By saying that he is not racist, he attempts to distinguish himself from what feminist scholar bell hooks refers to as "white supremacist capitalist patriarchy." Hogan lamented:

"This is not who I am. I believe very strongly that every person in the world is important and should not be treated differently based on race, gender, orientation, religious beliefs or otherwise," Hogan told PEOPLE. "I am disappointed with myself that I used language that is offensive and inconsistent with my own beliefs." (Kimble, L., July 24, 2015)

Reduce Offensiveness

Another way IRT strategies were used in Hogan's defense includes reducing offensiveness, which has two tactics: *bolstering* and *transcendence*. Transcendence occurred when Hogan told *PEOPLE* he will "use the situation to "improve as a person" and that he takes the matter as an "important learning experience," thus using bolstering to place himself in a more favorable light among stakeholders and viewers (Kimble, 2015). Minimization was employed during Hogan's appearance on the *Good Morning America* show when he claimed to not be a racist: "I'm not a racist, but I never should have said what I said. It was wrong. I'm embarrassed by it" (Khatchatourian, 2015).

Defeasibility

Hogan continued to use IRT strategies in his *Good Morning America* interview. For example, Hogan tried to evade responsibility through defeasibility when he stated that he grew up in an environment where the N-word "was just thrown around like it was nothing" (Khatchatourian, 2015). He said that he further employed blame shifting when he blamed his racist rhetoric on his upbringing, stating:

> "People need to realize that you inherit things from your environment. "And where I grew up was south Tampa, Port Tampa, and it was a really rough neighborhood, very low income. And all my friends, we greeted each other saying that word." (Khatchatourian, 2015)

Transcendence

Hogan admitted his transgression and said he felt terrible as he attempted to gain pity from stakeholders by adding that he was having suicidal thoughts around the time the sex act and racist rant were taped. He said in his first interview, since being fired by the WWE, with ABC News' Amy Robach that aired on August 31, 2015:

> "I was at the lowest point of my life to the point where I wanted to kill myself," Hogan said. "I was completely broken and destroyed and said, 'What's the easiest way out of this?' I mean, I was lost." (Chan, 2015)

Attack the Accuser

Hulk Hogan's lawyer David Houston told *Us* magazine that they were investigating the leaked audio. Houston said that Hogan had apologized to all his fans and that "we can only ask for forgiveness and understanding at this point" (Lee & Peros, 2015). Houston told *Us* magazine that the investigation was part of an ongoing trial centered on the sex tape. Houston said:

> We are investigating who leaked this audio and again, it is an especially suspicious circumstance realizing we are in a very contentious litigation with Gawker media. (Lee & Peros, 2015)

Further, Houston added:

> This tape surfaces through a transcript with *National Enquirer* at a time, when quite frankly some would say certain people would do anything. And as a consequence of this leak, we will do all possible to investigate who is responsible

and who again, after three years has passed, is once again attempting to attack Mr. Bollea [aka Hulk Hogan] and successfully sell. (Lee & Peros, 2015)

Corrective Action and Hogan

Caldiero, Taylor and Ungureanu (2009) in their study of image repair and fraud crises found that corrective action statements were most widely used to indicate the organization's intentions to "prevent incidents of these kinds from happening again" (p. 225). One day prior to the racist rant making its way into the public sphere, Hogan set the stage for its emergence in a cryptic tweet, alluding to a "storm" that will surface soon. He tweeted: "In the storm I release control." "God and his Universe will sail me where he wants me to be,one [*sic*] love. HH" (Lee & Peros, 2015). Hogan lawyer, Houston, tells *Us* magazine that Hogan made the comments and accepts ownership of those racist remarks. He stated:

"He does admit he made those comments and he accepts ownership," his lawyer adds. "This is something he dealt with three years ago and something he will deal with again. As we did then, we can only ask for the forgiveness and understanding of the general public and his fans. This is not acceptable behavior, and that is not something we would ever challenge. We only ask that people exhibit some understanding and realize that is not who he is and it's certainly not something that defines him. Throughout his career he has been, and continues to be, a different person. These comments were made under very, very extreme circumstances and as he has done in his press release, he sincerely apologizes." (Lee & Peros, 2015)

Corrective Action and WWE

WWE took action to disassociate itself from the racist scandal by terminating its contract with Hogan and removing any signs of the wrestler from its website. The famed ex-pro wrestler was scrubbed from WWE's website as if he never existed. Videos and photos were removed, including his removal from the online Hall of Fame. Rumors surfaced that Hogan was fired, but according to *PEOPLE*, his lawyer David Houston confirmed that he resigned. Houston said, "He decided to resign from WWE because he didn't want to put them or his family through this" (Kimble, 2015). WWE used corrective action strategy to contradict Hogan's "I stepped down" narrative in a statement:

WWE terminated its contract with Terry Bollea (a.k.a Hulk Hogan). WWE is committed to embracing and celebrating individuals from all backgrounds as demonstrated by the diversity of our employees, performers and fans worldwide. (Kimble, 2015)

MEDIA AND AUDIENCE RESPONSE

Audience response from Hogan's fiasco leaned toward redemption for Hogan, as evidenced in online polls. There were a small number of unscientific Internet public opinion polls on wrestling websites that were seeking audience engagement on whether Hogan should have his contract terminated or which wrestler is the most popular. Even Hogan engaged audience members on his YouTube channel to submit their thoughts under a specific post because he wanted to hear directly from his fans. This unscientific empirical data became indicators for gauging fan loyalty and demonstrated that forgiveness for Hogan's transgressions were plausible. The results from the various polls are summarized and include:

Poll No. 1

Cageside Seats, for Pro Wrestling and MMA fans conducted an unofficial poll to determine who is the most popular wrestler. The website boasts 780 votes, with the top three candidates including Hulk Hogan, Stone Cold Steve Austin and The Rock. Hogan was listed as No. 1 with 33 percent or as the most popular pro wrestler of all time; Stone Cold Steve Austin as No. 2 with 30 percent, and Dwayne "The Rock" Johnson as No. 3 with 21 percent (Mrosko, G., May 3, 2012).

Poll No. 2

Another unofficial Internet poll conducted on July 28, 2015, *The Jersey Journal* posed the question, "Did Hulk Hogan deserve to have his contract terminated by WWE?" Audience engagement in the poll suggest that the majority 315 out of 440 votes (71.59%) voted "No," while 125 voters or 28.41 percent voted "Yes" (The Jersey Journal, July 28, 2015). This demonstrates that his fan base is loyal and possibly forgiving of Hogan's transgressions, particularly in the N-word incident.

Poll No. 3

In a separate poll, Pro Wrestling News conducted an unscientific survey with its audience members on whether Hogan should be back on television after his racist remarks. The results determined that of 1,470 total respondents, 348 (24%) believed the WWE should never pay him or promote him as a role model or legend; 131 (9%) believed that maybe someday; 241 (16%) believed that he could come back if he expressed regret; 192 (13%) believed he should be brought back because fans can separate art from the artist; an

overwhelming 29 percent believe the incident was blown out of propor-
tion; while 129 (9%) said they don't care one way or the other (PWTorch
Pro Wrestling News, May 6, 2018).

YouTube Video/Poll No. 4.

A YouTube video posted on Hogan's official YouTube channel shows him
engaging his fans in a Q&A about the status of his future and asking them
to leave comments on what they think he should do. The website posted
Hogan's questions to the audience:

> "Now I got a question for you . . . from this point forward, with Hulk Hogan
> being in the prime of his career, with Hulk Hogan being the greatest beach bum
> ever with the greatest beach shop, what do you fans want to see me do with
> wrestling?"
>
> Hogan continued, "Do you want me to stay out of it? Do you want me to get
> back in it? Do you want me to tear the business apart? I want to hear from you
> guys. I want to get your replies. What do the fans want Hulk Hogan to do about
> wrestling from this point forward?" (Boone, M., September 2, 2017)

Hogan's YouTube channel has 9,524 subscribers and has 28,984 views of the
video targeted at fans. Audience members gave 749 thumbs up, 25 thumbs
down and 429 left comments that mainly supported the wrestler to continue
to pursue wrestling.

Although these polls are unscientific and are designed to encourage reader
discussion or engagement, the results are clear. Many of Hogan's fans believe
he deserves redemption and that while he made a mistake, they believe in his
"art" as a wrestler and believe that he doesn't deserve WWE's harsh punish-
ment. Hogan's use of mortification as an IRT strategy worked in his favor.
His pursuit of legal action against Gawker for this second offense gave the
wrestler a stronger defense for privacy invasion taking conversations made in
private spaces and making them public through media.

CONCLUSIONS AND IMPLICATIONS

This chapter began with discussing fighting words, that is, racist language and
asking three questions: "What image repair tactics did Hulk Hogan use following their racially charged incidents? How did media outlets and audiences
respond? What are the implications of this case study for IRT and critical race
studies? The results suggest that Hulk Hogan's strategies for repairing his
image and gaining redemption worked in his favor. Hogan employed multiple

IRT strategies addressing his use of racist language toward his daughter's African American boyfriend. The image repair tactics present one view of how Caucasian public figures realize the consequences of white supremacist ideology and the damage it causes to their reputations when they use hate speech to denigrate a person or race of people.

Hogan's two-minute racist rant about his daughter's African American boyfriend is indicative of the White privilege ideology of equating a black man's intrinsic value being tied to the stereotype of successful athletes and earnings versus basic respect for humanity.

Hogan chose to use the N-word to characterize his daughter's boyfriend. Ferber (2007) argues "Athletics and entertainment are the two primary realms in which we actually see Black men presented as successful in our culture, and they are consistent with the historical stereotypes and limited opportunities available to Black men" (p. 22). Hogan's ideology of African American men aligns with research on stereotypes of minority groups. Ferber (2007) states:

Black men have been defined as a threat throughout American history while being accepted in roles that serve and entertain White people, where they can ostensibly be controlled and made to appear non-threatening. Furthermore, within the contemporary context of color-blind ideology, the embrace of Black athletes helps White fans to assure themselves that America really is not racist after all. (p. 12)

Hogan needed to contain and control his crisis situation. Negative news about Hogan had already hit mainstream media, as he was already embroiled in legal drama in Florida against the gossip site Gawker Media when news of the transcript emerged. His legal team had filed a $100 million lawsuit against the popular site after its 2012 posting of video from a sex tape featuring Hogan, which was made in 2008. The published N-word footage became a hotbed discovery for the entertainment and mainstream press, catapulting Hogan into crisis management mode.

Benoit's IRT proposed 14 strategies and tactics, and Hogan used many of these during his self-imposed crisis. The image repair tactic of mortification was most frequently used in this study, as Hogan continually apologized in some way or another to seek forgiveness for his pejorative language, which was caught on tape.

Generally speaking, Hulk Hogan's image repair efforts are considered successful. Unscientific (random) poll data suggests Hogan gained public support, particularly in social media platforms. When searching Twitter using Hulk Hogan in the search about using the N-word, we found that there were 2,939 retweets and 4,101 likes from fans about this topic alone. This demonstrates that his fan base was engaged and supportive of the wrestling icon, indicating he did not lose credibility in the eyes of his base.

We believe this study is valuable for public relations professionals and others who study crisis management or race relations. There were small limitations to this study, however. For instance, we found only a handful of polls that addressed audience perception about the incident. And, while this story made national headlines, it was merely a footnote in the larger narrative about the leaked sex tape, which gained more media coverage due to the invasion of privacy lawsuit that followed against the Gawker Media. Thus, we focused on the more comprehensive news coverage from the sources listed in the chapter, particularly *Good Morning America*, *ABC News*, *PEOPLE* magazine and *Us* magazine.

Despite these limitations, we believe our findings demonstrate how a public figure will, depending on the crisis, employ various IRT strategies to repair a damaged reputation and image. The organization or public figure that contains and controls a situation early on in the crisis has a better chance at gaining favorable response from its target audiences, thus gaining back any respect that may have been lost. When Hogan told his side of the story in his own words, and then sued Gawker Media a second time for leaking the audio of his racist rant, he demonstrated that his private words were made public and deserved to be challenged in a court of law. He also used this crisis as an opportunity to show his imperfections, to challenge media giants on privacy issues and to capitalize financially in the end. His invasion of privacy became the prominent narrative in media stories and his racist speech eventually faded into the background. Despite the over $100 million verdict on the leaked sex tape, his white supremacist ideology and racist language is on the record and cannot be escaped or denied. The person or organization that is proactive in their response strategies is more likely to brave the consequences of their actions and have a favorable outcome.

NOTES

1. More than a century before the start of the Revolutionary War, slavery was woven into the fabric of the United States. In 1620, Puritans accepted "20 Negars" from a Dutch man-o-war vessel as payment for repairs. In subsequent years, the term "Negars" became "niggers" and forever derogatory in the lexicon of American speech (Holt, 2008). More than 150 years later, the founding fathers of the United States announced their independence from England via the Declaration of Independence that stated, in part, that "All men were created equal." However, all but one of the first five presidents of the United States, including the chief architect of the Declaration of Independence Thomas Jefferson, were slaveholders (Holt, 2008). In effect, the underlying intent of the document meant that all white, male, property holders were free

and created equal. Blacks, or "niggers," as blacks were called at the time, were only two-thirds of a person and counted only for taxation purposes. This characterization of blacks as second-class citizens permeated all aspects of American society until the end of the Civil War in 1865.

2. Black protests against racial epithets came to a head in 1933 and 1934 when both radio and film producers permitted the term's casual and frequent use. Sizeable Black protest greeted United Artists' Emperor Jones (1933), where both white and black men use the term "nigger" over 20 times in less than 90 minutes (Scott, 2014).

Part III

SEXUAL ASSAULT, DOMESTIC VIOLENCE, AND IRT

Chapter 8

The Fall of America's Favorite Dad

Bill Cosby's Image Repair Tactics

In the 1960s and 1970s, Cosby was an icon, a superstar. With the debut of the espionage drama "I Spy" on NBC, Cosby was the first African American actor to star in a dramatic series on American TV. In the 1990s, he was labeled America's favorite and funniest dad because of his lovable character on *The Cosby Show*. One of a handful of African American comedians to cross racial barriers in 1970s, Cosby's humor appealed to audiences of all races and ages.

By 2015, the Cosby brand was damaged when several women came forth claiming to have been sexually assaulted by the actor. People no longer saw him as the "king of the world" (Roig-Franzia et al., 2014). His pending NBC show was pulled, his Netflix special canceled and his various titles revoked (O'Connell, 2015). At first, Cosby remained silent and repeatedly denied claims through attorneys. He later appeared for various interviews and press events, but when asked about the sexual assault allegations, he simply shook his head and declined to answer questions.

Cosby's sexual allegations were highlighted in 2014 during Hannibal Buress's stand-up comedy show during which he challenged Cosby's integrity. Buress's comments sparked a public debate about the allegations (Pickert, 2014). Shortly after, alleged victims began to speak out publicly against Cosby. Accusations arose of sexual assaults that spanned Cosby's career. The famous television actor, comedian and the man known as "America's sweater-wearing dad," faced perhaps the biggest crisis in his long-standing career—rape allegations by "more than 50 women" and/or defamation by multiple women and repairing his image/brand (Begley, S., September 30, 2015).

In an interview with the Associated Press, Cosby repeatedly stated, "there is no response," before requesting that specific portions of the interview not be aired (Folkenflik, 2014). He then proceeded to attack the interviewer and the Associated Press' integrity for asking such questions (Folkentlik, 2014). Cosby's initial use of strategic silence only seemed to garner more media attention, instead of deflecting it, and eventually led to Cosby's disappearance from social media. One of Cosby's lawyers, Martin D. Singer, issued a statement the following statement (Rice, 2014):

> These brand new claims about alleged decades-old events are becoming increasingly ridiculous, and it is completely illogical that so many people would have said nothing, done nothing and made no reports to law enforcement or asserted civil claims if they thought they had been assaulted over a span of so many years.

IMAGE REPAIR AND INFIDELITY

The body of literature on infidelity and image repair is growing. Perhaps the most well-known case study involves Hugh Grant, who paparazzi spotted with a prostitute in the 1990s, apologized profusely and experienced success (Benoit, 1997; Grossberger, 1995). Grant, who was scheduled to appear on five talk shows to publicize the release of his new movie, *Nine Months*, strategically used these appearances to restore his reputation. Grant used *mortification*, bolstering, denial, and attacking one's accuser as consistent defenses to this incident and past risqué event on each guest appearance (Benoit, 1997). Grant kept it simple and, most importantly, admitted his mistake when he said, "I think you know in life what's a good thing to do and what's a bad thing, and I did a bad thing. And there you have it (Benoit, 1997)." Though his statement was basic, it fulfilled public interest enough to forgive him for his actions as he returned to his previous status in people's minds.

In another example, Xifra (2012) examined the interviews by the former Managing Director of the International Monetary Fund, Dominique Strauss-Kahn (DSK), after being declared innocent of sexual assault charges brought against him by New York's District Attorney. During his television appearance, DSK used some rhetorical and, more precisely, dramaturgical image repair strategies, but also combined them with other communication strategies. Xifra (2012) analyzed his strategies and suggests that image repair theory researchers must include other analytical elements, strategic as well as contextual, when researching responses to crises.

On May 14, 2011, a 32-year-old maid at the Sofitel New York Hotel, Nafissatou Diallo, alleged that DSK had sexually assaulted her after she entered his suite. DSK was formally indicted on 18 May and granted $1 million bail, plus a $5 million bond, the following day. A semen sample was found on the maid's shirt, and on May 24 it was reported that DNA tests showed a match to a DNA sample submitted by DSK. He was arraigned on June 6, 2011, and pleaded not guilty. On June 30, 2011, the *New York Times* reported that the case was on the "verge of collapse" due to problems with the credibility of the alleged victim, who had, according to sources within the New York City Police Department, repeatedly lied to the police since making her first statement. According to prosecutors, the accuser admitted that she had lied to a grand jury about the events surrounding the alleged attack. Diallo claims, however, that on June 28, 2011, the translator had misunderstood her. DSK was released from house arrest on 1 July.

In response to these events, DSK used image restoration strategies outlined by Benoit (2004), though not to *reduce the offensiveness* of the event, as for him it was clear that no criminal act had occurred. Xifra (2012) concluded the DSK case indicates it is possible to use other strategies than those of image repair discourse theory to construct and carry on with a new public image (Sheldon & Sallot, 2009). DSK used new strategies, such as modeling part of his discourse on a previous successful case, that of Bill Clinton, or strategies used by charismatic leaders, such as nonverbal communication and, mainly, dramaturgy. In sum, incorporating Goffman's theory of dramaturgy into this analysis represents a good step toward achieving this, as image repair is also a form of social interaction. In addition, cross-cultural analyses are also a good research perspective for improving the image repair strategies body of knowledge.

In another example, Gary Hart, a politician who underwent intense public scrutiny after journalists photographed him and a young woman on his yacht nicknamed "Monkey Business," failed to address the scandal truthfully. Rowland (1988) asserts that, "Hart concocted unbelievable stories and refused to answer questions and consequently undercut his credibility" (p. 8). Hart's decision to deny certain allegations that he had spent the night with Donna Rice coupled with his refusal to answer if he had committed adultery hurt his case. The media framed him as untruthful, an assumption that hurt his political career.

Tiger Woods experienced moderate success in his image repair tactics since the *National Enquirer* exposed his infidelity in 2009 (Husselbee & Stein, 2012). Woods apologized on his website for a "transgression"; however, he did not elaborate. By providing little information to the public, Woods reacted to speculations with defeasibility and minimization. Sponsors such as Gatorade and AT&T began backing out of contracts with Woods as soon as early December 2009. However, other sponsors, like Gillette and Tag Heuer, maintained their relationships with Woods as an athlete and support his family life remaining private (Husselbee, 2012).

More recently, Benoit (2017) analyzed Donald Trump's image restoration tactics used after *The Washington Post* posted a video of Trump "having extremely lewd conversation about women in 2005." Allen and Schouten's (2016) article reports Trump's remarks to Billy Bush from this video:

> "I did try and f*ck her," Trump tells Bush in reference to a married woman, while acknowledging he was unsuccessful. "I moved on her like a b*tch but I couldn't get there," Trump says. Later in the video, as Trump and Bush spot Arianne Zucker . . . the real estate mogul says: "I better use some Tic Tacs just in case I start kissing her," adding that he immediately starts kissing "beautiful" women when he encounters them. "I don't even wait," Trump says. "And when you're a star, they let you do it. You can do anything—grab them by the p*ssy." (para. 3–5)

Donald Trump was married to Melania Trump at the time, so these statements could imply that he was willing to commit adultery. This video and the firestorm of criticism it provoked threatened to derail his presidential run. In response, Trump and his wife Melania Trump used several image restoration tactics to repair his damaged image. Trump used *attack accuser* to deflect attention away from accusations of wrongdoing. Messages from others besides the accuser were important factors in his image repair effort. After accusations from other women surfaced, Trump used *denial* to respond to these attacks. He declared that these accusations had been "largely debunked." Benoit (2017) notes Trump's statement ("largely debunked") is not a particularly strong defense. It is not clear where they were debunked.

Benoit added that two things should be noted at the beginning of the evaluation of this image repair effort. "First, it is not sufficient to simply include an image repair strategy in a defense. A strategy must be developed persuasively to have any hope of being effective. For example, 'I didn't do it [wink wink, nudge nudge]' qualifies as an instance of denial, but it is unlikely to be convincing. Second, image repair can be helped or hindered by messages from others." Benoit adds (p. 243):

> In such a divisive context, the defense had no hope of repairing Trump's image with the general public (Trump lost the popular vote by 2.9 million). Even though he lost the popular vote, the business magnate won the Electoral College. We cannot say that the "Access Hollywood" video was solely responsible for Trump's poor popular vote showing, but it is clear that this defense did not completely dispel the cloud surrounding him.

These cases illustrate the importance of sincerity, openness and honesty, particularly in cases of infidelity. Transparency and publicly owning their indiscretions early on have helped celebrities successfully repair their image.

Conversely, those who waited to apologize or who tried to cover up their indiscretions were not as successful. These are all factors that play a role when successfully employing Benoit's image repair tactics. Such studies demonstrate the promise that image repair tactics offer for celebrities who use them. However, as mentioned in the introduction, it is important for scholars to continue to research the topic. Accordingly, we apply image restoration theory to Bill Cosby's response (or lack thereof) to rape allegations, his use of social media and how it backfired, and other factors in his attempt to contain and control the unfolding crisis.

REPRESENTATIONS OF BLACK MEN

According to Martindale (1990), mainstream press in the United States has presented minorities as outside, rather than a part of, American society. Historically media coverage of African American males in the media was inadequate or misrepresented; coverage of blacks in the media has been negative (Dates & Pease, 1994). Drummond (1995) adds that the portrayal of African Americans is routinely depicted as drug lords, crack victims, the underclass, the homeless and the subway muggers. The portrayal is more than just verbal and includes representation via images in the media. Media coverage of people of color is full of stereotypes, offensive terminology, biased reporting and a skewed interpretation of American society.

According to Smith, Yosso and Solórzano (2007), racial primes are a result of "a well-structured, highly developed, racially conservative, 'race-neutral' or 'color-blind' racial socialization process." The author argues that as a result children learn race-specific stereotypes of various ethnic groups. Throughout their life they continue to receive corroborating messages of anti-black stereotypes from adults, friends, games, folklore, music, television, popular media and the hidden curriculum—through both voluntary and involuntary means. The result of these forces in is black misandry; *Merriam-Webster* defines misandry as a hatred or contempt of men.

"Black misandry refers to an exaggerated pathological aversion toward black men created and reinforced in societal, institutional, and individual ideologies, practices, and behaviors." The study used focus group interview data from African American male students at four universities. It revealed that black misandric beliefs exist in both academic and social spaces in the collegiate environment. Based on their findings they concluded that using critical race theory as a framework, they were able to provide an interpretation of how racially primed black misandric beliefs influence the collegiate racial climate. These preconceived notions of black men were likely to play a role in how audiences received Cosby's image restoration tactics.

THE PRESENT ANALYSIS

Building on previous IRT studies, this analysis assesses Bill Cosby's image repair tactics during his crisis in 2015. Crisis is defined as "a specific, unexpected, and non-routine event or series of events that create high levels of uncertainty and threaten or are perceived to threaten high priority goals" (Seeger, Sellnow & Ulmer, 1998, p. 233). Benoit's image repair typology was applied in examining Cosby's tactics based on news and entertainment reports. For the purpose of this chapter, William Benoit's (1995) theory of image repair discourse is used as the theoretical framework in analyzing the Bill Cosby case.

To examine the extensive media coverage of the Cosby scandal, this analysis utilized a reading of media reports on the scandal and the defense Cosby has taken in addressing the sexual assault allegations. The present study is interested in examining the numerous strategies and tactics Cosby used to counter attacks on his established positive public reputation.

IMAGE REPAIR TACTICS

The allegations of sexual assault by Cosby date back years, but the Andrea Constand court case in 2005 is the lawsuit that brought alleged sexual assault charges into the public sphere and mentions 12 anonymous women as alleged victims, garnering minimal media coverage initially. In June 2005, the *Philadelphia Daily News* published a story identifying one of the anonymous women as Beth Ferrier, as mentioned in the Constand court papers. By November 2006, Constand and Cosby settled the lawsuit out of court (Pikert, 2014).

The controversy did not gain much mainstream media attention. However, in 2006 another woman, Barbara Bowman, told *People* magazine that Cosby mentored and sexually assaulted her in the 1980s. In February 2014, Gawker, a blog network, published a post summarizing old sexual allegations against Cosby and *Newsweek* published interviews with Barbara Bowman and Tamara Green, women who allege sexual assault allegations (Pikert, 2014). Cosby's career continued to flourish in 2014, as NBC revealed it was developing a new comedy show to star Cosby, and Netflix announced a Cosby stand-up special. Within a few months, Cosby faced a crisis that shook his "America's dad" image.

As stated previously, a comedic stand-up performance by Hannibal Buress in Philadelphia in October 2014 brought renewed interest in Bill Cosby's questionable past, particularly when he referred to the entertainer as a "rapist" and the clip went viral. The *Daily Mail* published a detailed account of

Barbara Bowman's accusations of rape, calling the entertainer a "monster" (Pickert, 2014). When the news of Cosby's alleged transgressions (re)surfaced, his immediate reaction was no response, a tactic known as strategic silence. This tactic is used in protecting one's image. In fact, Cosby utilized an integration of Benoit's image repair tactics including strategic silence, minimization, denial, bolstering and attacking the accusers. This analysis will closely examine the image repair tactics used by Cosby during his crisis.

During the controversy, Cosby initially maintained the majority of his media appearances. This would change, however, with cancellations on popular TV programs. An appearance on *The Queen Latifah Show* would be canceled, as well as an appearance on the *Late Show with David Letterman*. This was the beginning of the cancellation or postponement of projects, stand-up performances and new programs pulled from network lineups or cancellations of reruns on cable networks (Goodman, 2014).

Silence

Despite appearing for various interviews and press events, when asked about the allegations, Cosby would simply shake his head and decline to answer. Cosby's silence garnered uncontrollable media attention after his radio interview with NPR. Cosby's silence was intended to detract from the media attention, but seemed to have the opposite effect instead. This also led to the eventual disappearance of Cosby from social media in 2015 as well.

On November 6, 2015, Cosby showed up with his wife Camille for a joint interview with an Associated Press reporter. The reporter probed Cosby about the Buress segment and Cosby first refused to answer, but followed by stating:

> There's no response. There is no comment about that. And I'll tell you why. I don't want to compromise your integrity, but I don't talk about it. (Rhodan, November 19, 2014)

This is the first time Cosby had any verbal response, breaking his silence on the matter. In fact, Cosby asked reporter not to use the footage and even questioned the reporter's integrity for considering the release of the footage (Willis, 2014). He then proceeded to verbally *attack* the interviewer and the Associated Press' integrity for asking such questions (Folkentlik, 2014). Bill Cosby's lawyer, John P. Schmitt, issued a statement via Cosby's website that said (Associate Press, 2014):

> The new, never-before-heard claims from women who have come forward in the past two weeks with unsubstantiated, fantastical stories about things they

say occurred 30,40, or even 50 years ago have escalated far past the point of absurdity. These brand new claims about alleged decades-old events are becoming increasingly ridiculous, and it is completely illogical that so many people would have said nothing, done nothing, and made no reports to law enforcement or asserted civil claims if they thought they had been assaulted over a span of so many years.

The Associated Press went on to release the footage for the first time on November 19. As such, Cosby's attorneys resume the role of counsel, public relations gatekeeper, essentially Cosby's voice, when managing media inquiries. Attorney John Schmitt would represent Cosby's "voice" during press events and in any public communication. Cosby's attorneys would continue to serve as his "mouthpiece" throughout the open case.

Minimization

In addition, after the initial statement, Cosby kept some of his media appearances. He also was in the process of completing other career works, and seemingly attempted to avoid conversation about the incident. In January, Cosby used two strategies in his stand-up comedy routine in Ontario. He *minimized* the allegations made against him during a comedy show in Ontario, when he joked about women drinking around him. *Minimization* occurred when he provided context for the casual environment and alcohol consumption, yet he *shifted the blame* by merely implying that women under the influence are aware of their actions. A member of the audience even yelled at Cosby saying he was a rapist. Cosby attempted to *deny* the accusation, but the joke already made its impression upon the audience.

In a separate interview with Florida Today, Cosby defended his image stating: "I know people are tired of me not saying anything, but a guy doesn't have to answer to innuendos. People should fact-check. People shouldn't have to go through that and shouldn't answer to innuendos" (Roig-Franzia et al., 2014).

Bolstering

Another image repair strategy was the use of attorneys to *bolster* Cosby's image. Part of his legal strategy included hiring the best attorneys; however, the image repair strategy aligned with the legal strategy is to *reduce offensiveness*, which means to reduce the degree of negative feelings by audiences. When Cosby retained Monique Pressley, an African American, female attorney, to provide a rigorous public defense for he and his wife Camille, his appeal to the African American community and to women in general was evident. Pressley alongside attorney Brian McMonagle showed prominent public support for their client. Pressley's representation of Cosby *bolstered* his image due to her gender and race. Cosby's image was improved by virtue of having an African American female represent him face sexual assault allegations.

Months after the public scandal, Camille Cosby broke her silence and spoke in support of her husband. On December 25, 2014, Camille gave a statement to CBS News supporting her husband throughout the allegations and employed *attack the accuser* strategy, questioning the legitimacy of the accusations (Moraksi, 2014). Immediately after Camille's appearance, the couple's youngest daughter, Evin Cosby, posted a statement on Facebook to lovingly support her parents.

THE "RACE CARD" NARRATIVE

Bill Cosby's defense against serious sexual allegations of over 50 women gained international media attention and narratives of his innocence against accusations, his age, health and celebrity permeated mass media coverage for months. A particular narrative of race would emerge in this highly visible case. Bill Cosby's attempt at injecting race and gender in to the narrative as part of his defense was to first hire a high-powered African American female attorney. For the purpose of this study, we will focus on the race narrative and Cosby's use of the media's negative depiction of black men to build a case for doubt among fans and others.

The notion of identifying and classifying race matters in media is not a new phenomenon, as race is constructed across media from entertainment to sports. The mass media serves as a channel to reach millions of audiences at once. Cosby, whose rich history in entertainment as a leading African American male, has enjoyed a career of mainstream audience acceptance. Allegations depicting Cosby as a serial rapists contradicted his comfortable image of America's favorite sitcom dad.

According to cultural theorist Stuart Hall (1986), mass media are a source for articulating race and reinforcing white supremacy through hegemonic representations. Thus, media provide audiences with "representations of the social world, images, descriptions, explanations and frames for understanding how the world is and why it works as it is said and shown to work" (Hall, 2003, p. 91). Other scholars have discussed negative imagery of blacks in media and sports (Eastman & Billings, 2001; Sailes, 1996). Brown, Anderson and Thompson (2012) suggest that ongoing patterns of mediated images of black men as "wild, unruly, savage black men, further advancing and supporting this mythical common sense understanding of black men and their inclinations to be violent" (p. 72).

Sociologist Patricia Hill Collins (2005) postulate that black men have historically been characterized as deviants. In this context of black male representation in popular culture, Collins explains:

> Historically, African American men were depicted primarily as bodies ruled by brute strength and natural instincts, characteristics that allegedly fostered deviant behaviors of promiscuity and violence. The buck, brute, the rapist, and similar controlling images routinely applied to African American men all worked to deny Black men the work of the mind that routinely translates into wealth and power. (p. 152)

Collins (2005) posits that "the image of the feared Black male body also reappears across entertainment, advertisement, and news. As any Black man can testify who has seen a purse-clutching White woman cross the street upon catching sight of him, his physical presence can be enough to invoke fear, regardless of his actions and intentions" (p. 153).

When Cosby retained Monique Pressley, an African American female attorney, to provide a rigorous public defense for him and his wife Camille, his appeal to the black community and to women in general was evident. His appeal to key audiences, particularly blacks, would represent his need for moral support from this demographic. Pressley alongside attorney Brian McMonagle showed prominent public support for their client. Pressley's representation of Cosby *bolstered* his image due to her gender and race. Cosby's image was improved by virtue of having an African American female represent him as he faced sexual assault allegations. The legal representation by Pressley, however, would be brief.

Months later, in advance of jury selection, Bill Cosby once again employed the "race card" tactic in mass media responses to suggest that racism played a role in his felony sexual assault scandal (Roig-Franzia, Manuel, May 16, 2017). He was cautious in discussing legal issues, but said that he thinks racism and revenge could be behind the dozens of public allegations of sexual assault.

For instance, while speaking with Michael Smerconish on the SiriusXM POTUS radio channel, Cosby concurred with this daughter Ensa Cosby's recent statement that racism could have played a part in the allegations mounted against him. In a statement released by popular radio show, "The Breakfast Club," Cosby's daughter Ensa said, "racism has played a big role in all aspects of this scandal." Bill Cosby embraced and advanced his daughter's race narrative stating, "Could be, could be," when asked about Ensa's statement. "I can't say anything, but there are certain things that I look at, and I apply to the situation, and there are so many tentacles. So many different—nefarious is a great word. And I just truly believe that some of it may very well be that" (Gajanan, May 16, 2017).

Bill Cosby, as a black man and celebrity whose accusers are mostly Caucasian, advanced the race narrative by suggesting that his race would be a factor in his guilt or innocence in the court of public opinion as well as the court of law. The relevance lies in the evaluation of the victims, whose credibility was questioned because of the time passed before speaking out, or because many may have had a questionable past, or perhaps Cosby's popularity and mainstream acceptance. In this case, Cosby, a man whose public reputation counters empirical research on negative stereotypes of black males, finds himself in a unique position of defense because of his celebrity and uses race to redirect alleged sexual accusations in the public sphere.

Other IRT tactics, including *differentiation*, surfaced later in the Cosby case. For instance, sources mentioned Cosby's age and failing health, which served to encourage sympathy and support from the celebrity's fans. One anonymous source close to Cosby discussed his poor vision, age and failing health (Smith, 2016). The source stated, "Bill Cosby, 79, is blind, housebound and in his own personal hell with a degenerative eye." The source added, "He is confined to his house... Those who live with the condition usually experience blurred vision." *Differentiation* is used to distinguish from more offensive acts and to lessen audience negative feelings. Reporting his age and health issues align with this tactic.

CELEBRITY SUPPORT

An external factor that contributed to Cosby's image repair was celebrity endorsements. While Cosby did not rely on celebrity endorsements to *bolster* his image, they played a role in his image improvement. Grammy-winning artist Kanye West showed his support for Cosby on Twitter by tweeting, "BILL COSBY INNOCENT!" In a 2015 interview, Phylicia Rashad, Cosby's former on-screen wife, showed public support for Cosby. Rashad said "What you're seeing is the destruction of a legacy," she said. Keisha Knight Pulliam, better known as Rudy Huxtable, Cosby's former on-screen daughter, was five years old when she landed the role on the hit 1980s sitcom. During her interview on the *Today Show*, Pulliam looked back on those days now and considers that time of her life nothing short of "amazing" (Hines, 2015). In defense of her former TV dad, Pulliam said, ultimately, the assault allegation cases are "just that, allegations," (Bowie, D., July 8, 2015). She added: "You know, it's very much been played out in the court of public opinion.

But we're still in America, where ultimately you're innocent until proven guilty. I wasn't there. That's just not the man I know. So I can't speak to it."

Popular radio host Glenn Beck defended Cosby and accused the media, specifically the Associated Press, of "rape" after asking Cosby about rape allegations in the interview when they allegedly claimed they wouldn't ("Glenn Beck," n.d.). Beck said:

> You want to talk about rape? That's media rape right there. You said you would not do that. Since when does your 'no' mean 'yes'? Do you know the definition of 'no,' sir? You've just raped Bill Cosby. You said you wouldn't do it. You just did it and then you blamed it on him. My gosh, maybe we should have a lesson on rape.

Neo-soul music artist, Jill Scott, initially took to Twitter to defend Cosby, stating: "I'm respecting a man who has done more for the image of Brown people that almost anyone EVER. From *Fat Albert* to the *Huxtables*." She would later retract her support. Similarly, actress Stacey Dash, who worked with Cosby in the 1980s, said, "I worked with in '86 when I was 19. We were alone together many times. He was a perfect gentleman & became a mentor to me" (Bowie, D., July 8, 2015).

Worth noting is that the popularity of hashtag #metoo in 2017 was spurred by the Miramax cofounder Harvey Weinstein, who was accused by many women of sexual misconduct. Throughout 2017, an avalanche of similar accusations emerged implicating powerful men across occupations in sexual misconduct. In the aftermath of #metoo, dozens of men occupied the media spotlight after they were fired from major positions.

CELEBRITY CRITICISM

Worth noting is Cosby was not immune to public criticism by other celebrities. Hollywood director Judd Apataow was outspoken about the allegation and said: "I can understand why someone would say, 'Why does Judd care about this?' I don't know, I have two daughters. I'm a comedian. I see him a little bit as our comedy dad. It's like finding out your comedy dad is a really evil guy."

Actresses Amy Poehler and Tina Fey impersonated the entertainer at The Golden Globes, joking on the telecast that he was "putting pills in the people" (Howard, A., January 13, 2015). Similarly, Piers Morgan, Celebrity Apprentice winner and talk show host, criticized Phylicia Rashad for supporting Cosby. During an appearance on *The Meredith Vieira Show*, Morgan blasted Rashad, stating:

How many [women] have there been?" the former CNN host asked Vieira. "Twenty-five? 30? All saying exactly the same thing. All describing a very similar pattern of drug and sex related abuse by one of America's biggest stars and I don't think it's conscionable for anyone right now to be employing Bill Cosby while these allegations remain unresolved. He's going on tour. (Lee, E., January 8, 2015)

Piers Morgan continued to challenge Cosby to publicly address the issues (Lee, 2015): "I think if Bill Cosby, who is America's dad, this was his image. This is a man who lectured his own black community in America many times about their behavior, young black men in America about their behavior towards women. He is now have been leveled these incredibly serious charges. Go to camera, look that camera down, talk to America in the way you have many times before and go through these charges."

Scott, who had initially supported Cosby, reneged on her comments once the deposition was made public, stating: "About Bill Cosby. Sadly, his own testimony offers PROOF of terrible deeds, which is ALL I have ever required to believe the accusations" (Bowie, D., July 8, 2015). Radio shock jock, Rush Limbaugh, said someone was "setting him [Cosby] up, stating: "And I asked myself, what did Bill Cosby ever do to tick off some producer at CNN? Or some reporter? Or some assignment? What happened here?" (Bowie, D., July 8, 2015).

Most recently, Cosby's on-air daughter Lisa Bonet, who played Denise Huxtable, the second-oldest daughter on *The Cosby Show*, finally offered commentary in a published interview with *Net-A-Porter*, a premier online fashion destination, stating, "There was no knowledge on my part about his specific actions. There was just energy. And that type of sinister, shadow energy cannot be concealed. And if I had anything more to reveal then, it would have happened a long time ago. That's my nature. The truth will set you free" ("A life less ordinary with Lisa Bonet," March 9, 2018). Bonet, who admits having conflicts with Cosby over her involvement in various projects outside the show, has remained silent on the subject until recently, unlike many other actors on the show who demonstrated support of Cosby early on.

Public response to Cosby's allegations continues to mount in social platforms and polls.

For example, poll results regarding Cosby's sexual allegations were revealing. In response to a poll, which asked have the numerous allegations against Bill Cosby changed your perception of him, responses were mixed. Out of 42,000 votes, 24,000 people voted yes, the stories of his multiple accusers are damning. Compared to 10,000 who voted no, he's innocent until proven guilty. About 6,717 poll takers indicated Maybe, but we don't have enough information (Gruber, 2014).

CONCLUSIONS AND IMPLICATIONS

Overall, Cosby's integration of *denial, strategic silence, bolstering, blame shifting* and *attacking the accusers* were ineffective. Individuals who are considered to be on "moral high ground" seem to have a more difficult time restoring their image in situations similar to the Cosby case. Findings revealed *mortification* is the most useful tactic, but in Cosby's situation, *mortification* would result in higher perceptions of guilt. If Cosby is completely innocent, he should not apologize for the allegations especially regarding the legal concerns of this case. However, with 60 women coming forward alleging sexual assault against Cosby, his innocence remains in question.

Analysis of these texts reveals that Cosby's attempts to underestimate or redirect media attention based on his career, race, age and character is evident. *Strategic silence* is not one of Benoit's five image repair strategies, but as mentioned in the introduction, Cosby employed the strategy immediately following the resurfacing of multiple sexual allegations. *Strategic silence* in Cosby's campaign created doubt among his audiences about his innocence. The media portrayed his silence as guilt which created negative narratives of Cosby in traditional and social media. Cosby's disappearance from social media is another form of *strategic silence* which is considered ineffective for his campaign.

Initially, Cosby used humor to challenge individuals to create memes. This tactic demonstrates the comedian's lackluster approach to the seriousness of the allegations. One explanation for this approach is the statute of limitation had run out for the bulk of the cases. In addition, he may have found security in the accusers' lack of evidence or proof.

Media backlash played a critical role in the failure of Cosby's image repair campaign. Media have portrayed Cosby as guilty even though he has not been criminally convicted in a court of law. By contrast, several celebrities, including Kanye West, Keisha Knight Pulliam and Phylicia Rashad, responded to the allegations, offering support for Cosby despite his negative public perception by the media.

Limitations in this case analysis included the nature of the allegations and the ongoing legal issues in Cosby's case. His campaign will not be complete until all cases are finalized with a verdict of guilty or innocent. Since it has not been determined whether or not Cosby is guilty, these findings play an important part in crisis communication decisions. These are only the initial findings of the case but will be subject to further expansion through the duration of Cosby's legal cases. This case study contributes to the expansion of crisis communication theory and research. Suggestions for future studies would be to conduct new surveys and polls regarding Cosby's public perception and an examination of the post-trial image strategies utilized to rebuild or enhance his reputation. Since this case is ongoing, future researchers can analyze the final verdicts of his legal cases to compare and contrast his image repair tactics from the past to the future.

Our analysis revealed differences between Cosby's initial reaction to the sexual assault allegations as untruths juxtaposed to the one pending court case where he acknowledged drugging women in the deposition. By the time the deposition was made public, Cosby's strategic silence and blame shifting were no longer explicit strategies for avoiding the accusations. This would necessitate a new strategy to face the one pending court case that fell within the statute of limitations, thus challenging his notion of innocence.

Celebrity support is not likely to make a difference in the minds of publics, given the graphic nature of the detailed accounts given by the accusers, as well as the poorly executed PR tactics Cosby used during the crisis. In addition, the court of public opinion has decided that the popular sitcom dad's image has been tainted, possibly beyond repair, even if he's found not guilty.

Chapter 9

The Aftermath of #MeToo

Harvey Weinstein's Image Repair Tactics and Pinterest Representations

Individuals embraced the #MeToo movement in 2017 to denounce instances of sexual assault and harassment. During the avalanche of accusations that emerged, powerful media figures, high-profile politicians, actors, journalists and other executives were highlighted, including Bill Cosby, Bill O'Reilly, Charlie Rose, Kevin Spacey, Mark Halperin, Michael Oreskes and Leon Wieseltier.

However, the person who received the most coverage in the midst of the #MeToo movement was movie mogul Harvey Weinstein after *The New York Times* and *The New Yorker* published articles that cited numerous allegations of inappropriate sexual behavior by the producer. Dozens of actresses, models and film industry employees provided detailed accounts of sexual harassment and assault. In response to these allegations, Weinstein was expelled from various organizations, his name was removed from the Weinstein door and the company hired two ad agencies to create a new identity for his studio (Lafayette, 2017). Weinstein's highly publicized allegations created the need for him to repair his image.

Previous image restoration studies have examined the media's framing of issues of sex scandals, domestic violence and image tarnishing cases with public figures—primarily emphasizing traditional media platforms such as newspapers and magazines (Benoit, 2017; Garcia, 2011; Grossberger, 1995; Holtzhausen & Roberts, 2009). For instance, as mentioned in chapter 6, Cosby's image repair strategies included *denial, minimization, attacking accusers* and *strategic silence*, which was the actor's main strategy. In a another example, the Air Force Academy used *corrective action* to address the more than 140 sexual assault allegations that occurred over the course of a decade (Holtzhausen & Roberts, 2009).

Benoit's image repair theory (IRT) has also been widely used in classifying image repair discourse, particularly in cases of political sex-related scandal. Garcia (2011) analyzed the image repair tactics used by U.S. president Bill Clinton and Italy's prime minister Silvio Berlusconi. Both men were involved in highly publicized sex-related scandals during their respective stints in office (Garcia, 2011). Likewise, Benoit (2017) analyzed President Donald Trump's use of image repair after the release of the *Access Hollywood* video: "Grab Them by the P*ssy." These cases and others will be further explored in the literature review.

While these studies provide an overview of cases involving sex-related scandals, absent from the literature are cases that analyze image repair tactics used to address the onslaught of sexual assault cases that emerged during the #MeToo movement. Using a feminist lens, this study analyzes Weinstein's scandal within the context of previous sex scandals. Specifically, it fills a gap in the literature with an examination of sexual assault, the #MeToo movement, Weinstein's use of image restoration tactics and the audience response on Pinterest.

According to Pew, in 2018, around seven-in-ten Americans use social media to connect with one another, engage with news content, share information and entertain themselves. Explore the patterns and trends shaping the social media landscape over the past decade below (Smith & Anderson, 2018). Pinterest is of interest for this study because of its target audience—women. Pinterest is far more popular among women than men, and unlike some of its competitors it is popular across age brackets, including Millennials, Gen Xers and Boomers (Guimarães, 2014). Phillips, Miller and McQuarrie's (2014) analysis of 20 pin boards with 2,291 images indicated continued gender-related studies of this platform are important as women often use Pinterest to contemplate future purchases and identities. This study is particularly relevant as awareness of individuals use the new medium to share messages on #MeToo, feminism and the Weinstein case may offer scholars a deeper understanding of trends.

THE FEMINIST LENS

To explore Weinstein's use of image repair tactics, this chapter considers four strands of literature: feminist theory, representations of sex scandals, medium theory and image repair tactics. Feminist theory is concerned with the fundamental inequalities between men and women, as well as the sense of patriarchy it entails (hooks, 1984). Feminist theory encompasses work done in a broad variety of disciplines, prominently including the approaches to women's roles and lives and feminist politics. Ardener

(1975) posits that women and men within patriarchal, capitalist societies tend to form two distinct circles of experience and interpretation, one overlapping the other (Krolokke & Sorensen, 2006). The masculine circle converges with the norms of society, providing a masculine signature and overriding the feminine circle. Therefore, women's voices and perspectives are not openly articulated. Women can either try to translate their point of view into a masculine mode or try to separate alternate models of communication.

What feminist-informed methods have in common is they put gender and gender-related concerns at the center of analysis and highlight notions of power in different ways. In this chapter, feminism is used as the primary theoretical framework to help explain rape myth acceptance through patriarchal values. We highlight male oppression, or patriarchy, as the cause of gender inequalities, the emphasis being violence, both physical and psychological, as perpetrated by male-dominated institutions against females (Williams, Sawyer & Wahlstrom, 2012).

This study is particularly important as polls indicate sexual harassment is something many women experience during their lifetime (Edge, 2018). According to the study, more than half of U.S. women have experienced unwanted and inappropriate sexual advances from men, three in ten have put up with unwanted advances from male coworkers and a quarter have endured them from men who had influence over their work situation. A *Columbia Journalism Review* survey of journalists indicated 41 percent of staff journalists and 47 percent of freelancers had experienced sexual harassment in a newsroom. However, the study indicated 67 percent of staffers did not report the incident to HR.

Also relevant to this chapter is literature on rape culture, which refers to the broader, deeply entrenched cultural attitudes regarding biological sex, gender and sexuality that inform people's attitudes about rape (Rozee & Koss, 2001). The norms #MeToo revealed are often highlighted as being a part of the "rape culture" in the United States. Rape culture often excuses sexual violence as a fact of life and ultimately inevitable in society (Buchwald, Fletcher & Roth, 1993). Rape culture fosters and encourages an acceptance of male dominance, which takes many forms (Jaffe, 2018). For instance, many of the executives, artists and politicians touched by #MeToo were already known to be bullies or harassers (Schrobsdorff, 2018).

> Those open secrets didn't wreck their careers if they were making money for someone or fulfilling some need. Instead, the people around them suffered. Those who openly resisted men like accused rapist Harvey Weinstein say it was their careers that took a hit, and that standing up made it hard for them to rise in their field. (Schrobsdorff, 2018, p. 21)

In the feminist literature, scholars have turned their attention to new media platforms in the coverage of rape and sexual assault. Durham, (2013) found that bloggers and commentators quickly identified the patriarchal and victim-blaming aspects of *The New York Times'* coverage, resulting in an influential petition and an apology from *The Times.* Durham's (2013) analysis revealed bloggers and commentators engaged in feminist dialogue, raising awareness of patriarchal frames of sexual violence as well as fostering reformist actions. However, the study also pointed to a continued need for watchfulness and activism around sexual violence and child abuse.

Worthington (2013) attributes the reforms in gender violence coverage and online news to the increased need to update major stories on social media platforms. In her conclusions, she encouraged researchers to continue to study social media trends to remain current in the rapidly changing media environment.

MEDIUM THEORY

Online content offers a unique social experience. People share links, articles and videos on their Facebook walls or Pinterest feeds as a form of cultural currency. The nature of social media and UGC consists of users "re-posting, linking, 'tagging' (labeling with keywords), rating, modifying or commenting" (Goode, 2009). Some equate this use of user-generated content as a form of citizen or participatory journalism (Goode, 2009).

The focus of this study is the impact of new and social media on crisis communication, particularly sexual harassment and assault; therefore, it is important to discuss how the formation of digital communities on social media platforms such as Pinterest influences communication among online community members.

Scholars have long asserted that traditional media outlets function as the primary gatekeeper in disseminating news to the public (Snider, 1967; White, 1950). However, with the rise of social media sites such as Facebook, Instagram and Twitter, a varied group of gatekeepers emerge as numerous as those that use the medium (Curnutt, 2012). Pinterest is one of the newer social networking sites that launched in beta mode in March 2010.

In 2015, Pinterest had more than 100 million monthly active users (MAUs), according to *The New York Times* (Isaac, 2015). The site started out as an invite-only visual bookmarking platform, but changed in 2012. It is now open to anyone to join. Building on this review of the literature, this study seeks to answer the following research questions:

IRT and Sex Scandals

When public figures make mistakes, they often face public scrutiny for their actions. The media take the scandal that occurred, and spread information rapidly across multiple platforms. In this environment, image repair tactics are more crucial than ever for the redemption of a public figure facing a legal or social scandal. As a basis for this chapter, our literature review focuses on two themes: Benoit's image repair tactics and the effectiveness of those strategies in previous image repair campaigns.

Multiple studies from Benoit have asserted the importance of image repair for public figures, organizations, celebrities and athletes. As mentioned early in this text, Benoit describes the five categories of response strategy as: *denial, evasion of responsibility, reducing offensiveness, corrective action* and *mortification*. Due to the variety of available options to heal a damaged reputation, people commonly utilize a combination of tactics rather than focusing on a single strategy.

Some combinations of forms might be more effective or appropriate than single forms or than other combinations (Benoit & Drew, 1997). For this reason, a necessary step in IRT involves determining the appropriateness of each tactic in relation to his case. Following that, analyzing the effectiveness of tactic combinations from previous case studies assists in concluding the best method of image restoration for Weinstein.

As indicated in the introduction, image repair studies of cases emphasizing sexual assault are scarce, and IRT studies examining sex-related scandals are common. For instance, Hugh Grant is held up as the ideal of how to handle sex scandals. Grant made a full comeback after being found with a prostitute in 1995 (Grossberger, 1995). He apologized profusely on shows such as: *Live with Regis and Kathie Lee, The Tonight Show with Jay Leno* and CNN's *Larry King Live* (CNN, 1995). He never stopped talking about the situation and apologized right away. The media continued framing Grant as a relatable celebrity, as he went on *J. Leno* to say, "I think you know in life what's a good thing to do and what's a bad thing, and I did a bad thing . . . and there you have it." In the end, Grant's publics forgave him. His girlfriend forgave him and his movie *Nine Months* was a hit.

In a mega study of 24 sex-related political scandals, Moran (2012) applied a crisis communications lens to American political sex scandals using Benoit's IRT. All of the sex scandals occurred from 1987 to 2011 and received significant national attention. The study found *evading responsibility* to be most frequently used tactic, while *denial* was the least utilized tactic. The researcher concluded officials can no longer hide their discretions from the public by arguing the distinction between their public and private lives. The dramatic growth of media and Internet outlets in the last decade alone has called for an increased focus on communication and higher standards of accountability.

In a similar case study of the image repair tactics of politicians, Garcia (2011) analyzed the image repair tactics of U.S. president Bill Clinton and the current prime minister of Italy Silvio Berlusconi. Both men were involved in highly publicized sex-related scandals during their respective stints in office. Garcia (2011) concluded the effectiveness of image restoration strategies can vary greatly according to cultural, political and media variables of each country. The two leaders safeguarded their positions of power and managed to keep a significant percentage of the public opinion on their side.

In another example, the Air Force Academy mostly used *corrective action* to address the more than 140 sexual assault allegations that occurred over the course of a decade (Holtzhausen & Roberts, 2009). The study concluded a proactive approach was most effective in generating positive media coverage. *Bolstering* was the most effective image repair strategy and surprisingly *mortification* was ineffective. The study suggests a complexity approach to crises management might be more appropriate in image repair.

More recently, Benoit (2017) analyzed President Donald Trump's use of image repair after the "Access Hollywood" Video: "Grab Them by the P*ssy." The scandal occurred in October 2016, when Trump was in the midst of a hotly contested presidential campaign. Days before the second presidential debate, *The Washington Post* posted a video of Trump "having extremely lewd conversation about women in 2005." In response, Trump and his wife Melania Trump offered several messages to repair his damaged image. However, Benoit (2017) concluded the defense had no hope of repairing Trump's image with the general public. Although Trump won the election, he lost the popular vote by 2.9 million.

"We cannot say that the "Access Hollywood" video was solely responsible for Trump's poor popular vote showing, but it is clear that this defense did not completely dispel the cloud surrounding him."

The #MeToo Movement

The #MeToo moment is built on the work of longtime organizer, Tarana Burke, a survivor of sexual violence. In 2006, she used the social networking website Myspace to raise awareness about the issue by using two words: me too. Ten years later, her efforts spread virally after Alyssa Milano used the two-word hashtag on social media. The #MeToo movement was named *Time* magazine's Person of the Year for 2017. On its cover, *Time* called the people behind the movement "The Silence Breakers."

Burke had worked for decades with young women of color who survived sexual violence, and in 2006 she named her campaign "me too" as an expression of solidarity. When Burke found the words trending on social media in 2017, she worried that the movement was being used for something that she did not recognize as her life's work. Burke's "me too" campaign was designed to support survivors, to get them resources and to help them heal. Recently, the #MeToo movement has been less hinged on survivor stories, and has been more focused on outing the actions of perpetrators (Jaffe, 2018). Worth noting is while there is a fixation with trying to make #MeToo about the public shaming of celebrities; Tarana's campaign did not emphasize high-profile men (Douglas, 2018).

#MeToo has been translated or adapted into major languages including Arabic, Chinese, Finnish, French, Italian, Japanese, Russian and Spanish. In these ways, social-media reports of past abusive conduct have now spread into specific industries, including the art business world (Lydiate, 2018).

The movement has expanded beyond Hollywood, as activists support victims across the work spectrum. To help further the #MeToo cause, law professor and attorney Anita Hill, who accused then-U.S. Supreme Court nominee Clarence Thomas of sexual harassment during his 1991 confirmation hearings, is chairing a commission tasked with eliminating sexual harassment in Hollywood. Along with the president of the National Women's Law Center, Hill met with 150 top-level professionals to explore strategies to stop sexual harassment and promote gender equality (Ricker, 2018).

Similarly, high-profile attorney Tina Tchen, longtime chief of staff to Michelle Obama, is spearheading the *Time*'s Up Legal Defense Fund, which had raised more than $19.5 million by early February to help victims of sexual assault (Ricker, 2018).

Building on this literature review on sex scandals, the #MeToo movement and IRT case studies, this chapter expands the scholarship with an examination of image repair tactics Harvey Weinstein used immediately following media's coverage of his scandal. The goal of this study is threefold: (1) to introduce and explore the #MeToo movement, (2) to examine online image restoration tactics and (3) to expand feminist theory. The following three questions guide this study: (1) What image repair tactics did Weinstein use? (2) How did the media portray Weinstein before, during and after the scandal? (3) What was Pinterest users' response to Weinstein's image repair tactics before, during and after the scandal?

TEXTS ANALYZED

The climate created by the #MeToo movement offers a wonderful opportunity to analyze Weinstein's image restoration tactics following the 2017 accusations that flooded media outlets. Building on this review of the literature, this case study analyzes Weinstein's image restoration tactics within days of publication of *The New York Times* and *The New Yorker* articles followed by months of further damaging accusations.

This case study consists of an analysis of the statements Weinstein released immediately after his scandal broke and media coverage surrounding the incident and Pinterest pins shared in response to the scandal. Using the Google search engine, we collected full texts of public statements. Benoit's image repair tactics were used to code each statement (Benoit, 1995, p. 74). The sample Pinterest sample consisted of a pool of 100 Pinterest pins found by searching for the keywords "#MeToo" and Weinstein on Pinterest.

To get a sense of media and audience response, we relied on relevant newspaper articles and polls that highlighted their statements. Using this information, we were able to gauge audience and media response to Weinstein's image repair tactics.

#METOO AND HARVEY WEINSTEIN BACKGROUND

By all accounts Weinstein was a rock star. He boasted a rags-to-riches story as the man who turned little-known indie directors into rock stars—and, in the process, became one himself. Weinstein began his career as a rock promoter. The Weinstein brothers were 20-something concert promoters when in 1979 they started Miramax Film Corp., naming the company after their parents, Miriam and Max. Many tried to replicate their formula, but none could match Miramax's record of 249 Oscar nominations and 60 wins in just 15 years or deliver crossover hits such as *The Crying Game, The Piano* and *Pulp Fiction,* the first independent film to break $100 million at the box office (Rottenberg, Olsen & Whipp, 2017).

His empire would come crashing down after the #MeToo movement emerged on October 5, 2017, after the *New York Times* published a story accusing Weinstein of sexual harassment. Actresses Rose McGowan and Ashley Judd were among the dozens of women who came forward (Kantor & Twohey, 2017). The next day, the Weinstein Company announced it took the allegations "extremely seriously" and was launching an inquiry.

Gwyneth Paltrow, Angelina Jolie, Cara Delevingne and Uma Thurman were among the dozens of high-profile group of women who made claims against the movie mogul, which he unequivocally denied. Ashley Judd, 49, recalled an incident in which she expected to discuss business with Weinstein, 65, but instead was summoned to his hotel room. She claimed that Weinstein—wearing a bathrobe—then asked her if he could give her a massage, or if she would be willing to watch him take a shower (Wheatstone &

Baker, 2018). Judd sued him, stating she wanted former movie mogul to be held accountable for "illegal conduct" that caused her to lose money, status, prestige and power.

Likewise, Gwyneth Paltrow claimed Weinstein summoned her to his Beverly Hills hotel suite when she was 22 years old, where he placed his hands on her and suggesting they head to the bedroom for massages. Similarly, Angelina Jolie, 42, said she had a "bad experience" with the producer while at a junket for his film *Playing by Heart* in 1998. He was said to have made an unwanted advance and Angelina never worked with him again (Wheatstone & Baker, 2018).

After these cases, which had been covered up for decades, surfaced, the tarnishing of Weinstein's reputation was devastated following publication of personal revelations in the *New York Times* in October 2017. Weinstein's case illustrates how one's reputation is fragile. Legendary business magnate Warren Buffett described the fragile nature of a reputation: "It takes 20 years to build a reputation and five minutes to ruin it. If you think about that, you'll do things differently."

His remark is relevant to the explosion of social-media accusations of misconduct against Hollywood film mogul Harvey Weinstein (Lydiate, 2018). In the matter of a few days, Weinstein's lawyer Lisa Bloom announced her resignation and Weinstein was fired by the board of his company. On October 10, allegations from 13 more women were published in the *New Yorker* magazine, including three accusations of rape, which Weinstein strongly denied. Weinstein also lost awards and membership in various organizations, including BAFTA, the Oscars, the board of the Producers Guild of America. Harvard University stripped him of the Du Bois medal it gave him in 2014 for his contributions to African American culture (Farrow, 2017).

On February 11, after a four-month investigation, New York state prosecutors announced they had filed a lawsuit against the Weinstein Company on the basis that the studio failed to protect employees from his alleged harassment and abuse. On May 26, 2018, Weinstein turned himself in to the New York Police Department and Manhattan District Attorney's office. He was charged with rape, a criminal sex act, sex abuse and sexual misconduct for incidents involving two separate women.

Weinstein, who produced *Shakespeare in Love*, was once worth an estimated $240 million, but his net worth decreased during the #MeToo debacle. He spent millions of dollars on lawyers, private investigators and publicists after more than 100 women came forward accusing him of sexual abuse and rape (Mullin & Marsh, 2018). The Weinstein Co. filed for bankruptcy protection in March 2018 with a buyout offer in hand from a private equity firm.

Weinstein's Image Repair Tactics

In the aftermath of the articles accusing Weinstein of acts of sexual misconduct, several actresses spoke out and politicians distanced themselves from him. As soon as the story broke, Weinstein issued a statement of apology, took a leave of absence from his company and then threatened to sue the *New York Times* (Rottenberg, Olsen & Whipp, 2017). Weinstein responded to the allegations using statements and interviews. On October 5, 2017, Weinstein sent *The Times* a statement in response to its story about his treatment of women in Hollywood. In these statements, he used several image restoration tactics (Table 9.1).

Denial

The first tactic Weinstein used was *denial*. In a statement released by Weinstein's spokesperson Holly K. Baird, the movie mogul responded to Uma Thurman's claim of a sexual attack by releasing a series of photos that his team said "demonstrate the strong relationship Mr. Weinstein and Ms. Thurman had had over the years" (Evans & Patten, 2017).

The statement further claimed Weinstein made an "awkward pass" at Thurman "after "misreading her signals." Weinstein's team of publicists added that there "was no physical contact during Mr. Weinstein's awkward pass and Mr. Weinstein."

Weinstein's team also emphasized the length of time Thurman waited to release her allegation. They added that they were "saddened and puzzled as to 'why' Ms. Thurman, someone he considers a colleague and a friend, waited 25 years to make these allegations public."

In another display of *denial*, on October 6, 2017, Weinstein's attorney Lisa Bloom said in a statement that many of the accusations leveled against her client were "patently false," adding that he "does dispute many of the allegations" (White, 2018). She added that the married father of five children struggled with his temper and was "deeply bothered by his some of his emotional responses" (White, 2018).

A few months later, Weinstein outright denied allegations of sexual misconduct. He included the following paragraph in statement given to CNN:

> Any allegations of non-consensual sex are unequivocally denied by Mr. Weinstein. Mr. Weinstein has further confirmed that there were never any acts of retaliation against any women for refusing his advances.

Bolstering

Weinstein hinted at using bolstering by noting that "he and Thurman formerly shared an extremely close and mutually beneficial working relationship where they have made several successful film projects together" (Evans & Patten, 2017).

Table 9.1   Harvey Weinstein's Image Restoration Tactics

Strategy/Tactic	Key Characteristic	Example
Denial		
Simple Denial	Did not do act	Released photos that his team said "demonstrate the strong relationship Mr. Weinstein and Ms. Thurman had had over the years" His team also emphasized the length of time Thurman waited to release her allegation. They added that they were "saddened and puzzled as to 'why' Ms. Thurman, someone he considers a colleague and a friend, waited 25 years to make these allegations public"
Shift Blame	Another did act	
Evade Responsibility		
Provocation	Act was response to another's offense	
Defeasibility	Lack of information or ability	
Accident	Act was a mishap	Weinstein acknowledged making an awkward pass 25 years ago at Thurman in England after misreading her signals, after a flirtatious exchange in Paris
Good Intentions	Act was meant well	
Reduce Offensiveness		
Bolster	Stress good traits	Weinstein noted that he and Thurman have shared a very close and mutually beneficial working relationship where they have made several very successful film projects together
Minimize	Act not serious	
Corrective Action		
Normalcy	The individual can work to return things to the way they were before the incident in question	
Prevention of repeat offenses	The individual can make assurances of adjustments that will prevent any similar incidents from occurring in the future.	

(Continued)

Table 9.1   Harvey Weinstein's Image Restoration Tactics (Continued)

Strategy/Tactic	Key Characteristic	Example
Mortification		
Apology	The person admits responsibility for the actions in question and seeks forgiveness for them	Weinstein stated, "Georgina will be with Lisa and others kicking my a** to be a better human being and to apologize to people for my bad behavior, to say I'm sorry, and to absolutely mean it"

Evade Responsibility

In an example of *evading responsibility*, Weinstein acknowledged making an awkward pass 25 years ago at Thurman in England after misreading her signals during a flirtatious exchange in Paris, for which he immediately apologized and deeply regrets (Evans & Patten, 2017).

His spokespersons added that pictures taken throughout the history of their relationship tell a completely different story and that there would be more are detailed response later from Weinstein's attorney. The photographs released by Baird depict Weinstein in party surroundings with Thurman and others. One shows Weinstein and Thurman, John Travolta and Quentin Tarantino at a 20th anniversary party for *Pulp Fiction*.

Reduced Offensiveness and Mortification

Weinstein *reduced the offensiveness* of this act by using *minimization*. In an effective image repair tactic, Weinstein indicated he needed help. Weinstein's spokeswoman confirmed to CNN that he is heading to rehab. On October 5, 2017, in the statement Weinstein sent *The Times*, he apologized again, stating, "I came of age in the '60s and '70s, when all the rules about behavior and workplaces were different." He continued:

That was the culture then. I have since learned it's not an excuse, in the office—or out of it. To anyone. I realized some time ago that I needed to be a better person, and my interactions with the people I work with have changed. I appreciate the way I've behaved with colleagues in the past has caused a lot of pain, and I sincerely apologize for it.

I hope that my actions will speak louder than words and that one day we will all be able to earn their trust and sit down together with Lisa to learn more. Jay Z wrote in 4:44 "I'm not the man I thought I was, and I better be that man for my children." The same is true for me. I want a second chance in the community, but I know I've got work to do to earn it. I have goals that are now priorities.

Trust me, this isn't an overnight process. I've been trying to do this for 10 years, and this is a wake-up call. I cannot be more remorseful about the people I hurt, and I plan to do right by all of them.

In this display of *mortification*, Weinstein made assurances of adjustments that will prevent any similar incidents from occurring in the future. Weinstein indicated his wife was standing by his side. The statement included the following quote, "Georgina and I have talked about this at length," he said. "We went out with Lisa Bloom [an attorney who was advising him at the time] last night when we knew the article was coming out. Georgina will be with Lisa and others kicking my a** to be a better human being and to apologize to people for my bad behavior, to say I'm sorry, and to absolutely mean it."

Weinstein spoke too soon. His wife Georgina Chapman divorced him amid allegations of rape, abuse and other forms of sexual misconduct against him. The two, who had been married ten years, agreed on an eight-figure deal to end their marriage (Mullin & Marsh, 2018). The couple have two children, ages seven and four, and sources say she will get primary custody. In a statement to *People Magazine*, Chapman, his ex-wife, stated (Respers France & Selter, 2018):

My heart breaks for all the women who have suffered tremendous pain because of these unforgivable actions. I have chosen to leave my husband. Caring for my young children is my first priority and I ask the media for privacy at this time.

Corrective Action

Weinstein also demonstrated *corrective actions* in the October 5, 2017, statement. Weinstein indicated he was "going to need a place to channel that anger, so I've decided that I'm going to give the NRA my full attention." I hope Wayne LaPierre will enjoy his retirement party. I'm going to do it at the same I had my Bar Mitzvah. I'm making a movie about our president; perhaps we can make it a joint retirement party.

Weinstein publicized a scholarship he initiated. He stated, "One year ago, I began organizing a $5 million foundation to give scholarships to women directors at USC. While this might seem coincidental, it has been in the works for a year. It will be named after my mom, and I won't disappoint her."

Audience Response on Pinterest

To get a sense of audience response on a social media platform, we looked at Pinterest pins. In general, Pinterest pins fell into four categories: the movement's impact/success, its history, its victims/perpetrators and the fall-out from #MeToo and Weinstein's case.

Fallout from #MeToo and Weinstein's case. Many of the Pinterest pins emphasized news surrounding the #MeToo and Weinstein. For instance, there was an article about Weinstein turning himself in, the *Times* cover story designating #MeToo the story of the year and various other news items. Other pins detailed the success of the #MeToo movement and how it has surpassed other online campaigns.

Several of the pins highlighted Weinstein's relationships with various celebrities, including Oprah Winfrey. They questioned how she could speak negatively of him now when they were previously good friends. Winfrey was labeled as being part of the problem. I knew hashtag emerged indicating #SheKnew.

Pins also questioned the future of awards ceremonies that have previously carried the Weinstein stamp including Cannes festival and the Oscars. Pins linked to articles questioning what the fallout might be for these festivals. Another pin referenced a Cannes hotline to reporters' sexual harassment and assault. Most of the pins were anti-Weinstein; however, a few questioned if he could have a fair trial.

MEDIA AND AUDIENCE RESPONSE TO WEINSTEIN

After the *New York Times* article broke, no one publicly came to his defense. Instead, some in Hollywood admitted they were unsurprised by the stories of Weinstein's treatment of women, saying they had long been an open secret (Rottenberg et al., 2017).

Media coverage and polls indicate people did not accept Weinstein's apology. For instance, according to the results of poll commissioned by the Economist/YouGov Poll, Americans believed Weinstein was guilty with only 2 percent of individuals surveyed saying allegations are false, and 71percent saying they are true. The remaining respondents were not sure (Frankovic, 2018).

The *Wall Street Journal* listed Harvey Weinstein as one of the most hated public figures in the United States. They explained that the once darling of the American independent film movement in the 1990s, and the producer or distributor of over 80 Oscar-winning films, has been engulfed in controversy since the 2017 *New York Times* expose. Much of the public outrage over the growing scandal has been directed at the Weinstein Company's leadership, which may have been complicit in Weinstein's actions.

The rankings were based on a range of information, including major news events from the last year, customer survey results from the American Customer Satisfaction Index, employee reviews on Glassdoor, as well as our own annual customer satisfaction survey, 24/7 Wall St. identified America's most hated companies (Stebbens et al., 2018).

Also worth noting, Weinstein's influence had already begun to dim considerably in recent years. The Weinstein Co. has faced significant financial challenges, and new, deeper-pocketed competitors—including Amazon Studios, A24, Netflix and Fox Searchlight—have stolen the awards season spotlight.

Demonstrating the importance of the #MeToo movement and Weinstein's case, on April 16, 2018, *The New York Times* and the *New Yorker Magazine* won the Pulitzer Prize gold medal for public service. The two publications were honored for exposing Weinstein's sexual assault allegations. *The New Yorker* was honored for stories by Ronan Farrow, a contributing writer, and the *New York Times* was honored for articles written by Jodi Kantor and Megan Twohey (Pearce, 2018).

Another outcome of the revelations was *Citizen Rose*, which premiered January 30, 2018, on E Network to highlight Rose McGowan, one of the many women who spoke out against Weinstein during the #MeToo movement. Amy Introcaso-Davis, executive vice president of Development and Production at E!, describes the show as highlighting "Rose McGowan's courage in addressing sexual abuse and harassment in Hollywood ignited a conversation and inspired other women to speak out against their abusers."

Worth noting is a few women have come to his defense, including Jennifer Lawrence, who told Oprah Winfrey she had known Weinstein since she was 20 years old and said, "he had only ever been nice to me," and Meryl Streep, who stated publicly that Weinstein had always been respectful to her in their working relationship," the lawyers add (Sager, 2017). Jennifer Lawrence told Oprah, "We do have a responsibility to say something; we've all worked with him, but everybody needed a moment." Lawrence, 27, told Oprah Winfrey in the *Hollywood Reporter:*

> Just speaking for myself, I had known him since I was 20, and he had only ever been nice to me—except for the moments that he wasn't, and then I called him an a-hole, and we moved on," she explained. "He was paternal to me. So I needed a moment to process everything because I thought I knew this guy, and then he's being accused of rape. We all knew he was a dog, we knew that he was a . . . tough guy, a brute, a tough guy to negotiate with. (Sager, 2017)

CONCLUSIONS

This study combines IRT and feminist theories to explore user-generated content in the characterization of #MeToo and the Weinstein case. Specifically, this chapter addresses celebrity image repair strategies in sexual assault cases and the media's coverage of these strategies. Sexual assault and feminist theory are important concepts to consider in this analysis of Weinstein, #MeToo and his use of image restoration tactics.

Study findings are particularly important because of the prevalence of sexual assault cases. A March 9, 2018, NBC News poll concluded a majority of adults in the United States believed the spotlight on sexual assault and harassment has helped address gender inequality (Shabad & Perry, 2018). The survey indicated 51 percent of respondents believed reports about sexual assault have helped address the gender gap. On the other hand, 20 percent said that those same reports lead to the unfair treatment of men. Just over a quarter of adults said that those reports have made no difference in society (Shabad & Perry, 2018).

The Weinstein case is still unfolding. However, this chapter provides a look at the groundwork that has been laid for Weinstein to salvage his image. Weinstein used *mortification*, apologizing almost immediately. However, his apology was sandwiched between other tactics such as *bolstering* and *corrective action*. As part of his apology, he used his age and era he was born as an image repair tactic. He stated: "That was the culture then. I have since learned it's not an excuse, in the office—or out of it." This tactic was effective to individuals who could relate to his statement. His announcement that it was not an excuse was an important part of his overall image repair tactics. In sexual abuse cases, it is important for the perpetrator to take responsibility for his or her actions.

Weinstein's most successful demonstration of *corrective action* is his initiation of a $5 million foundation to give scholarships to women directors at USC. Weinstein's emphasis on awarding women scholarship funds is a step in the right direction and an attempt to empower women with an education.

Another positive image repair tactics was for him to indicate he was seeking counseling for his previous behavior. This tactic indicates not only was he admitting he was wrong, but he was seeking help to become a better person. This action indicates Weinstein truly has a desire to change.

Previous studies have indicated the role of familial support in these types of scandals is essential. A personal disadvantage in Weinstein's case was the decision of his wife to divorce him, considering the other cases mentioned in the introduction and literature review (i.e., Cosby and Trump), the accused kept their marriages intact.

This study of Weinstein's image repair tactics and audience response offers insight into how celebrities might respond to sexual assault allegations and expectations for audience response. The study has limitations due to the time frame this chapter was written. Future studies may look at the long-term effects of Weinstein's image repair tactics coupled with media and poll results to get a better idea of the effectiveness of his efforts.

As with all studies, this analysis of social media framing of #MeToo and Harvey Weinstein had limitations. The most prominent limitation is it does not analyze other popular social media sites such as Facebook or Instagram. It is also lacking feedback from persons who posted to the platforms analyzed. The authors selected Pinterest, for its different perspectives on the topic and target audience of women in the media arena. Even with these limitations, this study extends the feminist literature on #MeToo and IRT.

Findings indicate that celebrities must be careful to establish a carefully tailored persona on each social media site in order to garner the popular support of users. It is imperative for them to respond appropriately to such content and to maintain an active presence on various social media platforms.

Of particular interest for future research would be the development of IRT response framework aimed for celebrity sex scandals in the #MeToo era. Handling such cases is more complex as there is a complete movement against sexual harassment, assault and abuse.

Part IV

GENDER, RACE, AND IRT

Chapter 10

Passing for Black

An Analysis of Rachel Dolezal's Image Repair Strategies

Mia Moody-Ramirez and Endia Turney

In June 2015, Rachel Dolezal, 37, a civil-rights advocate and former instructor of Africana education at Eastern Washington University, made national headlines after her parents revealed she had misrepresented herself as black since 2006 (Ford & Botello, 2015; Gayle, 2015). In an interview, Dolezal's parents stated she is white and had changed her appearance over time to look black. "She chose to represent herself as an black woman or a biracial person, and that's simply not true," said Ruthanne Dolezal (Mataconis, 2015). Dolezal had served as the Spokane NAACP president and had been hired by her previous employer under the assumption that she is multiracial or black.

Within a few days of the revelation, citizens expressed their feelings about the incident via memes on social media. These memes covered a number of themes, including race, gender, politics and pop culture. They were an indication of how the public, not just the media, reacted to Dolezal.

In many instances, Dolezal was characterized as a white woman who stole something from the black community by assuming the identity of an black female. In her blog entry titled, "Your White Opinion on Dolezal is Probably Irrelevant," Nelson (2015) noted people of color have "varied and justifiable feelings on the matter." She added: "Most of the reactions I've seen and read have been negative ones. There are a slew of memes being passed around that mock Dolezal's "identification" clarification, and the hashtag #askrachel trended with tongue-in-cheek questions meant to determine just how black her life experience had been."

CONSTRUCTIONS OF RACE

Constructions of race in America at one time centered on the "one drop rule," which is a historical colloquial term for a belief among some people in the

United States that a person with any trace of African ancestry is black (Leland & Beals, 1997). The rule, which stems from slavery, was a way to ensure that the offspring of slaves and masters would remain enslaved.

Bell (1992) argues that slavery set the precedent for sacrificing black rights in order to maintain the status quo. However, racial meanings have shifted over time, and scholars have observed the fluidity of race (e.g., Hall, 1980; Omi & Winant, 2002). Race is often marked by physical and cultural traits by which people construct categories. Race is also marked by group solidarity, familial ties and empowerment. Omi and Winant (1994) stated, "For all its fungibility and flexibility, race continues to code the social locations and identities of individuals and groups and to influence social opportunities, resource distribution, educational outcomes, power relationships, ways of thinking, and much more" (p. 35).

The question of Dolezal's race first emerged in a 2010 story published by the Coeur d'Alene Press. The article reported Dolezal's resignation from the town's Human Rights Education Institute. A comment said, "The people who have known Rachel for years do not like seeing her fraudulently passing herself off as 'black' for the sake of 'the cause'" (Gayle, 2015). Dolezal hinted at her self-appointed racial identity in another Coeur d'Alene Press story, published in 2009, where she described herself as "transracial"—a description that with hindsight could be seen as similar to transgender (Gayle, 2015).

Dolezal's self-selection of race became an issue because of existing cultural narratives, stereotypes and representations of both black and women. Early analyses found media deeply implicated in the patterns of discrimination operating against all women, invisibility or gender stereotypes (e.g., Carter & Steiner, 2003; Enriques, 2001; Gallagher, 1981; hooks, 1992; Krolokke & Sorensen, 2006; Zoonen, 1994).

According to Shome (2001), white femininity is "an ideological construction through which meanings about White women and their place in the social order is naturalized ... and as sites through which otherness; racial, sexual, classed, gendered, and nationalized [identity] is negotiated" (2001, p. 323). On the other hand, poor and/or women of color are prepackaged using negative stereotypes, regardless of their actual behavior (Collins, 1990; Crenshaw 1988).

TEXTS ANALYZED

This chapter combines framing, Benoit's image restoration theory (IRT) and medium theory to explore Dolezal's use of image repair tactics following the revelation by her parents that she is not black. The textual analysis approach often outlines culture as a narrative or storytelling process in which particular texts or cultural artifacts consciously or unconsciously link themselves to larger stories in society.

To identify key visual and textual themes, researchers used constant comparative analysis (Eaves, 2001) to openly code images and text posted following the Rachel Dolezal incident (Lindlof & Taylor, 2011). We analyzed the following: statements regarding the crisis, Dolezal's Facebook posts, television, newspaper and magazine interviews, a TMZ Report, and interviews with NBC's Matt Lauer and *Vanity Fair*.

DOLEZAL'S USE OF IMAGE RESTORATION

Dolezal released several statements and was interviewed by numerous media outlets following her parents' revelation about her race. In general, the themes that emerged included the idea that she identifies as black, she has black brothers and she was a victim because of her circumstances. *Transcendence* is the image restoration tactic Dolezal used most frequently to *reduce offensiveness* by indicating there are more important considerations than the issue at hand. In Dolezal's letter to the Executive Committee and NAACP Members, she stated:

> Many issues face us now that drive at the theme of urgency. Police brutality, biased curriculum in schools, economic disenfranchisement, health inequities, and a lack of pro-justice political representation are among the concerns at the forefront of the current administration of the Spokane NAACP. And yet, the dialogue has unexpectedly shifted internationally to my personal identity in the context of defining race and ethnicity.

Dolezal added she is consistently committed to "empowering marginalized voices and believe that many individuals have been heard in the last hours and days that would not otherwise have had a platform to weigh in on this important discussion."

Other more important considerations than her race, according to Dolezal include "Criminal Justice & Public Safety, Health & Healthcare, Education, Economic Sustainability, and Voting Rights & Political Representation." These issues affect millions, often with a life or death outcome, she added. Dolezal concluded this paragraph with the sentence, "The movement is larger than a moment in time or a single person's story, and I hope that everyone offers their robust support of the Journey for Justice campaign that the NAACP launches today!"

This tactic continued in an interview with Sky News, during which Dolezal said to the original article that questioned her racial identity, "I don't give two shits what you guys think." She said it's more important for her to "clarify" this with the black community than to "explain it to a community that I, quite frankly, don't think really understands the definitions of race and ethnicity" (Workneh, 2015).

In an interview with CBS affiliate KREM 2 News, Dolezal maintained she is black. "Yes, I do consider myself to be black and that's because . . . you know, that's how I identify," she told the station. "I actually don't like the term 'African American.' I prefer the term 'black,'" she said. Dolezal said she has nothing to say to critics outraged by her racial identification. She also said any concerns people may have about misrepresentation of her race is something she'd rather discuss only with the black community (Workneh, 2015).

It's more important for me to clarify that with the black community and my executive board than it is to explain it to a community that I, quite frankly, don't think really understands the definitions of race and ethnicity. Dolezal encouraged critics to "maybe think about W.E.B Du Bois that said race is usually biological, always cultural."

NAACP STANCE

The NAACP helped *reduce the offensiveness* of Dolezal's case in their statement. The statement began with the sentence, "For 106 years, the National Association for the Advancement of Colored People has held a long and proud tradition of receiving support from people of all faiths, races, colors and creeds."

NAACP Spokane Washington Branch President Rachel Dolezal is enduring a legal issue with her family, and we respect her privacy in this matter. One's racial identity is not a qualifying criteria or disqualifying standard for NAACP leadership. The NAACP Alaska-Oregon-Washington State Conference stands behind Ms. Dolezal's advocacy record. In every corner of this country, the NAACP remains committed to securing political, educational and economic justice for all people, and we encourage Americans of all stripes to become members and serve as leaders in our organization.

Bolstering

Dolezal used bolstering to stress her good behavior (Table 10.1). She stated that she was delighted that "so many organizations and individuals have supported and collaborated with the Spokane NAACP under my leadership to grow this branch into one of the healthiest in the nation in five short months."

Table 10.1 Rachel Dolezal's Image Repair Strategies

Strategy/Key Characteristics	Description	Example
Denial		
	Simple denial Did not perform act	Dolezal denied that she needed to apologize.
	Shift the blame: act performed by another	She shifted the blame to her parents for releasing the information: "whitewash some of the work I have done and who I am."
	Stonewalling: by refusing to answer questions or by giving evasive replies	When asked if her father is an African American man, Dolezal responded: "I don't know what you are implying."
Evade Responsibility		
	Provocation: responded to act of another	X
	Defeasibility: lack of information or ability	X
	Accident: act was a mishap	X
	Good Intentions: meant well in act	X
Reducing Offensiveness of Event		
	Bolstering: stress good traits	Discussed her contributions to society via the NAACP
	Minimization: act not serious	X
	Differentiation: act less offensive	X
	Transcendence: more important considerations	Indicated there are more important considerations than the issue at hand. "I don't give two shits what you guys think." She said it's more important for her to "clarify" this with the black community than to "explain it to a community that I, quite frankly, don't think really understands the definitions of race and ethnicity" (Feldman, 2015).

(Continued)

Table 10.1 Rachel Dolezal's Image Repair Strategies (Continued)

Strategy/Key Characteristics	Description	Example
	Endorsement: support from a celebrity and credible source	Dolezal received support from both black and white celebrities. "Everybody has some type of African blood in them," added cohost Raven Symone. "And what makes a black person—just your skin?" As far as Dolezal is concerned, since there is technically no such thing as race, she merely selected the cultural group with which she most identifies. Who can blame her? Anyone who listens to Isaac Hayes' "Theme From Shaft" wants to be black—for a little while anyway (Abdul-Jabbar, 2015). "Look, just like people say 'I feel like I'm a man, I feel like I'm a woman, I feel like I'm this.' She wants to be a black woman, fine," Whoopi Goldberg said during an episode of *The View*.
	Attack accuser: reduce credibility of accuser	She attacked society for not accepting her genuine identification as a black woman. She attacked the accuser, or attempted to reduce credibility of the accuser—her parents. I have waited in deference while others expressed their feelings, beliefs, confusions and even conclusions—absent the full story."
Compensation	Reimburse victim	X
Corrective Action	Plan to solve or prevent problem	X
Mortification	Apologize for Act	She never apologized Dolezal said. "If people feel misled or deceived, then sorry that they feel that way, but I believe that's more due to their definition and construct of race in their own minds than it is to my integrity or honesty, because I wouldn't say I'm African American, but I would say I'm black, and there's a difference in those terms"

Source: Benoit typology (in Wilcox & Cameron, 2012, p. 267).

She also indicated that she had the NAACP's best interest at heart: "In the eye of this current storm, I can see that a separation of family and organizational outcomes is in the best interest of the NAACP. It is with complete allegiance to the cause of racial and social justice and the NAACP that I step aside from the Presidency and pass the baton to my Vice President, Naima Quarles-Burnley."

Dolezal emphasized her acquisition of a "beautiful office for the organization in the heart of downtown." She added that she helped bring the local branch into financial compliance and catalyzed committees to do strategic work in the five Game Changer issues listed above. According to Dolezal, she also launched community forums, increased membership numbers, and helped many individuals find the legal, financial and practical support needed to fight race-based discrimination. "I have positioned the Spokane NAACP to buttress this transition," she added. Dolezal highlighted that seeking justice is bigger than her crisis:

> I will never stop fighting for human rights and will do everything in my power to help and assist, whether it means stepping up or stepping down, because this is not about me. It's about justice. This is not me quitting; this is a continuum. It's about moving the cause of human rights and the Black Liberation Movement along the continuum from Resistance to Chattel Slavery to Abolition to Defiance of Jim Crow to the building of Black Wall Street to the Civil Rights and Black Power Movement to the #BlackLivesMatter movement and into a future of self-determination and empowerment.

Attack Accuser

As another tactic to reduce the offensiveness of the crisis, she *attacked the accuser*, or attempted to reduce credibility of the accuser—her parents. In her first interview after being exposed as a white woman pretending to be black, Dolezal rejected the notion that she had deceived anyone. She accused her parents, who first revealed her race charade, of trying to "whitewash some of the work I have done and who I am."

According to Dolezal, her parent's announcement damaged her personal and professional life. In an interview with *Vanity Fair*, Dolezal revealed that she had lost her job and many of her friends (Lara, 2015). "I've got to figure it out before Aug. 1, because my last paycheck was like $1,800 in June," Dolezal said after losing her position as the president of the Spokane, Washington, chapter of the NAACP as well as a part-time teaching job at Eastern Washington University. "[I lost] friends and the jobs and the work and—oh, my God—so much at the same time."

Stonewalling

Dolezal also used stonewalling, or the practice of delaying or blocking a request, process or person, by refusing to answer questions or by giving evasive replies. During a *USA Today* interview, when asked do you think it's fair for people to question what your relationship is and whether you are his actual mother, Dolezal stated, "I think that's between me and him. You know? So, no, I don't think that's fair. It's none of their business." When asked, do you feel like you have, in any way, misrepresented your relationship with him, Dolezal responded, "Um. The only degree to which, um—You know I would say, I would first say no because I'm his mom and I do see myself as [that]. He's not my brother. That's not our relationship, you know?" However, her adopted brother, Ezra Dolezal, contradicted her version of events and claimed she advised him not to expose her secret.

Mortification

Mortification is the most important, although final image repair tactic. Dolezal used several image repair tactics; however, *mortification* was not one of them. She *reduced the offensiveness* of her actions by focusing on her contributions to the community via her involvement in the NAACP. She used *attack the accuser* in her response to her parents' decision to release information about her identity to the press. Throughout the whole process, she maintained that her transracial identity is genuine.

Although Dolezal never used mortification, she stated, "I don't know. I just feel like I didn't mislead anybody; I didn't deceive anybody," Dolezal said. "If people feel misled or deceived, then sorry that they feel that way, but I believe that's more due to their definition and construct of race in their own minds than it is to my integrity or honesty, because I wouldn't say I'm African American, but I would say I'm black, and there's a difference in those terms" (Lara, 2015).

Dolezal added: "This is not some freak 'Birth of a Nation' mockery blackface performance. This is on a very real, connected level." She also told the MSNBC host Melissa Harris-Perry, "I have really gone there with the experience, in terms of being a mother of two black sons and really owning what it means to experience and live blackness." Dolezal has continued to state that she identifies as black. In a statement she made on *Today* in June, she said. "It's not a costume. I don't know spiritually and metaphysically how this goes, but I do know that from my earliest memories I have awareness and connection with the black experience, and that's never left me" (Lara, 2015). "I identify as black," Dolezal said, when Lauer asked if she was an African American woman. She insisted that people didn't understand the "complexity" of her identity. She offered no apologies for her identity switch.

It's not something that I can put on and take off anymore. Like I said, I've had my years of confusion and wondering who I really [was] and why and how do I live my life and make sense of it all, but I'm not confused about that any longer. I think the world might be—but I'm not.

Demonstrating the dual nature of the Web, on one hand Dolezal used statements released on TV shows, online publications and social media to explain and minimize her actions. Conversely, viewers utilized the Web to respond to the case. In many instances, comments supported Dolezal in her decision to "become black." Other media responses were not as positive.

Media Response

The media was split in its characterization of Dolezal's case. "Jeff Yang, a columnist for The *Wall Street Journal Online,* stated for many black Americans and other people of color, she is an example of how the shadow of white entitlement extends over just about every aspect of life in America—how it shrouds even the ability to determine the bounds of one's own culture and community rather than have it defined by the whims of others" (Ford & Botello, 2015).

Yang continued, "Dolezal is a distraction. Our country's problems with race run far deeper with much greater consequences for people risking more than just public embarrassment. Tara Setmayer, a former communications director for U.S. Representative Dana Rohrabacher and a CNN political commentator, discussed the dangers of lionizing a liar. "One thing is perfectly clear: Rachel Dolezal is a liar. She created a complex world of delusion and deception that she perpetrated for years. Whether that delusion stems from white guilt of the nth degree or some other pathology, it's dangerous to lionize a liar" (Ford & Botello, 2015).

Clarence Page, a noted columnist, stated in an opinion piece on the topic that of all the questions that Dolezal's chosen lifestyle raise, the biggest was from her father in an NBC interview (Page, 2015): "She's a very talented woman doing work she believes in. Why can't she do that as a Caucasian woman?" Why indeed? Blacks and whites have worked together in the NAACP since its founding more than 100 years ago. Why did she have to lie about her race?

Page added that as admirable as Dolezal's civil rights work may have been, the suspicions over her reported hate crimes cast a cloud over her organization's entire mission (Page, 2015). When her leadership became a bigger distraction than a benefit, she had to go. "Yet Dolezal's negrophilia raises intriguing questions, including the validity of 'transracial' as a description of her transformation. Many people raise the timely issue of whether Dolezal should be accepted as a self-made black person, much as Caitlyn Jenner wants to be accepted as a woman" (Page, 2015).

In a *Chronicle of Higher Education* article titled, *Rachel Dolezal Case Leaves a Campus Bewildered and Some Scholars Disgusted,* faculty members there who know her are shocked and befuddled, said Scott Finnie, director of the university's Africana-education program. Finnie, who is African American, said that news of Dolezal's deception had come as such a surprise because of how she presented her personal story. Dolezal said she was born in a teepee, encountered physical abuse from her parents, and set up a hair-braiding service to raise the self-esteem of black girls (Patton, 2015).

"It did create an abnormal shock, not only because of her appearance but because she presented herself as someone who had a strong intensity about blackness," Finnie said. "There was this apparent connection in life experiences, not just ideology."

Renee Graham, who writes regularly for the *Globe*, stated that regardless of where we (black women) were raised or our differences in age, we shared an innate commonality (Graham, 2015). "We learned similar lessons from our mothers and grandmothers about how to conduct ourselves, no matter whether those lessons were delivered with accents from South Carolina, Jamaica, or Kenya. Early conversations blossomed and birthed confidence and trust; soon, a knowing look shared wordlessly could speak volumes" (Graham, 2015).

Celebrity Endorsements

Celebrity endorsements were common in the strategies to support Dolezal. "Look, just like people say 'I feel like I'm a man, I feel like I'm a woman, I feel like I'm this.' She wants to be a black woman, fine," Whoopi Goldberg said during an episode of *The View*. "Everything that comes with that, she is prepared for. Okay."

"Everybody has some type of African blood in them," added cohost Raven Symone. "And what makes a black person—just your skin?" She also later likened Dolezal's changing hair texture to black women getting their hair straightened. "Black women straighten their hair all the time," Symone pointed out after cohost Rosie Perez mentioned that white women adopt black hairstyles.

On MSNBC, Professor Michael Eric Dyson claimed Dolezal, a white woman, is culturally "blacker" than African American Supreme Court Justice Clarence Thomas, among other ridiculous racial assertions (Ford & Botello, 2015).

A celebrity opinion piece by Kareem Abdul-Jabbar stated that at no time in history has the challenge of personal identity seemed more relevant

(Abdul-Jabbar, 2015). "Olympic champion Bruce Jenner struggled for years with gender identity and only at the age of 65, as Caitlyn Jenner, seems to have come to some peace with it. The same goes for many in the gay community who have battled to embrace their true selves. The difference is that these people face a biological imperative rather than a choice of orientation."

He continued, "What we use to determine race is really nothing more than 'haphazard physical characteristics,' cultural histories and social conventions that distinguish one group from another" (Abdul-Jabbar, 2015). As far as Dolezal is concerned, since there is technically no such thing as race, she merely selected the cultural group with which she most identifies. Who can blame her? Anyone who listens to Isaac Hayes' "Theme From Shaft" wants to be black—for a little while anyway (Abdul-Jabbar, 2015).

Dave Chappelle told *The Washington Post* that he was wary of Dolezal jokes and the attention the media is giving her. He mentioned Dolezal during his commencement address to the Duke Ellington School of the Arts in Washington, DC—Chappelle's alma mater. But when he spoke to *The Post*, he elaborated on how he views her behavior.

"The thing that the media's gotta be real careful about, that they're kind of overlooking, is the emotional context of what she means," Chappelle said. "There's something that's very nuanced where she's highlighting the difference between personal feeling and what's construct as far as racism is concerned. I don't know what her agenda is, but there's an emotional context for black people when they see her and white people when they see her. There's a lot of feelings that are going to come out behind what's happening with this lady."

Public Opinion

A national survey of 1,000 likely voters conducted on June 18 and 21, 2015, by Rasmussen Reports indicated most voters agreed that racial identity should be based on birth, not preference, but black voters are less critical than others of Rachel Dolezal, a white woman who identifies as black who recently resigned from her post at the NAACP. The national telephone survey finds that 63 percent of Likely U.S. Voters believed Dolezal was being deceitful by claiming she was black. Just 13 percent disagreed, while 23 percent were not sure ("Most Black Voters Don't Think Rachel Dolezal Should Have Resigned From NAACP," 2015).

However, while most white (65%) and other minority voters (68%) believed Dolezal was being deceitful, just 46 percent of black voters agreed. In fact, 52 percent of black voters thought Dolezal should have stayed in her position as president of a Washington chapter of the National Association for the Advancement of Colored People, a view shared by just 20 percent of whites and 32 percent of other minority voters. Majorities of the latter two groups thought she should have resigned from her post.

An EpicTimes poll indicated the vast majority of Americans thought the story of former NAACP leader Rachel Dolezal was both hilarious and an embarrassment for the NAACP. Ten percent of poll participants thought the story was hilarious, 7 percent of poll participants believed it was just an embarrassment for the NAACP, 12 percent thought it wasn't worth the coverage and 71 percent thought all of the above.

CONCLUSIONS AND IMPLICATIONS

Broadening the application of Benoit's IRT, this case study looked at the image repair tactics of Rachel Dolezal following the revelation that she is white in 2015. This textual analysis adds a new perspective to IRT literature by using a critical race lens to analyze how Dolezal presented herself through personal statements, online sources and interviews and the media's coverage of the case. Dolezal used several image restoration tactics—*bolstering and reducing offensiveness, stonewalling.* She *reduced the offensiveness* of her actions by focusing on her contributions to the community via her involvement in the NAACP. She used *attack the accuser* in her response to her parents' decision to release information about her identity to the press.

Throughout the whole process, she maintained that her transracial identity is genuine. This was a positive decision as at the first hint of crisis, individuals must come up with a viable image repair plan of action that they will utilize simultaneously across all of their online outlets. Whether the first step is *mortification, bolstering* or *attack of accuser*, consistency is imperative. Many individuals found these tactics believable as demonstrated through the celebrity endorsements and favorable feedback she received from other credible sources. The one caveat to Dolezal's case is she never used *mortification*. Because of her decision to postpone this image repair tactic, many people disagreed with her stance on race and the misrepresentations of her father as black and her brother as her son.

Based on the findings, the researcher identified successful applications of critical race theory (CRT) to IRT that might be applicable to individuals who find themselves in race-related crisis situations in the future. The potential benefits available through the appropriate use of media outlets as image repair strategies are virtually limitless. If an individual follows an appropriate combination of Benoit's (1995a) image restoration tactics, he or she will have a much better chance of repairing their image quickly, efficiently, and permanently.

The announcement of Dolezal's deception created a stir in many communities with discussions emphasizing race, sexual orientation and political inclination. Therefore, the case served as an ideal starting point for discussions on the intersections of race and IRT.

The Dolezal saga is ongoing. She shares her story in a forthcoming Netflix documentary titled, *The Rachel Divide*. In it, Dolezal discusses the incident with her biological son Franklin (who is still recovering from the incident), who states, "This is gonna affect more than just your life." To which Dolezal responds, "If somebody has hope, don't take that away from them, because maybe that's all they have." "Trust me, it is going to bite me in the a–," he responds back (Kevito, 2018).

Dolezal's book, *In Full Color: Finding My Place in a Black and White World* (Dolezal, 2017), describes the path that led her from being a child of white evangelical parents to an NAACP chapter president and respected educator and activist who identifies as black. She recounts the deep emotional bond she formed with her four adopted black siblings, the sense of belonging she felt while living in black communities in Jackson, Mississippi and Washington, DC, and the experiences that have shaped her along the way. In the book, she asks the question, "What determines your race? Is it your DNA? The community in which you were raised? The way others see you or the way you see yourself?"

Chapter 11

Spanning the Decades

An Analysis of Monica Lewinsky's Image Restoration Strategies During a 2015 TED Talks Appearance

Macarena Hernandez, Liz Fassih, and Mia Moody-Ramirez

Monica Lewinsky became part of history in 1998 when news broke that she had an affair with then president Bill Clinton between 1995 and 1997. A graduate of Lewis & Clark College, Lewinsky was hired to work as an intern at the White House during the first term of President Bill Clinton, 49. She was later an employee of the White House Office of Legislative Affairs. In 1995, Lewinsky, 22, confided to her friend and Defense Department coworker Linda Tripp, who secretly recorded their telephone conversations, that Lewinsky masturbated with a cigar while President Clinton watched and masturbated as well.

Lewinsky confessed to Tripp that she had in her possession a blue Gap dress that still had the semen stain that resulted from her administering oral sex to President Clinton. The incident led to Clinton's impeachment in 1998 by the House of Representatives (but not by the Senate). Clinton was later acquitted of perjury and obstruction of justice.

The Lewinsky-Clinton story made national headlines and stayed in the news cycle for dozens of months. The sexual relationship was also detailed in a prosecutor's 400-plus-page report. Citizens and the media were unforgiving in their use of "shaming" narratives to frame Lewinsky negatively. In response to these negative portrayals, Lewinsky chose to make very few public appearances.

Fast forward to 2015; Lewinsky appeared on TED Talks, a series of videos featuring charismatic speakers from all over the world. During Lewinsky's segment, she discussed several key issues including the Clinton-Lewinsky scandal, public shaming and social media's role in bullying.

Lewinsky's talk was particularly relevant as shaming has become common in social media platforms. Internet shaming sites, social media platforms and online gossip magazines offer a venue for Internet shaming that was not available when Lewinsky's case emerged (Solove, 2007). Lewinsky's speech on cyberbullying and shaming provided an excellent opportunity for the exploration of IRT within the realm of a speech and social media audience response.

While previous studies provide valuable insight into image repair management of men who have had affairs (e.g., Benoit, 1995; Blaney & Benoit, 2001; Grossberger, 1995; Rowland, 1988), few have addressed image repair strategies used by women in the same situation. Most image repair studies use case studies, so generalizations are difficult to make.

This IRT study uses a feminist lens to explore Monica Lewinsky's use of a TED Talks speech to counter shaming narratives that emerged in the 1990s and remained for several decades. This chapter is important as it adds a new analysis to the literature on shaming, image repair and representations of women in general. Solove (2007) describes the use of public shaming as a tool for social control reminiscent of past public punishments methods such as Hawthorne's scarlet letter. However, as Lewinsky discussed in her speech, today there is one key difference in shaming today—Internet shaming creates a permanent public record of a person's transgressions.

IMAGE RESTORATION THEORY

When looking at image restoration, the framing of an incident and audience response, it is important to look at previous studies. Former president Bill Clinton relied on *denial* and *bolstering* strategies after his first brush with major scandal during his 1992 campaign (Blaney & Benoit, 2001). He denied doing anything illegal during his period of draft eligibility during the late 1960s. In addition, he denied acting opportunistically within the letter of the law in order to *evade* the draft. He used *bolstering* to talk about his general patriotism and military leadership of the Arkansas National Guard.

When Clinton was accused of an inappropriate sexual relationship with Monica Lewinsky in 1998, his personal image had been under attack since his first day in office by women alleging sexual misconduct and inappropriate relations (Denton & Holloway, 2003). Along with Lewinsky, Gennifer Flowers, Paula Jones and Kathleen Willey stepped forward amid public pressure alleging Clinton had been involved with them in some manner. Clinton's wife Hillary Clinton stood beside him throughout the scrutiny and investigation into his personal life. White House staff and contacts like pollster Dick

Morris advised Clinton that covering up the affair with Lewinsky would be viewed more critically by the nation than his actual infidelity. Clinton lied to the nation but later apologized and took responsibility for his actions. Though Clinton's reputation was tarnished as a husband, the nation continued to support him after the Lewinsky scandal. His apology and image as a successful politician were enough to repair his image.

Hillary Clinton was also in need of image repair in the 1990s surrounding a whirlwind of crises including accusations of fraud and her husband's extramarital affair. Her efforts to *deny* accusations and *reduce the offensiveness* of her actions failed; however, her image was ultimately improved by her corrective actions and by standing by her husband (Oles-Acevedo, 2012).

Another important image restoration case involves the scandals of American Televangelist Jimmy Swaggart. In 1981, when a wealthy California widow died leaving almost her entire estate to the Swaggart ministries, his ministries were charged with preying upon her loneliness and illness to secure donations from her. Swaggart was also investigated for other allegations, including using donations improperly, threatening a man for having improper relations with his daughter-in-law and having sexually inappropriate relations with prostitutes (Kaufman, 1988).

Church leaders questioned Swaggart, and eventually admitted "he had paid her to perform pornographic acts, and that he had had a fascination with pornography since childhood" (Kaufman, 1988). Because of the scandals, the minister temporarily stepped down as the head of Jimmy Swaggart Ministries. He also publicly apologized. According to *People Magazine*, Swaggart's televised confession was the most tortured public display of contrition in recent memory (Kaufman, 1988).

In his public apology, Swaggart admitted to his wife, son and congregation that he had had "an encounter with a New Orleans prostitute" (Kaufman, 1988). This public apology was only the beginning strategy for his attempt to alter the public's opinion of him. Swaggart's image repair tactics also included restitution via donations, rehabilitation and leave from the church. Because of these image repair tactics, Swaggart repaired his severely damaged image. His ministries are still thriving.

In another example, Gary Hart was a Democratic senator from Colorado and presidential candidate in the elections of 1984 and 1988, until the media caught him in an extramarital affair. The *Miami Herald* has pictures of Hart and model Donna Rice on a yacht called Monkey Business, and another with Rice in Hart's lap. Rowland (1988) says the fall of Hart is attributed to poor judgment, media attention over political agenda and a failed apologia. Americans revealed in *New York Times*/CBS polls that they were less concerned with the actual affair and personal life of Hart, but rather his character, revealed in his lapse of judgment (Rowland, 1988). Sixty percent of

Americans agreed that these Miami journalists had overstepped the boundaries of good taste and professionalism (Rowland, 1988).

Hart denied that he spent the night with Rice; he refused to respond to accusations of adultery, then shifted blame to different theological definitions as he made up unbelievable stories that undercut his credibility (Rowland, 1988). Regarding his politics, he bolstered his credentials as a leader, transcended uncontrollable situations and differentiation of his maturity. Upon his return to politics, he mentioned the situation in the Concord speech, implying that his family had forgiven him, and encouraged his political campaign—as Americans should too—because he had truly grown and changed as a person. From that point on, his wife made joint appearances with him.

In similar situations, Rowland (1988) recommends an *apology*, and *denial* if applicable, to allow the press to see their mistake as a personal invasion of privacy. It is also important to hold unlimited press conferences for questions and an explanation.

Based on this review of the literature, this chapter addresses three questions: (1) What are the general themes of Lewinsky's TED Talks speech? (2) What image repair tactics emerged? (3) How did audiences respond on Twitter to Lewinsky's TED Talks speech?

TEXTS ANALYZED

To assess Lewinsky's image repair strategies, we analyzed a transcript of her speech that was posted to the TED Talks website. Because Lewinsky controlled what she included in her speech, it offered a comprehensive look of her viewpoints and a first-hand look at her personal image-restoration tactics. To assess how audiences responded, we analyzed 1,500 tweets posted on Tagboard tagged #MonicaLewinsky in response to the speech, which are noteworthy because they presented diverse viewpoints. This sample provided a sense of how people responded to Lewinsky's speech.

MONICA LEWINSKY TED TALKS THEMES

After keeping a low profile for several decades, in 2015, Lewinsky appeared on TED Talks. While Lewinsky briefly addressed the Clinton scandal and some of her struggles during the crises, she primarily focused on public shaming and the difference the Internet has made today. One of the more compelling statements of Lewinsky's speech is in this paragraph:

For nearly two decades now, we have slowly been sowing the seeds of shame and public humiliation in our cultural soil, both on- and offline. Gossip websites, paparazzi, reality programming, politics, news outlets and sometimes hackers all traffic in shame. It's led to desensitization and a permissive environment online which lends itself to trolling, invasion of privacy, and cyberbullying.

Other powerful words that emerged in Lewinsky's speech included "public humiliation," and "compassion" (Table 11.1). These words indicate the importance of understanding an individual's circumstance after an incident of public shaming has occurred. She encouraged listeners to have compassion for other people who may encounter similar circumstances. Lewinsky also used terms such as "empathy," "bullying" and "shame," to describe her initiative to help teenagers who are cyberbullied by their peers. To emphasize her key points, she discussed the implications of public shaming:

Public shaming as a blood sport has to stop. . . . In 1988, I was Patient Zero of losing a personal reputation on a global scale almost instantaneously. Today, the kind of online public shaming . . . I went through has become constant. (TED Talks, 2015)

Lewinsky also discussed the theory of minority influence, proposed by social psychologist Serge Moscovici, which states that even in small numbers, if there is consistency over time, change can happen. She encouraged individuals in her audience to be an impetus for change by taking action when necessary and to have empathy for victims of public shaming.

She provided anecdotes, statistics and encouraged audience feedback. Lewinsky encouraged her audience to think about society's responsibility in freedom of expression and to take action. "We all want to be heard, but let's acknowledge the difference between speaking up with intention and speaking up for attention."

Table 11.1   Words Used in Lewinsky's 2015 TED Talks Speech

Term	Occurrence
Public humiliation	12
Compassion	10
Bullying	10
Empathy	7
Shame	6
Public shaming	3
Culture of humiliation	3

LEWINSKY'S IMAGE REPAIR TACTICS

Lewinsky used many image repair tactics in this TED Talks speech, including *bolstering* and *transcendence*. First, individuals may use *bolstering* to strengthen the audience's positive feelings toward them and to offset the negative feelings connected with them. Individuals may describe positive characteristics they have or positive acts they have done in the past. Demonstrating *bolstering*, Lewinsky emphasized her work with victims of public shaming. She highlighted individuals who had considered suicide and discussed how her mother had worried about her committing suicide.

Another strategy is to try to minimize the negative feelings associated with the person. Humor was a prominent strategy used by Lewinsky. Within the first minute of her speech, she warmed up the mostly young, female audience by joking about being mentioned in almost 40 rap songs and getting "hit on by a 27-year-old guy" at a conference. His pick-up line: "He could make me feel 22 again." "I realized later that night," she continued, "I'm probably the only person over 40 who does not want to be 22 again." Lewinsky also received several chuckles when she referred to the red beret she often wore during the scandal. She stated, "Now, I admit I made mistakes, especially wearing that beret." At another point, she asked the audience for a show of hands, "of anyone who didn't make a mistake or do something they regretted at 22?"

Transcendence

Transcendence is an attempt to focus on considerations that are more important than one's transgressions (Table 11.2). Lewinsky used this tactic several times throughout her speech. She stated, "I lost my reputation and my dignity. I lost almost everything, and I almost lost my life."

Lewinsky hammered home the importance by placing the scandal in context. She said public shaming did not happen as much in 1998: "By this, I mean the stealing of people's private words, actions, conversations or photos, and then making them public—public without consent, public without context, and public without compassion."

Lewinsky also mentioned noted scholars such as Professor Nicolaus Mills, who penned the phrase culture of humiliation, and Brené Brown, a research professor at the University of Houston Graduate College of Social Work, who studies vulnerability, courage, worthiness and shame. Brown has one of the most popular TED Talks, amassing more than 19 million views since her speech about vulnerability was posted in 2010.

To hammer home her point, Lewinsky cited "staggering statistics" released by ChildLine, a UK nonprofit that focuses on helping youth, that between

Table 11.2   Lewinsky's Image Repair Tactics

Strategy/Key Characteristics	Tactic
Evasion of Responsibility Provocation: responded to act of another Attack accuser: reduce credibility of accuser	Lewinsky stated she was an intern who slept with the president of the United States. The media kept it in the news cycle. She describes people as bullies and mean. This invasion of others is a raw material, efficiently and ruthlessly mined, packaged and sold at a profit. A marketplace has emerged where public humiliation is a commodity and shame is an industry.
Reducing Offensiveness of Event Bolstering: stress good traits Transcendence: focus on more important considerations	Young and dumb Can I see a show of hands of anyone here who didn't make a mistake or do something they regretted at 22? Yep. That's what I thought. "Not a day goes by that I'm not reminded of my mistake, and I regret that mistake deeply." Described her suicide attempts I lost my reputation and my dignity. I lost almost everything, and I almost lost my life. Focused on victims of public shaming and person who had killed herself.
Corrective Action: Plan to Solve or Prevent Problem	Softened image, dressed conservatively, dressy black pants and a blouse with minimal makeup Used humor I joked with them that some might only have heard of me from rap songs. Yes, I'm in rap songs. Almost 40 rap songs. (Laughter) Now, I admit I made mistakes, especially wearing that beret. At the age of 41, I was hit on by a 27-year-old guy. I know, right? He was charming and I was flattered, and I declined. You know what his unsuccessful pickup line was? He could make me feel 22 again. (Laughter)

Source: Benoit (1997).

2012 and 2013 there was an 87 percent increase in calls and emails about cyberbullying.

By quoting scholars and citing statistics, Lewinsky attempted to elevate herself from a victim with a personal story to an expert with something to contribute to the discussion—one who earned a master's degree in social psychology from the London School of Economics, reminding the audience that she is smart, articulate and a capable spokesperson for shaming and anti-bullying campaigns.

Lewinsky's speech spanned the decades and described the difference in public shaming after the emergence of social media. She noted, "The land-scape has sadly become much more populated with instances like mine, whether or not someone actually make a mistake, and now it's for both public and private people. The consequences for some have become dire, very dire." In one particularly poignant anecdote, she discussed the death of a young man named Tyler, who was secretly videotaped with a web camera by his roommate while being intimate with another man. His roommate released the video online, and Tyler decided to take his life. Lewinsky stated, "When the online world learned of this incident, the ridicule and cyberbullying ignited. A few days later, Tyler jumped from the George Washington Bridge to his death. He was 18."

Lewinsky described her mother's pain during her ordeal. Following Tyler's death, she said her mother began to relive the 1998 tragedy. Lewinsky noted that "cruelty to others is nothing new, but online, technologically enhanced shaming is amplified, uncontained, and permanently accessible."

Lewinsky *reduced the offensiveness* of what happened in 1988 by building on the narrative that she was young and did not know any better. This was an effective strategy, since her target audience was young adults who might be able to relate to making mistakes, particularly when there is a dynamic in which the person involved is in a position of power. She asked, "Can I see a show of hands of anyone here who didn't make a mistake or do something they regretted at 22? Yep. That's what I thought."

Mortification

The closest thing to an apology is the comment in which Lewinsky stated, "Not a day goes by that I'm not reminded of my mistake, and I regret that mistake deeply." Although Lewinsky did not use *mortification*, which is often deemed the best image repair strategy, she demonstrated many strategies to *reduce the offensiveness* of the crisis.

One of her most effective strategies was her emphasis on empowering people who are dealing with an incident involving public shaming. If opponents or adversaries' credibility is damaged, the accused's image might be repaired. Lewinsky did not outright attack Clinton. However, she mentioned their age difference at the time the affair occurred. She stated, "At the age of 22, I fell in love with my boss, and at the age of 24, I learned the devastating consequences." By including her age in this comment, listeners might sympathize with her, as she was young when the incident occurred. She adds, "Unlike me, though, your boss probably wasn't the president of the United States of America. Of course, life is full of surprises." Lewinsky's word choice was also good.

The statement that she fell in love with her former "boss" who was the "president of the United States" was powerful. The inclusion of Clinton's title as the leader of the United States added a hierarchical dimension to the speech. Listeners might be able to relate to someone falling in love with someone in a position of power. Demonstrating this tactic, Lewinsky attacked the media for focusing on the case when it broke in 1998. She described the news media of the day: "It was the first time the traditional news was usurped by the Internet for a major news story, a click that reverberated around the world." Lewinsky went from being an unknown citizen to well-known person overnight. She describes herself as, "I was patient zero of losing a personal reputation on a global scale almost instantaneously."

Lewinsky also used this tactic in her discussion of social media for its role in public shaming: "In this culture of humiliation, there is another kind of price tag attached to public shaming." She stated that not only does public shaming hurt the victim because it humiliates him or her, but companies are also profiting financially from such incidents. "This invasion of others is a raw material, efficiently and ruthlessly mined, packaged and sold at a profit. A marketplace has emerged where public humiliation is a commodity and shame is an industry." As a solution to the problem, she highlighted the importance of discussing society's responsibility to freedom of expression: "We need to communicate online with compassion, consume news with compassion, and click with compassion. Just imagine walking a mile in someone else's headline."

Gender References and Personal Reinvention

Lewinsky included a few references to common gender stereotypes in her speech. She stated, "I was branded as a tramp, tart, slut, whore, bimbo, and, of course, that woman." Lewinsky also described her attitude and personality following the scandal with some unflattering adjectives such as "silly' and "churlish." She stated: "Scared and mortified, I listen . . . to my sometimes catty, sometimes churlish, sometimes silly self being cruel, unforgiving, uncouth; listen, deeply, deeply ashamed, to the worst version of myself." Referring back to the literature, mass media outlets often use such terms to frame women negatively. Lewinsky takes back the power of such words by describing how they made her feel. She demonstrates to her audience that while she was vulnerable, she succeeded in moving beyond the hurt caused by the use of these words.

Lewinsky wrapped up her poignant talk with a discussion on how she wanted to save more than herself. She assured, "Anyone who is suffering from shame and public humiliation needs to know one thing: You can survive it." Timing is very important in any image repair campaign. Lewinsky answered the question that many people asked, "Why now?" She stated, "The answer has nothing to do with politics. The answer was and is because it's time: time to stop tiptoeing around my past; time to stop living a life of opprobrium; and time to take back my narrative." She ended powerfully with another statement about the importance of compassion. This time, she emphasized the importance of having compassion for one's self: "Have compassion for yourself. We all deserve compassion, and to live both online and off in a more compassionate world."

Reaction on the TED Talks transcript included more than 800 comments. In general, the posts were positive, encouraging Lewinsky to continue to discuss her cyberbullying initiative and lamenting how she was taken advantage of as a young intern. For instance, one commenter posted, "Such an important subject that truly needs to be dealt with quickly. Thanks so much for your grace and courage Monica, great job!" Another person responded, "Well done. Brilliantly spoken, and I hope the cyber bullies realize how much their insidious comments destroy lives. You have my respect Monica."

The comments indicated listeners noticed some of Lewinsky's preferred themes, which is an indication that her image repair tactics are effective. Referring back to Lewinsky's statements on her age when the affair occurred, one person posted: "Thank you Monica for this courageous and honest talk. . . . Nobody didn't make a mistake at his/her early age as you said, and it is really a shame the someone is making money out of somebody's else suffering." The large volume of sympathetic posts is another indication that listeners noticed some of her preferred frames. One person apologized for not speaking up for Lewinsky at the time the scandal broke, writing "I did not analyze it at the time—instead joined in the gossip and laughter. . . . If I had stopped to examine my 'glee' in watching, I would have faced my own embarrassing, naive, hurtful & silly mistakes made around the same age as Monica." One listener also included the word, "compassion" in her post, which is a strong indication he or she agreed with Lewinsky: "As it was, my mistakes never made the world stage and I was not required to dig deep and find the courage, compassion and strength that Monica was forced by her circumstances to find." The same person even asked for forgiveness: "Please forgive me for the part I played in your pain—I had no right to. I am a similar, flawed human very grateful for the compassion others have shown to me."

Many commenters expressed gratitude and admiration for Lewinsky's efforts to show the negative effects of online bullying and shaming. Some pointed out that the slut shaming directed at Lewinsky was proof of gender inequality in a culture that handsomely rewards men and critically judges women. One person wrote: "I cannot fathom the crucible of hatred she endured and applaud her for her courage to shine a light on the petty ugliness of this aspect of our human condition." Another commenter wrote, "I have to say that listening to her has changed my perception of her role in that big mess of the 90's. Like she says i [*sic*] saw her, but i [*sic*] didn't know her."

Other public figures, including journalists and talk show hosts such as David Letterman and Bill Maher have expressed regret for how they treated Lewinsky during the height of public scrutiny. This was before the TED Talk took place.

Although online users posted negative comments, they occurred much less frequently than positive ones. Often, the posts that seemed to address Lewinsky's speech in a negative light were more skeptical of her approach than they were of her character. In many instances, individuals questioned the content of Lewinsky's speech. For instance, one poster wrote, "My only criticism is how Ms. Lewinsky blew off her affair as a youthful indiscretion. What is the bigger offense? Having an affair with your married boss or saying mean things online?" The poster added, "I feel she should spend more time on this speech showing contrition and acknowledging that her actions caused the spiral." Another commenter also expressed a mixed reaction. While he wrote the topic was "entirely noble and valid," he said he did "struggle with the rationalization of her particular circumstances that 'all 20-somethings have made mistakes.' Rather than re-open the 17-year old debate in which every opinion has already been voiced, I'll just try to focus on the positive message in this talk."

TWITTER RESPONSES

From the mass of tweets tagged #MonicaLewinsky, we analyzed 1,500 tweets. There were five major themes, as outlined in Table 11.3. The majority of users on Twitter were in support of Lewinsky's TED Talk; even if they did not particularly favor Lewinsky herself, they praised the positive message that her speech relayed. The users who were negative in their reaction ignored the content of the talk and focused on Lewinsky's character and intentions for delivering it instead.

Users, as a whole, trended toward forgiving Lewinsky for her relationship with former president Clinton, commenting on their own past mistakes and expressing gratitude that their own events had not been publically and globally exposed.

Support for Lewinsky

The majority of tweets outspokenly offered support to Lewinsky, including messages such as "@MonicaLewinsky You inspire. Power on and thank you." Many other users labeled Lewinsky as "brave and beautiful" and asked "how many could've risen from the ashes w/such grace." A great deal of tweets link to the video of the TED talk, citing it as "the most important

Table 11.3   Twitter Themes for Lewinsky

Support for Lewinsky	• Inspiration to other cyberbullying victims • Displays grace and confidence • Draws attention to unequal treatment of men and women by the media
Cautions to social media users and young professionals	• Be careful of unintentionally bullying others • Be aware that every action may have unforeseen, harsh ramifications
Support for victims of cyberbullying	• Call for internet users to focus on empathy before judgment • Offer of support to cyberbullying victims
Negative tweets	• Lewinsky acted wrongly and deserves the consequences. • Lewinsky is seeking profit and/or sympathy. • Lewinsky is attempting to belittle Hilary Clinton's presidential run.
Personal reinvention	• It is never too late to reinvent or reframe a narrative. • The effectiveness of reinvention comes down to the style in which it is done.

TED talk yet." Users went beyond supporting Lewinsky and praised the concept of TED talks for giving someone like Lewinsky a platform to speak out against social ills.

Users also noted how unfairly Lewinsky was treated in comparison with former president Bill Clinton at the outset of the scandal. Multiple users underscored the need for feminism in similar cases where the woman involved is publicly "slut shamed," in contrast to the man who often receives nothing more than a light warning. A tweet reads, "I watched Bill Clinton attempt to personally destroy Monica Lewinsky with lies and commit perjury. I also watched the media protect him."

Cautions to Social Media Users and Young Professionals

In light of how Lewinsky was treated during the initial scandal, Twitter users voiced their concerns for the present, social-media obsessed generation. Users believe that the bullying Lewinsky received would have been much harsher in the era of social media. Lewinsky's case is used as a cautionary tale; one user tweeted "Every young woman should study @MonicaLewinsky case & aftermath. It badly damaged and altered her life. At age 22. #TedTalks #Consequences."

Another tweet cited Lewinsky's issues as a reason to refrain from certain social media platforms: "Monica Lewinsky's TED Talk has solidified my reasons to stay away from Snapchat. . . . The more shame, the more clicks." Young professionals are cautioned against making the same mistakes that Lewinsky made and to observe proper workplace professionalism. Tweets containing statements such as "Any of us could have been you" showcase users' empathetic yet wary reaction to Lewinsky's actions.

Support for Victims of Cyberbullying

Many tweets focused on the implications of Lewinsky's speech for the cyberbullying issue, rather than reacting to Lewinsky's particular case. Users fault themselves for being a part of the "culture of humiliation" and encourage others to take a moment to discern whether their comments are hurting or helping others. One such tweet reads, "Take 20 minutes & PLEASE do listen to #MonicaLewinsky. Something to keep in mind when we tweet or comment mindlessly."

The tweets including the hashtag #cyberbullying offer support to victims of the phenomenon, and often share links to resources where victims can reach out for help. Even the tweets condemning Lewinsky's character clearly stated that they were not in support of cyberbullying.

Negative Tweets

The negative tweets that existed were grouped into two categories: Lewinsky's character and Lewinsky's hidden intentions in delivering the speech. Tweets focusing on Lewinsky's character argued that, although cyberbullying is harmful, Lewinsky needs to face the ramifications of her wrongful actions. A user tweeted "So I just feel like, I would feel a lot more sympathetic to #MonicaLewinsky if she did more w/ her life than talk about her blow job." Others state, "I wish #MonicaLewinsky would stop #bullying people's marriages" and "#MonicaLewinsky is no victim. Stop it people. She was a grown woman that decide to sleep with a married man. #hardball #msnbc #Lewinsky".

The other set of negative tweets honed in on the political timing of the TED Talk, and believed Lewinsky was seeking profit or attention by coming forward. A user states, "Monica Lewinsky needs to shut up. She got a $20 million book deal and says she doesn't want to get publicly humiliated. You started it." In the same line of thinking, another tweet reads "Sleeps with married president. Gets caught. In public eye. Writes book. Performs speaking engagements. Gets paid. Victim?#MonicaLewinsky."

Believing Lewinsky's goal is to humiliate Hillary Clinton before the 2016 presidential election, users tweeted statements including: "I have no problem w/ #MonicaLewinsky criticizing folks for shaming her but it seems like she only wants to do that when there's an election" and "I think #GOP paying #MonicaLewinsky to appear where the #Clintons are. Repugs R dirty."

Another Twitter user asked "Which GOP PAC group is paying #MonicaLewinsky to speak now? It was Forbes that paid for her 'anti-bullying' speech 4 months ago. @vicenews." An image that has been popularly retweeted is a bumper sticker using Lewinsky to put down Hillary Clinton. A smaller subset of tweets posited that Lewinsky is a blight on the image of feminism, stating, "The sad part is #MonicaLewinsky is trying her BEST to represent feminism but she doesn't get that she committed Adultery."

Personal Reinvention

The last section of tweets emphasized the importance of reframing a narrative, or reinventing one's image. Users agreed, however, that the success of this tactic depends on the methods in which the narrative is reframed. One user tweeted, "Monica Lewinsky has obviously hired herself a great publicist" while another praises Lewinsky for her "confidence and not arrogance."

The *New York Times*, noting the change in image, tweeted "once vilified as a 'predator' White House intern, Monica Lewinsky has re-emerged." The *NYT* Styles section followed suit, tweeting "burn the beret and bury the blue dress, and meet Monica Lewinsky anew."

The popularity of these tweets is evident in the thousands of users who have favorited or retweeted the posts. Other users claim: "It's never too late to change your narrative. In tears from this," or "you can insist on a different ending for yourself @MonicaLewinsky."

CONCLUSIONS AND IMPLICATIONS

This article analyzed the image repair tactics presented in Lewinsky's speech in comparison with comments following the event. Lewinsky said she is not attempting to restore her image, but she wants the world to know the "real" her. Her speech was effective in addressing the shaming narratives that emerged following the 1988 scandal, in which citizens and media outlets often crucified her for having an affair with the president of the United States—a person who was older and in a position of power.

The *New York Times* article leading up to her TED speech called the talk "her most public appearance to date." The reporter, Jessica Bennett, shadowed Lewinsky for a month even as she practiced her heavily revised TED talk with her speech coach listening in on Skype from Great Britain.

Findings indicate the former intern used TED Talks skillfully to discuss timely topics such as Internet shaming, suicide and bullying. While Lewinsky opted not to use *mortification*, she *reduced the offensiveness* of what happened in 1988 by building on the narrative that she was young and did not know any better. This was an effective strategy because her target audience during this speech was young adults who could relate to person becoming involved with a person in a position of power such as the president of the United States. Lewinsky encouraged her listeners to practice compassion and empathy and to think of how they might feel if they were on the receiving end of shameful content. Lewinsky wrote the speech herself, but consulted with a cabinet of people, according to *The New York Times*.

In gender studies, appearance is normally part of a woman's image repair plan. It appears, Lewinsky played it safe in her attire, hair and makeup. Perhaps to counteract frames depicting her as promiscuous, Lewinsky's corrective actions included changing her makeup and style of dress and focusing on being down to earth. She wore very little jewelry and her style of dress— button-down black top with three-quarter sleeves and black slacks.

The image-repair strategies used in her speech were diverse. It is interesting to note that the typical gender frames were not displayed: Twitter users did not analyze Lewinsky's clothing during the TED talk, nor did they pick apart her appearance, portray her as too masculine or too feminine, and so on. One tweet stood out from the rest by focusing on Lewinsky's weight, arguing that she made "a fantastic reinvention though it'd never work if she were thin." Additional gender-specific comments focused on the importance of feminism in defending women who are being "slut shamed," emphasizing the difference in the way media treated Lewinsky and Clinton.

Many of the audience members responded favorably when she asked them if they had made a mistake or done something they regretted at age 22. A number of TED Talks commentators apologized on behalf of the United States, society and men in general. Her audience applauded her for taking a stand against public shaming and often noted the imbalance of power between a 22-year-old intern and the president of the United States. Reactions often included personal anecdotes of public shaming, with some comments reflecting on how we react differently to men and women. Humor was an effective strategy as Lewinsky received a great response from her jokes in reference to the scandal.

Study findings provide crucial insights regarding the ideas and positions individuals are likely to embrace about women in general. They also demonstrate that historical representations were not as strong as expected in the gender narratives used in comments found in Twitter and TED Talks comments.

They further indicate feminist scholars have produced many profound changes in our culture in the past 30 or so years and substantial inroads are reflected in comments regarding Lewinsky. Future studies may add a survey or in-depth interview component in which the researchers talk to creators of user-generated content to find out their uses and motivations for commenting on social media platforms regarding shaming.

An important question that demands exploration is how audiences respond via other social media platforms to this particular crisis. Such a study might look at gender narratives used in comments found in Twitter and TED Talks comments. Future studies may add a survey or in-depth interview component in which the researchers talk to creators of user-generated content to find out their uses and motivations for commenting on social media platforms regarding shaming. An important question that demands exploration is how audiences respond via other social media platforms to this particular crisis. Such a study might look at comments in response to blog posts, Tumblr and Facebook posts to assess the effectiveness of changing public opinion via social media. A longitudinal study of Lewinsky's image repair tactics might also be of interest.

Also valuable would be articles that offer exercises and suggestions for literacy courses on shaming. Such studies are even more important as gossip and shaming have become more common online. As mentioned earlier, research on social media has become particularly important as "slut shaming," or "victim blaming," trends have become more widespread in recent years (Alaniz, 2013). Findings are enlightening and provide a powerful springboard for future studies on image repair, shaming, social media and framing.

Since Lewinsky's TED Talks appearance and first writing an article for *Vanity Fair*, she has made the rounds at benefits, bullying workshops and conferences. She appeared on ABC's *The View* to talk about her anti-bullying campaign. Lewinsky has also written four articles for *Vanity Fair*, including one about how the "Online Rebuttal is the New Black." By stepping into the public sphere, Lewinsky leaves little doubt that it is important for her to speak out and disrupt the singular narrative about the young naïve, beret-wearing intern that slept with the president.

Part V

POLITICS AND IRT

Chapter 12

Taming of the Shrew and Rock Star

Media Framing of Senators Hillary Clinton and Barack Obama during the 2007–2008 Presidential Primaries

Mia Moody-Ramirez and Tina Libhart

Hillary Rodham Clinton has battled media negativity since her husband, former president Bill Clinton, entered politics. News coverage often portrayed her as a hindrance to his public image. Warner (1993) described her years during Clinton's early political office in this manner: "Her look had changed little since her left-leaning college days. She wore no makeup, hid behind thick glasses, dressed in big shapeless sweaters and sack-like skirts, and did little to tame the mousy, meandering waves of her hair" (pp. 5–6). When Clinton became first lady of the United States in 1992, the media's criticism continued. She received critiques of her style of dress, hairstyle and assertiveness.

In 2007, Clinton threw her hat into the Democratic presidential primary race, making history as the first viable female Democratic candidate. She was a noteworthy contender with a background filled with accolades and firsts. However, she had the difficult job of convincing voters she was tough enough as a woman to handle issues such as war, finances and health care, yet feminine enough to fulfill the preconceived notions people often have about women. Troubles surrounding Clinton's background, particularly her gender, were a challenge that she found very difficult to combat, and in the end, it may have lost her the 2008 presidential nomination.

Former senator Barack Obama faced many of the same adversities as Clinton with regard to societal perceptions of people of color. Pollsters and political commentators speculated on the role that race and gender played in the Obama and Clinton campaigns, respectively. The racial picture of Obama's campaign was complex and not only raised questions about whether Whites would support him, but also whether blacks would—especially black women. On the other hand, the gendered pictured of Clinton's campaign was not one of whether women would support her candidacy but whether men would (Parks & Rachlinksi, 2008, p. 3).

Research indicates historical stereotypes might prime whites' negative racial attitudes about black candidates and therefore may be a significant barrier to the electoral success of minority candidates (Caliendo & McIlwain, 2006). For instance, although Obama was the fifth African American senator in U.S. history, media coverage often focused on negative perceptions including doubts about his reliability because of his age/experience, rumors about his citizenship, religion and liberal views. His so-called "star power" both helped and hindered him as he fought to make voters take him seriously during the presidential primaries. According to Herrnson and Stokes (2001), white voters tend to hold positive stereotypes of white candidates and negative stereotypes of minority candidates. These stereotypes are particularly detrimental to state- and federal-level candidates whose districts are large enough to include a significant number of white and minority voters (Herrnson & Stokes, 2001). Frames and stereotypes found in media coverage of political candidates are of interest because journalists and editors draw maps or internal story patterns for their readers, and these maps or frames serve to outline public debate and influence readers' level of information (Gamson & Lasch, 1983).

Previous IRT studies have focused on the nature of image repair strategies of athletes, politicians and religious leaders (e.g. Benoit, 2006; Brewer, 2009; Kroon & Ekstrom's, 2007; Oles, 2012; Yioutas & Segvic, 2003). While they provide valuable insight into image repair management, few have addressed social media and image repair strategies used by black and female politicians. The topic is particularly relevant today.

Using Benoit's (1995) image repair theory (IRT), this chapter analyzes Obama and Clinton's personal, online communication strategies. Benoit's approach to image repair operates under two major premises: an assumption that communication is a goal-oriented activity, and the primary communication goal is to maintain a positive image (Benoit, 1995; Blaney & Benoit, 2001). In this case, the researcher used the theory to help determine whether Obama and Clinton's online communication efforts were effective and to what extent cultural narratives and media frames of politicians, race and gender played a role in media coverage of Clinton and Obama.

This chapter is important for several reasons. First, it analyzes the image repair strategies of two candidates who media covered along the lines of gender and race and offers a glimpse into the historically significant 2008 presidential primary in which an African American man and an Anglo woman competed for the presidential nomination of the Democratic Party. Scholars must continue to test all communication paradigms in new media environments.

Secondly, broadcast news coverage of presidential elections continues to be an important information source for voters, whether it is network, cable or digital news formats. A 2004 Pew survey following the 2004 election revealed that television news was the primary source for news for 76% of respondents; 29% said network news, while 40% said cable news was a primary source (Pew, 2004).

The news outlet is also a concern in discussions of gatekeeper and framing functions. Most studies have concluded cable news outlets present dichotomous viewpoints (e.g. Conway, Grabe & Grieves, 2007; Pew, 2004; Selepak, 2004; Weatherly et al., 2007). Media outlets' influence in campaigning, voter decision-making, leadership selection, and more generally, the American democratic process, has spurred a growing interest in cable news as a tool for political campaigning.

Lastly, this study adds to the growing body of knowledge seeking to identify and understand the role race and gender of a candidate plays in a voter's decision of how to vote. The framing of gender and racial images used in the media's coverage of politics is of concern because overall, careless and insensitive coverage of racial groups might actually promote racial stereotypes and resentments (Entman, 1991; Shah & Thornton, 1994). Additionally, stereotypes in popular culture help citizens make sense of the world around them, especially for depictions of people of a different gender or ethnicity.

STEREOTYPES, IRT AND REPRESENTATIONS OF GENDER AND RACE

Researchers have examined media coverage of gender and other minority racial groups for decades. Three broad areas of research are frames, gatekeeper theory and stereotyping. A literature review exploring these topics provides a framework for understanding the present study. The concept of stereotyping is useful in an analysis of media coverage of Obama and Clinton. Lippmann (1922) defined "stereotype" as a form of perception that imposes ways of seeing. Stereotypes often target race, gender, age, disabilities and sexuality. Members of the dominant group or cultural elite often use stereotypes to dehumanize other cultural groups that differ in values, beliefs or physical characteristics to maintain its own political power and social control (Lassiter, 1999).

Stereotypes provide clues to how voters should view an issue and influences them on how they should vote, which is often times based on stereotypes. Winter notes, for example, the different stereotypes applied to welfare versus Social Security: While stereotypes of welfare typically emphasize themes of laziness, lack of personal responsibility and perverse incentives, discussions of Social Security have typically focused on hard work and legitimately earned rewards. These frames generally overlap with stereotypes of African Americans and Anglos. As such, characterizations of race schema include hostile "in-group/out-group" competition.

Such stereotypes are of interest because studies have also demonstrated that the framing of issues may directly influence political debate. For instance, Kim, Scheufele and Shanahan (2005) found that issue framing, along with demographic characteristics, could influence voter decision making because they often use such information to formulate positions and opinions about candidates and to determine how they will vote. Having Clinton in a race against all men provided the opportunity to explore gender differences in what was presented in the media.

Stereotypes are of concern because media help citizens make sense of the world around them, especially for depictions of people of different backgrounds. Audiences often form their opinions on race relations based on the media (Domke et al., 2003). Additionally, stereotyping is a social control tool that builds group solidarity and creates an "us versus them" mentality. Stereotypes persist because "they fulfill important identity needs for the dominant culture" thereby maintaining the status quo and preserving hegemony (Mastro & Behm-Morawitz, 2005, p. 112). According to Smith (2009), children begin learning race-specific stereotypes of various ethnic groups at an early age, and they continue to receive corroborating messages from adults, friends, music, television and other popular media through both voluntary and involuntary means.

Because people typically use stereotypes to fill in missing information (Entman, 1991), one can assume that stereotypes and frames have an effect on the media coverage of an election in which candidates are not the norms for U.S. presidential races. It is essential to continually analyze and address media perceptions of women and people of color to underscore unbalanced information and to build upon existing theories and test their validity in today's news environment.

With its inclusion of a white woman and a black man, the 2007–2008 presidential primaries provided a great opportunity to advance the literature on media coverage of race and gender in political competitions. The 2007–2008 Democratic presidential primaries provided a platform to study both demographics. In the end, cultural narratives, frames and stereotypes send audiences hidden messages that suggest a group's importance in society.

Framing Politics

Framing, according to Goffman (1974), offers a way of explaining "what is going on" and determining "what is salient" in a given event or experience. According to Gans (1979), it is impossible for anyone to work in any environment without values, which he suggests in the news industry may manifest themselves as subjectivity in coverage, which leads to framing. Entman (1993) defined framing as selecting "some aspects of a perceived reality and make them more salient in a communicating text, in such a way as to promote a particular problem definition, causal interpretation, moral evaluation, and/or treatment recommendation" (p. 52).

The framing body of work shows that socioeconomic status, race and education can make a difference in how reporters frame certain issues. As a macroconstruct, the term "framing" refers to modes of presentation that journalists and other communicators use to present information in a way that resonates with existing underlying schemas among their audience (Shoemaker & Reese, 1996). Frame analyses provide a means through which one can study different aspects of a topic. For example, a "pro-life frame" will use terms such as "baby," "abortionist," "unborn," "murder" and so on, whereas, the "pro-choice frame" might use "fetus," "doctor," "woman" and freedom to describe the same situation (Hertog & McLeod, 1999).

The gatekeeper approach (Tuchman, 1978) is also pertinent to the study of Clinton and Obama because race and culture play a key role in what reporters and editors perceive as important. Gatekeeping theory describes the role of initial selection and later editorial processing of event reports in news organizations. Undoubtedly, gatekeepers at different outlets will have a different idea or perception of what is important and what journalists should cover.

The gatekeeper process illustrates that the gatekeeper's role is biased and based on his or her own set of experiences, attitudes and expectations. For example, in the study, "White News: Why Local News Programs Don't Cover People of Color," Heider (2000) observed two newsrooms, one in Honolulu, Hawaii, and one in Albuquerque, New Mexico, and found that even in areas where people of color account for the majority of the population, those persons in charge of the news programming did not reflect the makeup of the population covered. The researcher's subsequent findings clarified that although people of color sat in news meetings in both newsrooms, their positions did not include leadership authority.

Gatekeeping coupled with framing allows elites to exert power over the public opinion. News articles containing certain frames help the ideas of those in power become the basis of public opinion. This is a critical concept when analyzing news coverage of controversial issues that the average reader will likely encounter through the media.

FEMINIST THEORY AND MEDIA STEREOTYPES

To understand the cultural narratives reporters used to cover Clinton, it is important to study the tenets of feminist theory and stereotypes of women. Historically, Ardener (1975) posited that women and men in patriarchal,

capitalist societies tend to form two distinct circles of experience and interpretation, one overlapping the other (cited in Krolokke & Sorensen, 2006).
The masculine circle converges with the norms of society, providing a
masculine signature and overriding the feminine circle. Therefore, women's
perspectives are often not openly articulated.

Other feminist theorists argue mass media serve as instruments to trans-
mit stereotypical, patriarchal and hegemonic values about women, which
in turn make hierarchical and distorted sex-role stereotypes appear normal
(e.g. Carter & Steiner, 2004; Hartmann, 1981; Vavrus, 2009). Van Zoonen
(1994) summarized this transmission model as a media reflection on society's dominant social values that symbolically belittle women, either by not
showing them at all or by depicting them in stereotypical roles (p. 17). As a
result, their expression is muted (e.g., Collins, 2000; Orbe, 1998). Muted
group theory sees language as excluding and demeaning women based on
several factors, including words to describe them. For example, "stud" and
"playboy" are popular words to depict promiscuous men. Conversely, people
use less appealing words, such as "slut," "hooker" and "whore" to describe
promiscuous women.

Previous research has shown that although media give men and women
candidates an equal quantity of coverage, they do not give them the same
type of coverage. Typically, coverage of male candidates focuses on their
policy and history in office, while coverage of female candidates focuses
more on their personality and appearance rather than their stances on various
issues (Devitt, 2002; Freedman & Fico, 2005). Likewise, other scholars have
found the media focus more attention on female candidate's gender, children and marital status, framing their ability to hold political office in terms
of their roles as mothers and wives. Echoing earlier findings, Semetko and
Boomgaarden (2007) found the media give female candidates less coverage,
assess their electoral prospects more negatively and focus reporting on "soft"
issues.

Banwart (2010) determined to what extent voters use gender frames in
evaluating female and male candidates, particularly after exposure to campaign communication run on behalf of the candidates. Through an experi-
mental design, researchers exposed participants to candidate's advertising in
two mixed-gender congressional races from the 2008 election cycle. Results
indicate that traditional trait stereotypes continue, according to the evaluation
of female candidates, although the generations of policy stereotypes are more
complicated.

Kanter (1977) identified four common archetypes of professional women:
"sex object," "mother," "pet" and "iron maiden." "Sex object" stereotypes
refer to both sexuality and often include references to clothing, appearance, behaving and speaking in "feminine" ways. Conversely, the "mother"

stereotype presents a dichotomous representation of women. On one hand, they are caring and understanding; on the other hand, they are scolding, nagging and shrewish. The "pet" or "child" stereotype depicts women as mascots or.cheerleaders (see Wood, 1994, p. 264–265). In such situations, women are too weak, naïve and unprepared to handle difficult tasks without a man's help. As a result, men treat them like a child, which diminishes their capacity to fill leadership positions. Conversely, the "iron maiden" is excessively strong and overpowering, the opposite of the mother archetype. However, mass media deem the iron maiden too powerful and pushy to be an effective leader (Carlin & Winfrey, 2009). All four stereotypes of women surfaced to some degree in media portrayals of Clinton.

Additionally, feminist studies indicate journalists stereotype women with "gendering" frames in particular, as they are not usually as visible in political positions. For example, Devere and Davies (2006) found that international research reports demonstrate a consistent "gendered" framing of media coverage, which highlight a person's gender when it is not particularly relevant to the context. Similarly, Heldman, Carroll and Olson (2005) found that news reports on Elizabeth Dole in her bid for the presidential nomination demonstrated a heightened attention to her personality and appearance. Likewise, Ross (2002) found media concentrated on what she termed as "stupid, little things such as clothes and hair." News reports described women as "feisty, perky, small and lively" in coverage of women running for legislative office (Poole, cited in Ross 2002, p. 153).

In sum, it appears that female politicians still have a difficult time convincing their constituents to elect them to office than their male counterparts, although female voters outnumber male voters (Jamieson, Shin & Day, 2002). Media scrutinize their lives, public and private, in minute detail, considering more than just "the issues" in their election to political office.

Race and Politics

Like Clinton, Obama fought negative media coverage continuously throughout his political career. Various negative stereotypes dominate news media's portrayals of minorities, including the idea that they are violent, lazy and untrustworthy and lack intelligence (e.g., Collins, 2004; Dates & Barlow, 1993; Dates & Pease, 1995; Martindale, 1990; Poindexter, Smith & Heider, 2003; Rowley, 2003; West, 2001). In the 1980s and 1990s, stereotypes of black men emphasized images of drug lords, crack victims, the underclass, the homeless and subway muggers (Drummond, 1990).

Entman (2000) found that African Americans were more likely to emerge as perpetrators in drug and violent crime stories on network news. Such images often result in black misandry, which the *Merriam-Webster* defines as a hatred or contempt of black men. Black misandry refers to an exaggerated pathological aversion toward black men created and reinforced in societal, institutional, and individual ideologies, practices and behaviors.

These representations often spill over into coverage of politics. Historically, Chaudhary (1980) found that black elected officials received longer stories, averaging 300 words compared to 225 for white officials, but, significantly, more stories that are negative appeared for black elected officials than for whites. Conversely, Zilber and Niven (2000) analyzed the news coverage of black members of the Congress and found that media devoted equal coverage to all candidates; however, they were more likely to mention the race of black candidates, typically ignoring the race or ethnicity of white candidates.

In their study of congressional candidates, Huddy and Terkildsen (1993) found the news discussed racial issues much more when black candidates were involved. Conversely, Tripathi (2003) found that mainstream society might view women and blacks as too radical if they stand on a center-left platform (Tripathi, 2003). The researcher asserts that this explains why many history-making women and black politicians such as Condoleezza Rice and Colin Powell were either Republican or supported by established conservative politicians.

CNN and FOX News were selected for a comparison of coverage because each outlet represents a politically contrasting viewpoint—FOX News Network represents a conservative viewpoint on politics, while Cable News Network (CNN) represents a more middle of the road or liberal viewpoint. According to Accuracy in Media (2004), viewers consider FOX News the most credible source of news for Republicans and CNN News as the most credible source for Democrats. Statistics showed that FOX News had a credibility rating of 29% for Republicans, while CNN News had 26%, and FOX News had a credibility rating of 24% for Democrats, while CNN News had 45% (Selepak, 2004). Previous studies conclude cable news outlets present dichotomous viewpoints (e.g., Conway, Grabe & Grieves, 2007; Pew, 2004; Selepak, 2004; Weatherly et al., 2007).

POLITICS AND IMAGE REPAIR

Image repair studies have addressed the ways presidential candidates have used a variety of communication platforms and technological developments to shape their images. For instance, following the 2008 campaign, Benjamin Warner et al. (2011) looked into the issue of the ability of presidential candidates to shape their image through televised debates. They found that most of the public already has a perception of candidates before the debates even begin. Because of this, it's highly improbable that candidates will be able to alter public opinion of them through anything they say in the debates. They can reinforce positive views and try to minimize negative views, but, for the most part, viewers already have formed opinions.

Studies looking at image repair of politicians note they use different strategies with varying degrees of success. Image issues surrounding President George W. Bush during the 2004 election provide a good example of the use of image restoration tactics. Bush was accused of failing to fulfill his role as a president, and he, in turn, ineffectively used *denial* and *defeasibility* to defend his image. Benoit (2006) concluded the use of *defeasibility*, or attributing failure to lack of information or ability, may actually be destructive to politicians because it undermines their trustworthiness.

Conversely, John Edwards' strategy of *admittance* and *apologia* were good for his image restoration after his sexual scandal was unearthed during his 2008 presidential race (Friedman, 2011). Edwards began an affair with Rielle Hunter in 2006, finally admitting to the affair in 2008 (Friedman, 2011). One of the biggest controversies surrounding this affair was Edwards lied about being the father of Hunter's child until January 2010. The other biggest part of the controversy was with Edwards' attempt to cover up the controversy by spending large sums of money. In 2010, Edwards apologized and admitted that his actions were wrong and that what he had originally said was not true.

Another interesting political scandal featured Anthony Weiner and the inappropriate photographs that were "tweeted from his account to a Seattle woman." According to the ABC News Timeline of Representative Anthony Weiner's scandal, he began the series of photographs sent via email in April 2011, and continued communication with Meagan Broussard until May 27, 2011 (Dwyer, 2011). Once these photographs were made public, Weiner had to perform considerable image control, especially after he lied about the accusations.

The media frenzy that surrounded his scandal propelled the accusations and controversy into the limelight. Many other women came forward with proof that Weiner had contacted them after they had commented on his Facebook or Twitter accounts. This inappropriate use of social media as a means to exploit himself was exceedingly harmful to his reputation.

One of the strongest image repair tactics that Weiner used was his admittance to sending "'hundreds' of suggestive photographs and messages to at least six women he had met online, and then repeatedly lying to cover up his actions. Though he claimed no physical contact ever took place, he did not deny having had phone sex with some of the women" (Cheever, 2011). Another action that has significantly helped Weiner's image repair was his announcement in early June 2011 "that he was going to receive treatment for his problem" (Cheever, 2011).

In another example, former president Bill Clinton relied on *denial* and *bolstering* strategies after his first brush with major scandal during his 1992 campaign (Blaney and Benoit, 2001). He denied doing anything illegal during his period of draft eligibility during the late 1960s. In addition, he denied acting opportunistically within the letter of the law in order to evade the draft. He used bolstering to talk about his general patriotism and military leadership of the Arkansas National Guard.

Bauer (2008) also analyzed the various image repair issues that President Clinton underwent during his time in office. Clinton had to "go immediately to the public in a display of willing openness . . . he broadcast a televised statement explaining his grand jury testimony. He had to confess that his previous denials of a sexual relationship with Lewinsky were incorrect; a sexual relationship had indeed existed" (Bauer, 156). According to the *Washington Post* article, "Clinton: 'There Is No Improper Relationship,'" Clinton expressed his view that he thinks "[H]ardly anyone has ever been subject to the level of attack I have. You know, it made a lot of people mad when I got elected president. And the better the country does, it seems like the madder some of them get" (Washington, A13).

Clinton did not act in a way, according to the *Washington Post*, that was exactly indicative of his innocence and "his repeated assertions that the relationship was 'not improper' had led to unceasing speculation . . . that there might be 'loopholes in the President's denials.'" This *denial* and *evasion* strategy was one of the main things that Clinton focused on during the Lewinsky scandal.

The next strategy that Clinton used was openness. He began implementing this strategy to save his reputation on August 17, 1998. According to Bauer (2008), Clinton's fourth statement on the matter, and the first to admit any kind of fault other than a bad memory—was widely viewed by the media as a failure. This final admittance of guilt was only somewhat addressed to the extremity of the matter. Clinton, according to Bauer, used "words, such as 'misled' and never addressed the lies he had told by denying any existence of a relationship" (Bauer, p. 157). This public admittance of guilt was exceedingly damaging to Clinton's reputation as an authority figure, but it was also a public relation strategy to begin to make the public trust him again because of his openness.

Clinton further expanded his strategy for regaining the public's trust with his speech on the 35th anniversary on the March on Washington. One of the topics of his speech was forgiveness, where he explained to the audience at Union Chapel in Oak Bluffs, Massachusetts (1998), that he has "become quite an expert in . . . forgiveness. . . . It gets a little easier the more you do it. And if you have a family, an administration, a Congress and a whole country to ask you, you're going to get a lot of practice." This image repair tactic was one of the smarter things that Clinton did during this scandal. The admittance to the people that he was in the wrong was the first step to regaining the citizens' of the United States trust in not only him but also the presidency.

Benoit (2016) analyzed the image restoration tactics of former president Obama during the 2008 presidential campaign after the ABC News story broke about Senator Barack Obama's pastor, Reverend Jeremiah Wright. Obama was accused of racism using guilt by association with his pastor, Reverend Wright. This news report portrayed an attitude that he was not patriotic, reporting that "an ABC News review of dozens of Reverend Wright's sermons, offered for sale by the church, found repeated denunciations of the U.S."

Quotations from Reverend Wright included: "The government gives them the drugs, builds bigger prisons, passes a three-strike law and then wants us to sing 'God Bless America.' No, no, no, God damn America, that's in the Bible for killing innocent people." This attitude would likely evoke condemnation in much of the audience.

Following the revelation, Obama used *denial* to repair his reputation and used *bolstering* and *provocation* to repair Wright's reputation. Obama gave a speech to repair his image. Obama also attempted to repair his image using *denial* and *differentiation*; however, Obama did not repudiate Wright entirely. Instead, Obama engaged in third-party image repair, using *attack accuser, bolstering,* and *differentiation* to repair Wright's reputation. The study concluded self-defense can be combined with third-party defense and that the accused does not have to use the same strategies to defend self and others. This case study also provides an example of a response to an attack using guilt by association.

In another study on Obama, Benoit (2014) analyzed the former president's health care initiative HealthCare.gov, which went live on October 1, 2013. The program was plagued with problems. Republicans seized the opportunity to attack the president, his administration, and his health care program. Obama's approval rating waned.

On November 7, Obama was interviewed by Chuck Todd and on November 14, 2013, Obama held a press conference to try to mend his image. His defense during both events relied heavily on *mortification, corrective action* and *minimization*. They also contained instances of *defeasibility, bolstering* and *transcendence*.

Overall, President Obama wanted to lower expectations about HealthCare. gov's performance; however, he did want not to create expectations that its performance would be bad. These expectations were important to his image as well as his legacy. Benoit concluded Obama's argument contributed to a generally well-designed image repair effort.

PLATFORMS AND IMAGE RESTORATION

Although televised debates, websites and blogs have been studied as platforms to shape public opinion on a candidate, the recent development and prevalence of social media has yet to be studied as a tool for image repair and improvement. This chapter aims to fill in the gap by analyzing the specific ways in which Clinton and Obama tried to shape or enhance their image.

With the digital age, presidential candidates have another platform for presenting their images: campaign websites. Verser and Wicks (2006) studied the new abilities this gives to a candidate by looking at the 2000 election. They found that an online presence allows candidates to counter negative messages from the media by highlighting the positive aspects of their campaign. Momoc (2011) concluded that candidates primarily use blogs as tools for presenting what they have to offer, not for attacking their opponents (2011).

With the digital age, presidential candidates have another platform for presenting their images: campaign websites. Verser and Wicks studied the new abilities this gives to a candidate by looking at the 2000 election (Verser & Wicks, 2006). They found that an online presence allows candidates to counter negative messages from the media by highlighting the positive aspects of their campaign. Another technological innovation available to presidential candidates is the blog. Momoc found that candidates primarily use blogs as tools for presenting what they have to offer, not for attacking their opponents (2011).

TEXTS ANALYZED

This chapter addresses two questions: (1) How did the media frame Senators Barack Obama and Hillary Clinton during the 2007–2008 presidential primaries? (2) What image repair tactics did the two candidates utilize in their online news releases and blogs during the 2007–2008 presidential primaries? This chapter is two-pronged: it provides an examination of (1) the media's coverage of Senators Barack Obama and Hillary Clinton during the 2007–2008 presidential primaries and (2) a review of their image repair tactics.

To assess the media's coverage of the two senators and their image repair tactics, the researcher analyzed CNN and FOX News transcripts, their official blogs and online news releases. Because candidates control what they include in their online news releases and blogs, these texts provide a comprehensive look at their viewpoints and image restoration tactics.

Transcripts were retrieved from LexisNexis that aired on CNN and FOX News during the period of September 1, 2007–February 29, 2008, using the keywords, "Obama," "Clinton" and "presidential primaries." The unit of analysis was the entire transcript, news release or blog entry. This method of analysis provided the framework for understanding the way in which cable television news framed Senators Obama and Clinton in the months of the 2007–2008 presidential primaries and how the two candidates responded using image repair tactics.

EXPLORATIONS OF THEMES

Researchers noted that most broadcasts tended to give the same amount of time to both Obama and Clinton. Many times, this involved airing clips containing one candidate's statement followed by the other candidate's rebuttal. Guest commentators had strong opinions about individual candidates' strength or weaknesses, but there were only a few glaring examples of the actual news anchors or hosts taking sides. In addition, both networks aired a balance of email and phone call commentaries with both candidates getting the same amount of airtime.

Gender was more salient than race in how journalists framed candidates in their coverage of elections. Gender frames were laced throughout network coverage of Clinton in prominent themes such as family, health care and education issues. Clinton received mixed reactions from commentators and voters. In interviews, some people stated they believed that a woman should not run for president. Others expressed that having a woman as president for the first time would be revolutionary, and they would support Hillary in the election. The other common viewer perception was that she is too hard, or she does not sympathize with average people and comes off too strong. Similarly, journalists played up patriarchal representations of Clinton, choosing to focus on trivial issues such as attire, hairstyle and mannerisms. Race-related frames were not as prominent in Obama's campaign coverage. When used, race frames focused on external factors out of his control such as negative comments made by the Reverend Jeremiah Wright and Obama's biracial heritage.

CNN and *FOX* differed in their use of frames. While transcripts from both outlets were neutral, CNN tended to have more references to gender issues overall, with an emphasis on appearance and attire. Such transcripts often talked about the disparity in media's coverage women politicians, which boosted the network's use of gender-based frames. The network was also more likely to discuss Clinton in the context of her role as mother or wife.

The former first lady inherited some animosity from her actions during her husband's tenure as president. Her ideas about her role as first lady raised eyebrows especially when she announced indignantly that she did not want to "stay at home, bake cookies, and give teas" as part of her effort to demonstrate her value as a member of her husband's administration (Marin, 2009). She also faced societal concerns that a woman lacks strong leadership qualities Americans desire in a president, especially at a time of economic unrest and the war on terror. Jeff Gordon's analysis of the 2008 election sums up the media's portrayal of female candidates with this quote: "From Photoshopped pictures of a rifle-toting Sarah Palin in an American-flag . . . to hearing pundits criticize everything about Hillary Clinton—her tears in New Hampshire to short haircuts or the color of her pantsuits—it's been glaringly obvious that women are treated differently than men" (Gordon, 2007, p. 12).

In other instances, conversations about Obama turned into a discussion of Clinton's appearance. For example, on CNN, February 25, 2008, during an exchange about a photo of Obama dressed in Somali garb, former Bill Clinton advisor, Dick Morris, interjected, "Has anyone seen the old photos of Hillary? Anybody seen the ones with the Coke bottle glasses and the brown hair and the brown eyes and the pre-shall we say- heavily made up face?" (*Obama Photo Firestorm; Interview with Arizona Governor Janet Napolitano; McCain Iraq's Fear*).

How well the candidate was aging was also a concern for some commentators. After a photo of a tired-looking Clinton appeared in *The Drudge Report*, Rush Limbaugh opined that "as you age—and you know women are hardest hit on this. . . . America loses interest in you." Thus, the question for voters became, "Will this country want to actually watch a woman get older before their eyes on a daily basis?" (Shea, 2008).

To spotlight this trend, CNN's *Reliable Sources'* commentator Michelle Cottle on December 23, 2007, raised the issue of how women in politics get their appearance analyzed more than men (*The Drudge Factor; How are Media Treating Hillary?* 2007). "I have talked to people from rival Democratic campaigns, journalists, whatever, who sit and obsess about this woman's ankles. I mean, it is absolutely a double standard." In the same transcript, *Washingtonpost.com* political reporter Chris Cillizza agreed: "I don't think anyone blinks an eye when someone writes a story about 'she's changing from pantsuits' or that her hair has changed."

I've never read a story about what kind of shoes John Edwards has on. What Hillary Clinton wears, what—her changing hairstyles, all of those things have become part of what has become acceptable political discourse.

SENATOR CLINTON'S IMAGE REPAIR TACTICS

Senator Clinton's image repair tactics varied (Table 12.1). Her main strategy was to gain support by showing that she was qualified. Demonstrating bolstering, Clinton emphasized her philanthropy work and her outstanding career as a New York senator. Her blog featured campaign ads and personal supporter testimonies. One campaign tactic highlighted women who campaigned for her. For instance, the New Hampshire for Hillary campaign included names of more than 3,500 women who supported her. In one blog entry, she highlighted an ad depicting children sleeping with the voice over saying, "It's 3 a.m. and who do you want answering the phone at the White House?"

Demonstrating *transcendence*, Clinton's news releases focused on hot button issues like strengthening the middle class, providing affordable health care, ending the war in Iraq, energy and global warming, helping veterans, caring for parents and children and women's rights. News releases also focused on geographical issues such as families in the areas she campaigned. For instance, on November 25, she released information about a Nevada initiative that stated, "Clinton's plan will extend the Family Medical Leave Act to cover 13 million additional workers across the country, and will ensure that 635,000 Nevadans who do not receive paid sick days will receive a minimum of seven days a year." On October 23, 2007, she released a statement

Table 12.1   Senator Hillary Clinton's Image Repair Strategies

Strategy/Key Characteristics	Tactic
Evasion of Responsibility	Attacked opponents
Provocation: responded to act of another	Clinton announced she was sick of being a punching bag for Barack Obama and former North Carolina senator John Edwards and that she intended to fight back.
	After you have been attacked as often as I have from several of my opponents, you cannot just absorb it. You have to respond.
Attack accuser: reduce credibility of accuser	Attacked Obama and Bush
	There's a lot that voters don't know about Barack Obama.
Reducing Offensiveness of Event	Focused on political strengths
Bolstering: stress good traits	Discussed campaign strategies
Transcendence: focus on more important considerations	Blog featured her recent ads and personal testimonies by people who know her and believed she would be a great president.
	In the "Morning HUBdate," she included a section that corrected candidates if they made statements that were either false or inaccurate.
Corrective Action: Plan to Solve or Prevent Problem	Softened image
	Cried
	Dressed differently
	College tour

Source: Benoit (1997).

about the fires in Southern California, "I have been following the news about the wildfires that are affecting seven counties in Southern California. My heart and prayers go out to the families who have been displaced, have lost their homes, businesses or worse-have lost a loved one to these ravaging wildfires."

Several releases focused on the candidate's support of veterans. If elected president, she stated she would provide affordable and quality health care, guarantee the benefits they have earned extend hiring preferences to veteran-friendly contractors and reduce homelessness among veterans. One a radio advertisement aired on her blog focused on how she would continue to fight for those who have represented America in past wars. In the ad, Clinton explained that her parents are veterans and how they have served their country. In a corresponding news release, Kimberly Fulton stated, "Hillary has worked hard to guarantee our young men and women serving here and abroad are well cared after. I know my family is greatly appreciative of the work she has done in the Senate and we know she'll continue these efforts as President of the United States" (Hillary Airs Third Radio Ad Focusing on Support for Veterans, 11/15/07).

She also announced politicians and constituents who supported her and could attest to her character. For instance, on October 16, after former governor Bob Holden endorsed Clinton, he said, "This country needs change, and Hillary Clinton has the strength and experience to deliver it. She is uniquely qualified to hit the ground running on her first day in the White House." Blog entries and news releases also laid out her plans for things that would be important to American citizens like health care.

Attack-accuser Strategy

If an opponent or adversaries credibility is damaged, the accused's image might be repaired. Demonstrating this tactic, Clinton used the attack accuser strategy. In December, she focused on the Bush Administration's handling of the War in Iraq, stating, "George Bush's faulty and offensive historical analogies aren't going to end the war in Iraq, make America safer or bring our troops home." Clinton also attacked George Bush's actions surrounding the mortgage crisis. One news release stated, "Throughout the foreclosure crisis President Bush has ignored the crisis for help. President Bush's plan takes the heat off the mortgage industry but leaves homeowners to sink" (Hillary Clinton's Response to Bush Foreclosure Plan, 12/6/2007).

Later, she turned her attention to Obama. For instance, one news release included the following statement, "There's a lot that voters don't know about Barack Obama. And one thing they don't know—we found out this week—is that he has been using and operating a so-called leadership PAC, in apparent contravention of campaign finance laws, taking in money from lobbyists despite the fact he said he doesn't take money from lobbyists" (Clinton Campaign Calls on Obama to Shut Down PAC, 12/2/07).

Other negative news releases varied. For instance, in one, Clinton's Deputy Communications Director, Phil Singer, attacked Obama's foreign policy and began the string of releases openly attacking Obama's electability versus Clinton's electability. With the critical foreign policy challenges America faces in the world today, voters will decide whether Senator Obama, who served in the Illinois State Senate just three years ago and would have less experience than any president since World War II, has the strength and experience to be the next president. Senator Clinton, who has traveled to 82 countries as a representative of the United States and serves on the Armed Services Committee, is ready to lead starting on Day One (Response from Clinton Campaign on Senator Obama's Foreign Policy Forum Today, 11/27/07). Clinton's news releases attacked Obama's electability several more times in December, usually strengthening claims with links to news stories published about him. One release stated:

> If You Read One Thing Today: The Politico uncovers a 1996 voter questionnaire that then-state senate candidate Obama filled out that raise serious questions about his electability. Obama, who is making an issue of his opponents' consistency while touting his own, embraced a number of positions in that 96 questionnaire—like banning handguns—that he abandoned as he rose to political prominence. (Morning HUBdate: Obama Gets Hit With Electability Questions, 12/11/07)

Another image repair strategy Clinton started in December was a series of releases titled "I've Switched to Hillary." These releases featured statements from former Obama supporters who "switched" to Clinton for various reasons. Several posts in December included quotes from supporters who stated that Clinton was ahead of other candidates.

Along with the *attack opponent* strategy, Clinton practiced *evasion of responsibility*, which focuses on *provocation* or the response to an act of another person. She announced in an interview with CBS that she was sick of being a punching bag for Obama and former North Carolina senator John Edwards and that she intended to fight back. For instance, both Edwards and Obama criticized Clinton's support of Bush and the war. Obama criticized Clinton for voting in favor of the war. In another news release, Romney stated, "She couldn't get elected president of France, let alone president of the United States." He also attacked her plan to put people on government health insurance and raise Social Security taxes (Romney criticizes Clinton, 2007).

In response to these attacks and many others, Clinton responded, "After you have been attacked as often as I have from several of my opponents, you cannot just absorb it. You have to respond" (Couric, 2008). Clinton's husband chimed in that he had never seen anyone treated so badly as his wife just for running for office.

A Softening of Clinton's Image

Mid-election, Clinton softened her image. Her blog included highlights of this transformation. To increase her appeal as a "normal" person, she began to smile more, wear pastel colors and more makeup. On one campaign stop, she even had a beer with local blue-collar workers. Clinton also made an appearance on the *Tyra Banks Show* and discussed how she met Bill. She kicked off "Our Voice, Our Future" tour in Florence, S.C. The event highlighted two high-profile actors, America Ferrera and Amber Tamblyn, who both endorsed Hillary earlier that month. To show her motherly side, which might aid in the softening of her image, her daughter, Chelsea campaigned for her by visiting colleges.

However, the biggest news items to aid in her transformation were the two times she displayed emotion publicly. For example, on January 7, 2008, she became visibly emotional at a New Hampshire campaign event after a friendly question from a voter, inquiring about how she handles her hectic schedule and hair. Similarly, in early February of 2008, Clinton became teary-eyed during an event at the Yale Child Study Center. She welled up after an introduction by Penn Rhodeen, a public interest lawyer who worked with Clinton when she was in college. Rhodeen praised Clinton's efforts as a college student.

After these brief displays of emotion, the media seized the opportunity to discuss Clinton's new softer side. Once criticized for being too cold and unemotional, journalists speculated on whether Clinton was really feeling emotion or just using the "gender card" to garner votes. While at the beginning of the election process many felt Clinton did not display enough feminine qualities, it did not take long for the pendulum to swing too far to the other side. News coverage portrayed Clinton as being too expressive. "And just like that . . . gender-transcendent Hillary morphed into a disrespected, mistreated victim" (Cottle, 2008). FOX commentator Alan Colmes agreed: "She's (Clinton) been raked over the coals for showing emotion, for showing some—she was accused of sobbing" (*Discussion of the New Hampshire Primary Results; Clinton Victory Speech,* 2008).

MEDIA RESPONSE

In the end, many journalists believed Clinton played the victim to receive more votes. CNN political analyst Bill Schneider felt that a rise in support for Clinton could have been solely because she showed some emotion and voters felt sorry for her. "Victimhood is a very easy thing to play . . . people will feel bad for her. And she actually went up in the polls against Obama" (*Political assault against Hillary Clinton*, 2008).

This type of response illustrates the difficulty Clinton had creating a good, balanced image in the eyes of mainstream voters. When she was strong and forceful, the media portrayed her as cynical and overbearing. On the other hand, when she was emotional, the media depicted her as weak and vote-hungry. Taking a cue from her news releases, the majority of negative-toned CNN and FOX News broadcasts dealt with Clinton's take-charge tactics in which she appeared to do whatever was necessary to get into the White House again. For example, on "Fox Hannity & Colmes," Jonah Goldberg, author of *Liberal Fascism* stated the "Clintons have always been very good at having a public face—a nice public face, while working very cut throat inside game" (Hillary Clinton Makes Questionable Remark at End of Debate).

In other news segments, Democrats and media pundits rebuked Clinton's attacks on Obama. They discussed her comments surrounding the political debates in which she accused Obama of ducking the debates. Journalists discussed Clinton fostering the same old politics with phony charges and false attacks. For instance, Nina Easton on "The Big Story with John Gibson" stated she felt that Clinton's negative tactics were a big reason for Clinton's lack of success at the polls (*Obama vs. Clinton out West? Will Oscars be Held this Year?*, 2008).

Journalists accused the Clinton camp of shameful and offensive fear mongering by circulating a picture of Obama in African garb while visiting Kenya in 2006. For instance, on a February 25, 2008, Fox News segment titled, guest Dick Morris said the tactic was an attempt to cast Obama as something outré and foreign and removed from the normal pale of American life. "He's black, and that's why they're showing him in an African costume. If they showed him in an Asian costume that he might have donned to appear before the King of Siam or something, Thailand, then that wouldn't have any political relevance." Morris said the ploy was an attempt to "ghettoize" him (*Senator Clinton on Attack, 2008*).

Some commentators emphasized a comparison that Clinton made likening Obama to former president George W. Bush. On CNN, February 25, 2008, The Situation Room, Candy Crowley said it was the unkindest cut of all in reference to Clinton's comment: "We have seen the tragic result of having a president who had neither the experience nor the wisdom to manage our foreign policy and safeguard our national security. We can't let that happen again" (*Obama Photo Firestorm; Interview with Arizona Governor Janet Napolitano; McCain Iraq's Fear, 2008*).

After analyzing articles and transcripts about Clinton, critics at *Mediamatters.com* asserted that members of the media often implied Senator Hillary Clinton displayed "mood swings," "could be depressed," "[r]esembl[ed] someone with multiple personality disorder," and "has turned into Sybil" (*Media Matters for America, 2008*).

While Clinton's change in appearance and display of emotion helped her gain momentum temporarily, it was too little, too late. In the end, she lost the bid for the 2008 Democratic presidential nomination, leaving most people to speculate if it was because of her gender. Renowned feminist Gloria Steinem characterized this sentiment in her op-ed statement in the January 8, 2008, issue of *The New York Times:* "Gender is probably the most restricting force in American life, whether the question is who must be in the kitchen or who could be in the White House."

Obama's Coverage

Conversely, Obama's coverage rarely made mention of his emotions, clothing, or appearance. Instead, the media played up his experience, change campaign and charismatic qualities often leaving out his scholarly and political achievements. Pundits often discussed Obama's pledge for change within the context of Clinton's assertion of her experience. Clinton and journalists also criticized Obama for using rhetoric and words rather than informing voters about his actual records or stands on particular issues. In a February 20, 2008, discussion with NPR's political editor Ken Rudin, Lynn Neary spoke of the rhetoric controversy:

> NEARY: . . . And we want to turn now to the longstanding American tradition of lofty political rhetoric. John Kennedy had the gift so did Ronald Reagan. Many say Barack Obama has that same ability to inspire those who hear him but last night, both John McCain and Hillary Clinton took jabs at Obama's speaking style. (*Momentum and Rhetoric*)

Image Repair Tactics of Senator Obama

The theme of "experience versus change" was prevalent in Obama's campaign tactics. Many quotes in his news releases focused on his pledge for change in Washington and Clinton's assertion of her experience. Demonstrating attack accuser strategies, Obama criticized Clinton for voting for the United States to go to war in 2002 (Table 12.2). When Clinton criticized him about his lack of experience with foreign policy, he charged, "On what I believe was the single most important foreign policy decision of this generation, whether or not to go to war in Iraq, I believe I showed the judgment of a commander-in-chief and I think that Senator Clinton was wrong in her judgments on that" (*Highlights of Obama-Clinton Texas Debate, 2008*).

Attack Accusers

Obama's negative releases about Clinton were often statements posted by his campaign manager, David Plouffe, regarding Clinton's campaign tactics. In a November 17 release, Obama said:

> in the interest of our party, and her own reputation, Senator Clinton should either make public any and all information referred to in the item, or concede the truth: that there is none. She of all people, having complained so often about 'the politics of personal destruction,' should move quickly to either stand by or renounce these tactics. I am prepared to stand up to that kind of politics, whether it's deployed by candidates in our party, in the other party or by any third party." (*Obama Statement on Report of Clinton Campaign Tactics*)

In a later release, Plouffe made a statement about Clinton's continued "mudslinging" tactics (Plouffe: Latest Clinton attack "increasingly desperate'). The Obama camp stated that "attacking other Democrats is the 'fun part' of this campaign, and now she's moved from Barack Obama's kindergarten years to his teenage years in an increasingly desperate effort to slow her slide in the polls." They added that Senator Obama plans on winning this campaign by focusing on the issues that actually matter to the American

Table 12.2 Senator Obama's Image Repair Tactics

Strategy/Key Characteristics	*Tactic*
Attack accuser: reduce credibility of accuser	Attacked Clinton's previous decisions/ foreign policy Challenged Clinton to stand by or renounce her previous actions. Discussed Clinton's mudslinging
Reducing Offensiveness of Event	Focused on change
Bolstering: stress good traits	Discussed campaign strategies
Corrective Action: Plan to Solve or Prevent Problem	
Endorsements	Many celebrities and news outlets frame Senator Obama favorably

people. On CNN, Democratic strategist Jamal Simmons stated: "And what we're watching is a Democratic campaign where one candidate is fighting the other candidate as is if they're fighting against the other party . . . and we've seen Hillary Clinton's negative numbers skyrocket because of that" (*Countdown to Pennsylvania Showdown; single women and the presidential campaign,* 2008).

The three issues most discussed on all three networks made up another frame for this study called, "Health Care/Taxes/Economy." Both Clinton and Obama supported health care for all Americans. However, they differed on how to do it. Clinton wanted health care to be mandatory, whereas Obama wanted it to be optional so those who felt they could not afford to have more taken out of their paychecks could make the choice themselves (*Highlights of Obama-Clinton Texas Debate,* 2008).

Clinton was criticized for not addressing successfully the health care issue when her husband appointed her to that task while he was in office for eight years. She did help create the State Children's Health Insurance Program that covered millions of children (*Can McCain Rally Conservatives?* 2008), but she and her advisors did not come up with a solution for universal health care. Former Virginia governor Douglas Wilder commented on a February 11, 2008, broadcast of CNN's *The Situation Room:*

> WILDER: . . . Since it's been brought up, Mrs. Clinton would have you believe that she had absolutely nothing to do with it, when she talks about the need for health care. I remember—I was a governor—when we went and said, OK, you are in charge of health care. She was made the czar of health. (*Can McCain Rally Conservatives?* 2008)

Although Clinton had little to say regarding taxes, Obama stated he was in favor of tax breaks for working-class families and keeping tax rebates and Social Security supplements in order to spur the economy (*Obama Criticizes Bush Stimulus Plan,* 2008). He also stated he wanted to take away tax breaks to companies who outsource job overseas (Ballot Bowl "08, 2008"). Obama criticized Clinton's plan to freeze mortgage rates stating, "A blanket freeze, as she's proposed, will drive rates through the roof on people who are trying to get new mortgages to buy or refinance a home. Experts say the value of homes will fall even more, and even more families could face foreclosure. Well, that's why one economic analyst calls her plan disastrous" (*Political Headlines,* 2008).

Race and Image Repair

The issue of race was more prominent in coverage of Obama than of Clinton. While the candidate did not refer to himself as black, newscasters and political analysts discussed it on both networks mostly to portray him as the first viable African American candidate. On January 23, 2008, *FOX Special Report with Brit Hume*, commentators discussed the question of media outlets portraying Obama as somebody who really can only win where there is a huge black turnout and it overwhelms the other vote.

On February 27, 2008, *FOX Hannity & Co*, guest Alan Kirsten Powers discussed the hard sell with Barack Obama. "When you look at him—He has not run as the black candidates." However, Colmes responded "he does not have to run as a black candidate, society will make him into a black candidate" (*Discussion of the Media's Treatment of Sen. Hillary Clinton,* 2008). Conversely, on a CNN October 11, 2007, report, Ann Coulter said, "I think Democrats have hit on the perfect candidate with Barack Obama or as I call him, B. Hussein Obama (*Barack Obama Criticizes Hillary Clinton,*" 2008). "B. Hussein Obama is half-white, half-black, so there's somebody for every Democrat to vote for," she added.

> The candidates did not refer to one another's race in a negative light. The only real race critique Clinton made was in regard to her comments about Martin Luther King, Jr., rallying for civil rights, in which she stated it was Lyndon Baines Johnson who made it actually happen.

Race was an issue early in the competition, as blacks had to decide whether they were going to support an African American man or the wife of former president Bill Clinton, who is still revered in some circles.

A December 12, 2007, NPR report detailed this dilemma among African American women voters given this was the first time both a woman and a black candidate were running:

> CONAN: . . . We're going to change directions a bit and focus on an issue facing many African-American voters, especially African American women—who to vote for? For the first time in history, an African-American and a woman are among the frontrunners for the Democratic nomination for president. Not to disparage the other candidates, but opinion polls show most African-Americans support either Hillary Clinton or Barack Obama. ("Debates Lead Up to Iowa Caucus")

Another instance in which race became a big issue is when TV stations covered Obama in relation to other people such as the Reverend Jeremiah Wright, who made derogatory comments about the United States and included black liberation theology in his sermons. On Fox, Sean Hannity, one of the more negative commentators toward Obama, played up the Wright scandal frequently on his appearances. In a March 1, 2007, interview, Hannity interviewed Wright in order to gain a better understanding of his seemingly racist remarks. The two were not able to see eye to eye on Wright's teachings,

which he says are geared toward empowering the black community. Obama
was even asked to denounce his former pastor. Other comments by O'Reilly
and Hannity laced throughout many transcripts included, "he is not ready,"
"he cannot win," "he doesn't like America" and "he pulled off his United
States flag pin."

The issue of race transcended to Clinton on a few occasions. Commentators often spoke of a dilemma among black women voters given this was the
first time both a woman and a black candidate were running. They also noted
that both Latino and black voters supported Clinton. On January 30, 2008, on
CNN's *The Situation Room*, Terry Jeffrey, editor in chief, Cybercast News
Service, said: "The Democrats clearly now face an historic choice. And it's
not just whether they're going to nominate the first possible black president of
the United States or the first possible woman. There's the question of whether
they really want to put a Clinton back in the White House" (*John Edwards
Suspends Campaign; Giuliani Exit Expected; Interview with Senator Claire
McCaskill*, 2008).

Endorsements and Image Repair

Much of Obama's image repair was executed by endorsements and coverage
from media outlets and celebrities. At one point during the primaries, journalists accused the Clinton camp of shameful and offensive fear mongering by
circulating a picture of Obama in African garb while visiting Kenya in 2006.
On a February 25, 2008, FOX News segment, guest Dick Morris said the tactic was an attempt to cast Obama as something outré and foreign and removed
from the normal pale of American life (*Senator Clinton on Attack*, 2008).
"He's black and that's why they're showing him in an African costume.
If they showed him in an Asian costume that he might have donned to appear
before the King of Siam or something, Thailand, then that wouldn't have any
political relevance." Morris said the ploy was an attempt to "ghettoize" him.

Many unfavorable transcripts dealt with Clinton's take-charge tactics in
which commentators claimed she appeared to do whatever was necessary
to get into the White House again. Others stemmed from her actions during
her husband's stint as president. For example, on "FOX Hannity & Colmes,"
Jonah Goldberg, author of *Liberal Fascism* stated: The "Clintons have always
been very good at having a public face—a nice public face, while working
very cut throat inside game" (*Hillary Clinton makes questionable remark at
end of debate*, 2008).

In other segments, commentators and media pundits rebuked Clinton's
attacks on Obama. They discussed her comments surrounding the political debates in which she accused Obama of ducking the issues. Easton on
stated she felt that Clinton's negative tactics were a big reason for her lack of

success at the polls (*Obama vs. Clinton out West? Will Oscars be Held this Year?* 2008).

Similarly, guest Nina Easton on "The Big Story with John Gibson" stated she felt that Clinton's negative tactics were a big reason for her lack of success at the polls (*Obama vs. Clinton out West? Will Oscars be Held this Year?* 2008). On CNN, Democratic strategist Jamal Simmons concurred, stating: "And what we're watching is a Democratic campaign where one candidate is fighting the other candidate as is if they're fighting against the other party . . . and we've seen Hillary Clinton's negative numbers skyrocket because of that" (*Countdown to Pennsylvania Showdown; Single Women and The Presidential Campaign,* 2008).

MEDIA RESPONSE

Media also emphasized the idea that journalists were easier on Obama than they were on Clinton. For example, on *FOX News Network* February 27, 2008, commentator Alan Kirsten Powers said journalists such as Tim Russert were aggressive with Clinton in a way that they were not with Barack Obama. Powers explained that reporters let Obama slide on difficult issues, but expected much more from Clinton, "There is a different standard and I just think you have to hold them both to the same standard (*Discussion of the Media's Treatment of Sen. Hillary Clinton,* 2008)."

CNN special reports reporter, Jeanne Moos, spotlighted the media's obsession with Obama on February 25, 2008. During one news report, an unidentified female said, "I myself have been clinically diagnosed as an Obama-maniac." In the same segment, Moos referenced a *Saturday Night Live* clip that parodied a CNN debate, with Obama getting hard-hitting questions such as "Are you comfortable?" "Is there anything we can get for you?" (*Obama Photo Firestorm; Interview with Arizona Governor Janet Napolitano; McCain Iraq's Fear,* 2008).

On February 20, 2008, CNN *The Situation Room* analyst, Deborah Feyerick, said, "Style vs. substance always comes up in politics, even between men, but voters judge personality traits differently between men and women." She described how a number of feminist groups see the Clinton/Obama race: "a highly qualified woman running for president against a younger candidate with captivating style" (*Powerful Union Endorses Obama; McCain Blasts Obama: Addresses Issue of Experience,* 2008). In agreement, guest Martha Burk, former chair of the National Council of Women's Organizations, added, "Were he female, put lipstick and long hair on him, I don't think he would be anywhere near the presidency of the United States right now."

An October 29, 2007, study by the Project for Excellence in Journalism and the Joan Shorenstein Center on the Press, Politics and Public Policy found that through the first half of 2007, Obama had received by far the most favorable media coverage of any of the 2008 presidential candidates, with 47% of stories having a favorable tone towards him, 16% having an unfavorable tone, and the balance neutral. In terms of amount of coverage, Obama had been the subject of 14% of all campaign coverage, the second largest amount after Clinton.

After a self-critique, many journalists owned up to showing favoritism for Obama. They discussed the idea that maybe they had been too hard on Clinton in their coverage of the election. Toward the middle of the race, journalists self-analyzed this shortcoming, focusing on the double standard regarding emphasis on Clinton's appearance and personality. The consensus was that women are scrutinized at a higher level than men in regards to appearance and the media portrayed a bad physical image of Clinton compared to other candidates.

IMPLICATIONS AND SOLUTIONS

Both Senators Barack Obama and Hillary Clinton were noteworthy candidates with backgrounds filled with accolades and firsts. In 2000, Hillary was elected to the United States Senate from New York where she continues to serve today. Barack Obama was the fifth African American senator in U.S. history and the only current African American on the Senate. The two faced very different challenges. Clinton had the difficult job of convincing voters that she is a woman attuned to issues that concern Democrats such as abortion, childcare and health care, while also avoiding implicit concerns that a woman lacks the leadership qualities Americans like to see in a president at a time of economic unrest and of war. Our findings indicate she did a good job of presenting these issues to the press as they made up a very large percentage of the frames covered.

Conversely, the biggest challenge that Obama faced was his race and the question of whether America is ready for a black man as president. Obama walked a line between being "Black enough" for the black community while avoiding issues and statements that might trigger racial stereotypes, fears and resentment that some whites harbor against blacks (Parks & Rachlinksi, 2008). In the end, gender was more salient in media coverage. The media mentioned gender repeatedly in its coverage of Clinton. Gender presented a challenge that Clinton found very difficult to battle, and in the end, it may have lost her the Democratic Presidential nomination. Renowned feminist Gloria Steinem said in the *New York Times* that women still have a more difficult time getting ahead than men. "Gender is probably the most restricting force in American life, whether the question is who must be in the kitchen or who could be in the White House." Transcripts often cited instances in which Clinton was supported more by older women than younger women did because younger women are not as familiar with sex discrimination. Additionally, there is the idea that men will not vote for a woman because they feel threatened. There was also discussion of a double standard regarding comments about Clinton during her campaign with regard to her clothing and her haircuts.

Gender may not have been the only culprit. Some of the animosity directed at Clinton may have been inherited from constituents who harbored a distaste for her husband and for the positions of his administration. Many voters remembered that Clinton stood by her man in light of the Monica Lewinsky scandal and she worked on a health care package during his presidency that did not come to fruition. To demonstrate her value as a member of her husband's administration, she announced indignantly that she did not want to "stay at home, bake cookies and give teas" (Marin, 2009).

Prior to this analysis, it was speculated that issues regarding race would be prominent in the coverage of Obama. However, findings indicate this was not the case. Though Obama openly embraced being black man, he did so in a way that did not alarm non–African Americans. He often noted that although his father was from Kenya, his mother is a white woman from Kansas. The fact that he is biracial helped him allude a stereotyped image. Issues of interest to Obama's campaign included taxes, education and finances, all of which he managed to catapult into the media spotlight. Other factors that worked in his favor: he is well educated, calm under pressure and from a hard-working background.

Several implications are worth noting. First, candidates may use an assortment of image repair tactics to improve their reputations; however, they must be consistent and believable. Early in the primaries, Clinton evaded responsibility, attacked accusers and reduced the offensiveness of the event. Later, she shifted gears, projecting a softer nicer appearance on one hand, while attacking her running mates on the other. Media highlighted her inconsistencies and suggested she had split personalities. In other words, while her appearance morphed into a more desirable persona, her campaign tactics did not. Obama, likewise, used fewer tactics in the preservation of his image—including, attack accuser and bolstering. However, endorsements from celebrities and journalists were helpful in repairing his image. Media and individuals often framed him as a "rock star" and "charismatic."

The second implication is although candidates provide news releases and other content to help reporters write stories, in the end journalists control mass media content such as network news, magazines and newspapers. Initially, Obama and Clinton's news releases were informative, tactful and well written. Fact sheets reinforced their statements and were supported by quotes from high-level political figures and corporate representatives. However, media did not always cover their preferred frames or topics presence in personal news releases.

A follow-up study might include interviews with editors and reporters to determine whether news releases influenced the type of stories published in newspapers or network news. One might also pair such a study with an agenda-setting paradigm to find out how consumers used such information to make their decision. Another follow-up study would be a comparative analysis of how many instances candidates did not have equal coverage among the network news organizations. Since this study was limited to just Clinton and Obama and their campaign for the Democratic Party vote, such a comparative analysis could determine who among Democrats, Republicans and Independents received more coverage, and if that was based on the political leanings of the network or the reporters/analysts.

Furthermore, scholars might encourage public discussions and essays such as this one, which will help keep issues of race, class and culture on people's minds. Tolerance should be encouraged that allows all people to run for office without the fear of being stereotyped. Such portrayals must constantly be challenged by alternative visions in a meaningful, consistent fashion. Without alternate perspectives, negative stereotypes targeting women retain their accepted place in American culture. Politicians in crisis would be wise to develop extensive and effective public relations media plans that include traditional and new media outlets to foster positive framing. This study may serve as a tool to help public relations and crisis communications practitioners understand that role social media can play in image repair. Findings provide a powerful springboard for future studies on image-repair, social media and framing.

Chapter 13

Image Repair and Online Media Framing of Hillary Clinton During the 2016 Presidential Race

Mia Moody-Ramirez, Hazel James
Cole, and Mayra Monroy

Senator Hillary Rodham Clinton, who confirmed on April 12, 2015, she was running for president in 2016, announced her candidacy in a video and on her Facebook page. The former secretary of state, senator and first lady stated, "Americans have fought their way back from tough economic times. But the deck is still stacked in favor of those at the top. Everyday Americans need a champion, and I want to be that champion" (Miller, 2015).

Scholars have captured the ongoing relationship between women and American politics (Gaffney & Blaylock, 2010; Huddy & Terkildsen, 1993; Khan, 1992; Kittilson & Fridkin, 2008; Larson, 2001; Lawless, 2004; Meeks, 2012, 2013). Research suggests that media coverage becomes increasingly hostile as women politicians aim for higher public offices (Huddy & Terkildsen, 1993; Kittilson & Fridkin, 2008; Meeks, 2012). Atkeson and Krebs (2008) found "little evidence of gender bias in the press coverage of mayoral campaigns with race context on issues, traits, appearance and electability" (p. 249). However, Kittilson and Fridkin (2008) described the gender differences in press treatment as "more dramatic for presidential candidates" (p. 373). In 2008, a national study revealed that only one out of five respondents held that belief (Banwart, 2010).

Oles-Acevedo (2012) concluded as Hillary Clinton evolved from a first lady known into a prominent political figure, people's perceptions of her changed. Clinton was criticized because she overtly took a nontraditional approach to her role as the wife of an American president, creating her need for image repair (2012, p. 34). Oles-Acevedo (2012, p. 34) adds:

Clinton is a moving target who has reinvented herself from political bumbler to U.S. Senator, to viable presidential candidate, to Secretary of State. Most perplexing about her political trajectory is the direct attacks that she has undergone

179

and the scandals that she has survived. Clinton's gender and image-related issues created the need for her to use image restoration or maintenance tactics, which will be analyzed in this study that looks at both the 2008 and 2016 elections

Previous studies indicate people who use social media as a source to help repair their image (or to focus on other occurrences in their life) have been more successful in their image repair tactics than those who were belligerent, accusing and refused to take responsibility and apologize. Such studies have focused on the nature of image repair strategies of athletes, politicians and religious leaders (e.g., Benoit, 2006; Brewer, 2009; Kroon & Ekstrom's, 2007; Oles, 2010; Yioutas & Segvic, 2003).

While these studies provide valuable insight into image repair management, few have addressed social media and image repair strategies used by female politicians. This chapter provides an examination of Clinton's image restoration tactics with a look at how she used her personal blog to improve her image during the 2016 presidential races. Benoit's approach to image repair operates under two major premises: an assumption that communication is a goal-oriented activity, and the primary communication goal is to maintain a positive image (Benoit, 1995; Blaney & Benoit, 2001). In this case, the researcher used it to help determine whether Clinton's communication efforts were effective and to what extent cultural narratives and media frames of politicians and gender played a role in her media coverage. Many studies in this area use rhetorical criticism, or case studies, so generalizations are difficult to make. Clinton's use of online media during a political race provided a good opportunity for exploration of IRT within the realm of a relatively new medium.

With the increased use of social media and number of female politicians, the topic is particularly relevant today. Blogs, in particular, have become a vital role in communication between the author and readers in the past few years. Sweester and Metzgar (2007) found that "there has been much attention to the use of blogs as an emergent public relations tool. Blogs seem ideally suited for crisis communication situations. Because blog writing style lends itself to more frequent publishing in its shorter statements through a personal/human voice, it seems logical that organizations could deploy crisis blogs as a means of quickly communicating during a crisis."

This study is important for several reasons. First, media provide historical content that researchers may use to analyze trends in the reporting of gender. The framing of gender is noteworthy because, overall, careless and insensitive coverage of groups might actually promote stereotypes and resentments (Carlin & Winfrey, 2009; Heldman, Carroll & Olson, 2005; Ross, 2002). Therefore, it is essential to continually analyze and address media perceptions of women to offer insight and solutions.

Second, the growing usage of the Internet as a source of political information has spurred a growing interest in the medium as a tool for political campaigning. While traditional communication has been top-down giving greater influence to elites, the Web opens up the possibility of horizontal communication without gatekeepers. Wright and Hinson (2008) note that "the potential impact of blogs on public relations and corporate communications is phenomenal" (p. 4).

Finally, this chapter offers a longitudinal investigation of the 2008 and 2016 U.S. presidential elections to assess the similarities and changes in Clinton's image maintenance/repair strategies. Study findings may prove useful for social media and candidate crisis/scandal management and provide insight into the best strategies for improving scarred public images in today's rapidly changing media climate.

PREVIOUS POLITICAL IRT STUDIES

The term "image" is defined as the perception of a communicative entity shared by an audience (Benoit, 1995). One's image must enable him or her to portray certain characteristics like power, trust, leadership and name recognition. In politics, this is especially important. Mayer (2004) concluded "The power of the president to realize his agenda in Washington and indeed around the world is directly affected by his standing with the public." Image includes both reality and perception, and public perception is not necessarily controllable.

Benoit asserts that it is easier for the public to forgive an actor than it is to forgive a politician because of the responsibilities of their career. Three reasons, according to Benoit (1997), are due to politicians with opponents to initiate attacks, partisans who control the time they stay in the public eye and the nature of impact upon more people's lives. An actor is paid to act and entertain, affecting their audiences' lives less seriously and significantly. Referring to a politician, "This is important because whenever a person admits to making a mistake, auditors may think about what might happen if the rhetor makes another mistake in the performance of their job" (Benoit, 1997).

Previous studies on political cases indicate mortification, or an apology, can be the most effective tactic after a crisis (e.g., Benoit, 2006; Grossberger, 1995; Kennedy, 2010; Sheldon & Sallot, 2009). However, Sheldon and Sallot (2009) assert apologizing has its limits. "It is more effective than corrective action, but no better than emphasizing past good deeds when the politician is trying to convince the public to believe his version of the faux pas, think well of his character, and recognize his concern for others" (p. 44). Sheldon and

Sallot (2009) assert that openly admitting mistakes may be more difficult for politicians than others because "greater future costs are at risk."

Former president Bill Clinton relied on *denial* and *bolstering* strategies after his first brush with major scandal during his 1992 campaign (Blaney & Benoit, 2001). He denied doing anything illegal during his period of draft eligibility during the late 1960s. In addition, he denied acting opportunistically within the letter of the law in order to evade the draft. He used *bolstering* to talk about his general patriotism and military leadership of the Arkansas National Guard.

In another example, Valenzano and Edwards (2012) analyzed the image restoration tactics used by Newt Gingrich during the South Carolina primary, which represented a pivotal moment for the presidential candidate's campaign. Leading up to the primary the evangelical base of the Republican Party, which constituted a large portion of the South Carolinian electorate, had split their votes between Gingrich and Santorum. The news that his ex-wife was slated to air an interview where she would cast major aspersions regarding the former speaker's behavior during their marriage exacerbated problems Gingrich had with this core constituency.

Valenzano and Edwards (2012) concluded Gingrich combined three strategies of image repair rhetoric to deflect attention from his own personal failings, encourage forgiveness for his transgressions, and shift the focus of the issue from him to the conduct of national news organizations. Gingrich vaguely admitted faults in his past relationships, but made them appear as nothing more offensive than what other Americans may be guilty of doing. In addition, he *denied* the specific comments his ex-wife was set to make before she even made them, and *attacked* the news media for focusing on his former marriage during a presidential election cycle.

In another example, Sheldon and Sallot (2009) used fictional character, Senator Davis, to analyze perceptions of image restoration tactics. In the study, Senator Davis made a speech praising a senior politician for opposing the civil rights movement. The study indicated the different outcomes for *mortification, corrective action and bolstering.* The strategy that met most success was *mortification* (Sheldon & Sallot, 2009). Out of the three strategies used, *mortification* suited the situation best.

However, *mortification* is not always the best strategy based on situational factors. For example, U.S. Senator Joseph Biden, a presidential candidate in 2007–2008, used *transcendence* (reducing offensiveness of the event) as a strategy when faced with a crisis situation (Davis, 2008). Biden, Hillary Clinton, Chris Dodd and John Edwards were Democratic presidential candidates who voted to authorize U.S. military force in Iraq and voted for subsequent bills, which funded the war. This presented a situation for these candidates, especially among Democratic primary voters, who strongly opposed the war and wished its end. Davis found Biden's *transcendence* strategy proved the most successful for image repair out of all the candidates in the same situation.

Stereotypes and Gender

The study of gender and IRT are useful in an analysis of media coverage of Clinton because of the media's dual ability to reinforce unequal status quo relationships, as well as to circulate new ideas and help set political agendas leading to change. The promotion of gender stereotypes and resentments toward women can be detrimental in political campaigns. Stereotyping, misrepresentation and underrepresentation occur because of overall, insensitive coverage of women or symbolic annihilation or the lack of coverage (Entman, 1991; Hermant & Thornton, 1994).

As mentioned in chapter 12, previous research indicates that although media offer men and women candidates an equal quantity of coverage, they do not give them the same type of coverage. Typically, coverage of male candidates focuses on their policy and history in office, while coverage of female candidates focuses more on their personality and appearance (Devitt, 2002; Freedman & Fico, 2005). Likewise, other scholars have found the media focus more attention on female candidate's gender, children and marital status, framing their ability to hold political office in terms of their roles as mothers and wives. Similarly, studies indicate journalists depict women with "gendering" frames. For example, Devere and Davies (2006) found that international research reports demonstrate a consistent framing of media coverage, which highlight a person's gender when it is not particularly relevant to the context.

Čičkarić (2015) asserts political coverage has always been viewed as men's struggle to win power. "The levers of power are designed, managed and controlled by men" (p. 95). She adds that the 21st century demonstrates a more common perception advocating for an "increased women's participation in political institutions that might significantly change the nature of representative democracy, revive and improve the system of management and decision making." Čičkarić (2015, p. 96) adds:

> Women doubt their capacity, knowledge and experience and rarely enjoy party allegiance. These findings are significant ones since they suggest that women, despite equal qualifications, education and social capital they possess just like men do, are primarily of low self-confidence and lack the wish to risk and compete. Even women with good political connections in parties are not ready to repeat candidacy and win the support of voters.

Butler (1999) asserts that gender is a product of performativity rather than a product of a person's sex. Gender is performative and not a fixed point of agency as identity emerges from the repetition of stylized gender acts. She adds that "performativity, in this sense, is used to understand how people behave and the power associated with performing certain social roles" (Butler, 1999, p. 179; as cited in Oles, 2012, p. 35).

In previous analyses of Hillary Clinton's image repair tactics, Oles-Acevedo, (2012) concluded the combination of *denial* and *reducing offensiveness* was Clinton's main approach to image repair. The researcher critically analyzed image damaging incidents that Clinton faced in the 1990s, including Clinton's defiance of traditional models of first ladies, the Whitewater Land Investigation, and the Monica Lewinsky scandal.

A common theme that appeared in each of Clinton's repair attempts is *denial*, not denial of having been involved in the particular incident but *denial* that her words or actions were designed to cause damage to either the president or the symbolic position of first lady. During her initial comments about Tammy Wynette and baking cookies, Clinton *denied* that her comments were intentionally malicious in nature toward traditional womanhood.

Clinton also denied that Whitewater was solely of her doing since it was her idea to partner with the McDougal's. In the end, *denial* was ineffective because of the time span from when the allegations were first made and the couple was cleared of wrongdoing. The author also noted that during the Lewinsky affair, Clinton began to act as a more traditional first lady, which in the end led to an improved personal image because for the first time she was the supporting wife.

In a similar study, Davis (2013) concluded Hillary Clinton used the 2007–2008 presidential primary debates to defend her decision to vote in favor of authorizing and funding the war in Iraq. The author concluded Clinton employed image repair strategies of *differentiation*, *defeasibility* and *mortification*. However, the politician's contradictory and inconsistent combination of *defeasibility* and *mortification* was ineffective because inconsistent and contradictory rhetoric violates democracy's expectations of consistent and responsive leadership.

During this campaign period, Clinton responded to accusations of reversing positions or flip-flopping (Davis, 2013). Clinton was in the U.S. Senate in 2002 and 2003 and had voted on October 11, 2002, to authorize the use of the U.S. armed forces against Iraq (U.S. Senate, 2002). Further, on October 17, 2003, Clinton voted for the supplemental appropriations bill for operations in Afghanistan and Iraq (U.S. Senate, 2003). Clinton, as the Democratic Party's early front-runner, had to provide excuses for her votes so as to repair her image in the eyes of Democratic primary voters.

In the end, Clinton's support for the Iraq War and her refusal to apologize for that vote likely hurt her chances with voters who had the alternative to vote for Obama, who did not vote to authorize the war and did not have to make such an apology. Further, Clinton's contradictory declaration that she was adequately briefed by the CIA further weakened the effectiveness of her use of *defeasibility* and *mortification*. Ultimately, these factors may have led to Clinton's loss of the primary nomination to former president Barack Obama.

Based on a review of the literature, the following questions guided this analysis: (1) What common themes emerged in media coverage of Clinton during the 2008 and 2016 U.S. presidential races? (2) What image repair/ maintenance tactics did Clinton use in her online news releases and blogs during the 2008 and 2016 U.S. presidential races?

TEXTS ANALYZED

To assess Clinton's online image repair strategies, this study used a qualitative content analysis of Clinton's rhetoric during the 2016 presidential elections. Specifically, we analyzed the blog entries posted on her official campaign website during this race. Clinton's blog posts are of interest because they were heavily used to help spread the word about the political race and her campaign platform. Bichard (2006) defines blogs as, "online diaries wherein information is electronically posted, updated, and presented in reverse chronological order." Sweetser and Metzgar (2007) add that blogs seem ideally suited for crisis communication situations because blog writing style lends itself to frequent publishing, shorter statements and a personal/ human voice.

The study sample included the top 100 blog entries posted to Clinton's official web page in 2016 (for a total of 100). Each blog post was selected by scrolling down the pages of Clinton's website with search results and the post was copied and pasted into a Word document as well as any links to connected posts, reaching a total of 100 posts total in the sample. We also referred to articles published online by CNN, the *Washington Post*, the *New York Times* and *USA Today*, as these were heavily shared and cited by other news outlets and citizens. We developed a coding protocol based on Benoit's IRT to place the posts into categories related to the most prominent image restoration themes: *denial of the accusation, evading responsibility of the act, reducing the offensiveness of the accusation, offering corrective actions* and *mortification* (Table 13.1).

Table 13.1   Benoit's Image Restoration Tactics

Strategy	Actions
Denial	"I didn't do it"
	"It didn't happen"
	"They did it"
Evade responsibility	Provocation
	"I was provoked by an untoward act directed at me"
	Defeasibility
	"I didn't know; I couldn't control myself/the situation"
	Accident
	"It was an accident"
	Good intentions
	"I meant well"
Reduce offensiveness	Bolstering
	"I'm a good person"
	Minimization
	"This isn't so bad" Differentiation
	"I'm not slandering, I'm discussing"
	Transcendence
	"My actions were true to my beliefs"
	Attack the accuser
	"They framed me"
	Compensation
	"I will pay for my error to those I hurt"
Corrective action	"This will not happen again"
	"I am a changed person"
Mortification	"I am wrong"
	"I deeply regret my actions"
	"I seek forgiveness"

Source: Benoit (1995).

To identify image repair strategies, the analysis included the reading and identification of themes identified in the review of the literature. Reading the posts multiple times and cycling through the posts, the researchers were able to see similarities and differences in thematic elements. A pattern emerged, which provided the evidence for an argument about the nature of Hillary Clinton's blog posts in 2008 and 2016. This method of analysis provided the framework for understanding Clinton's image restoration strategies during the 2008 and 2016 presidential races.

BACKGROUND

Throughout the 2008 and 2016 presidential races, critics often focused on Clinton's character flaws rather than her campaign platform. In 2008, many media outlets played up patriarchal representations of the candidate, focusing on her emotions, appearance, personality—often overlooking her skills. One of the most prominent characterization of the former senator was she was "unapproachable, unattractive and shrill."

Clinton's 2016 U.S. presidential campaign emphasized many of the same issues that emerged during her 2008 run for office; however, several new ones emerged that proved detrimental to her election. Clinton placed the blame for her Electoral College loss on factors such as media coverage, sexism, fake news and the Democratic Party's infrastructure. She stated that she would have won if not for "an influence campaign" directed by Vladimir Putin to undermine her during the election. Clinton also emphasized Comey's decision to notify Congress on October 28 that the FBI would review additional emails in connection with an investigation into her personal email server. The FBI announced on the eve of the election that the emails would not affect the outcome of the investigation (Foran, 2017).

Evasion of Responsibility and Provocation

Clinton used evasion of responsibility as an image restoration tactic immediately following the election (Table 13.2). She stated that her presidential campaign was flawed, but largely pinned the blame for her defeat on factors beyond her control, including Russian interference in the election, and actions taken by FBI Director James Comey (Foran, 2017).

Clinton primarily focused on the Comey scandal, addressing it throughout the campaign. In July, Comey concluded a year-long investigation into Hillary Clinton's emails and decided not to move forward with any charges—saying it wasn't even a close call. "No reasonable prosecutor," he noted,

Table 13.2   Hillary's Clinton's 2016 Image Repair Strategies

Strategy/Key Characteristics	Tactic
Evasion of Responsibility	Clinton stated that her presidential campaign was flawed, but largely pinned the blame for her defeat on factors beyond her control, including Russian interference in the election, and actions taken by FBI Director James Comey.
Attack accuser: reduce credibility of accuser	Attacked Trump, Comey and CIA
Reducing Offensiveness of Event	Focused on political strengths Discussed campaign strategies
Bolstering: stress good traits	Blog featured her recent ads and personal testimonies by people who know her and believed she would be a great president.

Source: Benoit (1997).

would have chosen to pursue the case. Clinton's campaign originally praised the FBI director for his initial findings in the email case. In an interview on CNN's "Situation Room" in July, Clinton press secretary Brian Fallon went after Republicans for criticizing Comey after the FBI concluded it would not press criminal charges against Clinton (Lee & Merica, 2017).

Closer to Election Day, Clinton stated the timing of such a move was "unprecedented" and "deeply troubling." After the election, Clinton told donors on a 30-minute conference call that Mr. Comey's decision to send a letter to Congress about the inquiry 11 days before Election Day thrust the controversy back into the news and had prevented her from ending the campaign with an optimistic closing argument (Chozick, 2016).

Bolstering

Bolstering from key people emphasized Clinton's positive traits throughout the campaign. Her blog posts included an endorsement from former president Barack Obama and several large newspapers in Texas and Pennsylvania. A blog post included the statement below:

> Texas may be a historically red state, but this year, the race is tight—and newspapers across the state are urging voters to back Hillary Clinton. (That includes *The Dallas Morning News*, which hasn't endorsed a Democrat in 76 years)

Attack Accuser

Clinton demonstrated the attack accuser strategy in her handling of Trump during the presidential campaign. Blog posts emphasized Trump's handling of issues such as race, gender and socioeconomic status. She mentioned Trump's wealth, and that he was out of touch with his constituents. In one blog post, Senator Elizabeth Warren, a guest contributor on the Clinton blog, discussed why she was planning to vote against Trump.

> Just look at how a man like Trump can take advantage of the system: He inherited a fortune and kept it going by cheating and scamming people. Time and again, he's preyed on people in debt, people who have fallen on hard time, he's preyed on people in debt, people who have fallen on hard times. He's conned them, defrauded them, ripped them off.

Following the election, Obama and his senior aides attacked the media, which they asserted often focused on "right, shiny objects at the expense of serious policy" (Cillizza, 2016). When asked about the Russian hacking of the Democratic National Committee in Hillary Clinton's campaign, Obama offered a media critique:

> This was an obsession that dominated the news coverage. So I do think it is worth us reflecting how it is that a presidential election of such importance, of such moment, with so many big issues at stake and such a contrast between the candidates came to be dominated by a bunch of these leaks.

Demonstrating bolstering and attack accuser, Obama, again offered a media-focused answer when asked whether Clinton's loss could be blamed on the Russian hack (Cillizza, 2016):

> I couldn't be prouder of Secretary Clinton, her outstanding service, and she's worked tirelessly on behalf of the American people, and I don't think she was treated fairly during the election. I think the coverage of her and the issues was troubling.

In a less common image repair tactic, Clinton used *endorsements* to attack her opponent. In one blog post, the Clinton campaign discussed the endorsements that Trump had received that were perceived as unfavorable. Donald Trump, on the other hand, has received an unprecedented lack of support. But yesterday, Trump did receive a new backer: A prominent Ku Klux Klan newspaper called the Crusader announced their support for a Trump presidency.

Accepting Blame

While Clinton did not use mortification as an image restoration strategy, she addressed the campaign issues that surfaced by accepting blame. "Did we make mistakes? Of course, we did. Did I make mistakes? Oh, my gosh yes," Clinton told CNN's Christiane Amanpour at a "Women for Women International" event in New York, "but the reason why I believe we lost were the intervening events in the last 10 days" (Foran, 2017).

Clinton's campaign press secretary Brian Fallon asserted that the news media often covered Trump in a more positive light, which often placed Clinton on the defensive (Logan, 2017). The article notes:

> The election stretched on and the Clinton campaign and its surrogates sought to capitalize on Trump's frequent missteps, Clinton often had to address unflattering headlines about the Clinton Foundation, her corporate speeches, her health, and her record as Secretary of State. Logan also notes the former press secretary believed the cumulative events added to the downfall of the campaign, characterizing it as "irreparably damaging to Clinton's already battered second bid for the White House."

Other political analysts asserted Clinton's narrow loss to Donald Trump was influenced by complacency driven by polls. Analysis of final results in the three Rust Belt states—Michigan, Pennsylvania and Wisconsin—suggests Clinton may have lost because she failed to show up in crucial counties where she might have made a difference. Clinton lost the three states by a total of 77,759 votes (Cannon, 2016).

In response to the idea that racism is to blame for Trump's success with white working-class voters, several of Clinton's losses in Pennsylvania came in mostly white counties that had twice supported former president Barack Obama (Cannon, 2016).

CONCLUSIONS AND IMPLICATIONS

This chapter analyzed Clinton's image repair tactics presented in 2008 and 2016. Throughout both races for president, the Clinton campaign team published hundreds of entries that focused on her campaign strategies and why she was the best candidate for U.S. presidency. Overall, her blogs were effective at the beginning of the political race. During the early months, journalists noted her clean campaign tactics. By remaining positive, Clinton hoped to be seen as drastically different from other candidates. However, her outlook changed after Obama and Trump gained momentum. In 2008, she widely criticized Obama and the Bush administrations and then explained how her policies were better. Although she explained her negativity as a measure to fight back, the public did not buy it. Clinton did not fit the stereotype of the traditional US presidential candidate. She was strong-willed, well known and highly qualified for the position.

Clinton approached her loss differently in 2016, acknowledging that her presidential campaign was flawed, but largely pinning the blame for her defeat on factors beyond her control, including Russian interference in the election, and actions taken by FBI Director James Comey (Foran, 2017). Clinton also placed the blame for her Electoral College loss on other factors, including media coverage, sexism, fake news and the Democratic Party's infrastructure.

In both instances, although Clinton used several strategies, she did not use mortification, which previous studies have shown is the most effective. In 2008, instead of apologizing for her negative comments, Clinton defended her actions by saying she was fighting back. Instead of gaining long-term sympathy and media support, the media did not respond favorably to her mixed messages because of her attack campaign strategies. This finding alludes to the idea that journalists are less sympathetic when candidates do not adhere to clean campaign strategies. By making offensive comments, on one hand, and trying to project a more positive, friendly persona on the other, she lost credibility. The media began to portray her as untrustworthy and willing to win by any means necessary. In the end, she was unsuccessful in gaining sympathy. Journalists and constituents thought she was insincere because of her negative attacking rhetoric.

While Clinton accepted responsibility for her loss in 2016, she blamed misogyny and Russian President Vladimir Putin's interference with the election (Estepa, 2016). She primarily emphasized Comey's decision to send a letter to Congress about the inquiry 11 days before Election Day, which thrust the controversy back into the news and ultimately prevented her from ending the campaign on an optimistic vantage point.

Several implications are worth noting. First, candidates can use an assortment of image repair tactics to improve their reputations; however, they must be consistent and believable. Early in the 2008 election, Clinton evaded responsibility, attacked her accusers and reduced the offensiveness as image repair strategies. Later, she shifted gears, projecting a softer, nicer appearance on one hand, while attacking her running mates on the other.

In 2016, Clinton was similarly split in her image repair strategies. Her campaign handled Comey's decision to write to congressional leaders about emails uncovered in the bureau's probe differently throughout the campaign. Close to Election Day, Clinton stated the timing of such a move was "unprecedented" and "deeply troubling." However, the attacks on Comey were a sudden turn for Clinton's campaign, which originally praised the FBI director for his initial findings in the email case. In both instances, media highlighted her inconsistencies.

Secondly, study findings provide crucial insights regarding the ideas and positions voters are likely to embrace about female politicians. Historical narratives of women are still strong and have an impact on coverage of female politicians. In 2008, journalists played up patriarchal representations of Clinton, focusing on her lack of emotion, looks, overbearing personality, and often overlooking her skills. Evidence points to gender as the one remaining area where stereotypes and societal beliefs stay the same. Toward the middle of the race, journalists self-analyzed this shortcoming, focusing on the double standard regarding emphasis on Clinton's appearance and personality. Many journalists and political pundits agreed there was a double standard when it comes to coverage of male and female politicians. The general consensus was that women are scrutinized at a higher level than men in regards to appearance. Media outlets portrayed a negative image of Clinton compared to other candidates. In the end, journalists tried to make amends by covering the election in a more unbiased manner.

Media gatekeepers must be willing to evaluate their unconscious or conscious decision to frame men and women politicians differently. Media's reliance on stereotypes of women candidates not only hinders the reporting of issues that are more important but also helps determine how people choose to vote. Alternative portrayals can help change such misconceptions. Feminists can seek to decenter the patriarchal voice by providing alternative feminist discourses to help supplant the traditional views of women and politics.

Findings are enlightening and provide a springboard for future studies on image repair, politics and gender. Future studies might include a comparison of several blogs maintained by candidates in crisis. Other media sources such as social media platforms and newspapers offer are also of interest. An important question that demands exploration is how politicians use social media platforms such as Instagram and Facebook during a crisis.

Audience response is another area that must continue to be developed across media platforms. Future studies might look at comments in response to blog posts to assess the effectiveness of changing public opinion via social media.

In both 2008 and 2016, Clinton had the difficult job of convincing voters she was tough enough as a woman to lead the United States. Her blog entries, personal statements and endorsements from high-level political figures and corporate executives provided a favorable portrayal of the presidential candidate. However, in the end, Clinton's campaign strategies were not enough. Clinton received mixed reactions from commentators and voters. In interviews, some people stated they believed a woman should not run for president. Others expressed that having a woman as president for the first time would be revolutionary, indicating they would support Hillary in the election.

These two campaigns together reveal the great strides against sexism that America has achieved. Clinton experienced success on the campaign trail that no woman would have dreamed of decades ago. Clinton's gender has not kept her from attaining many firsts in her lifetime. However, the presidency of the United States was one glass ceiling that she was unable to break after two noteworthy attempts.

Chapter 14

Conclusions and Future Directions in Image Repair Theory

Although in different settings, many of the case studies included in this book analyze situations that have sexual or racial overtones that necessitated image repair tactics. Undoubtedly, the media played a vital role in keeping the debates alive, perhaps to sensationalize the topics or to engage in a debate about freedom of speech, a debate that has been ongoing for many centuries. Eventually, each scandal dropped out of the news cycle. However, clearly, they served as a jump-start to good discussion on critical race theory (CRT) and image repair theory (IRT).

First and foremost, the case studies in this text reveal individuals may engage in various image restoration tactics to repair his or her image. Many of the cases indicate social media can either be one's solution or problem. Depending on how social media is used, a person can successfully repair a tarnished image.

Furthermore, the case studies in this text add a fresh perspective to the IRT literature by using a critical race lens to analyze how individuals present themselves through personal statements, online sources and interviews and the media's coverage of each case. Previous examinations of race-related incidents have primarily focused on media framing through analysis of traditional platforms such as print and broadcast mediums.

We identified successful applications of CRT to IRT that might be applicable to individuals who find themselves in race-related crisis situations in the future. The potential benefits available through the appropriate use of media outlets as image repair strategies are essentially limitless. If an individual follows an appropriate combination of Benoit's (1995) image repair tactics, they will have a much better chance of repairing their image quickly, efficiently, and permanently.

Many of the cases in this text demonstrate that the post-racial society that many had hoped for has not materialized. The cases created a stir in many communities with discussions emphasizing race, sexual orientation and political inclination. Therefore, the case served as an ideal starting point for discussions on the intersections of race and IRT.

IRT AND SOCIAL MEDIA

Information and opinions can be released within seconds of a story breaking. Journalists and publications, specifically those with a mass following, hold the power to ruin reputations with just a press of a button. The growing usage of the Internet as a source of information has spurred a burgeoning interest in the medium as a tool for image repair. Social media has become the communication practitioner's essential tool in image repair. When implementing an image repair campaign, social media is the best tactic to communicate with a vast audience.

The cases included in this text indicate social media provide a viable platform for celebrities to repair a tarnished image while at the same time allowing audiences to express their viewpoints in an interactive environment. The rise of social media as primary tools for communication has fostered the demise of the mediating role of traditional media between celebrities and publics. Not surprisingly, the gatekeeper-audience dynamic cultivated in social media has raised questions about its value in image repair planning.

Self-presentation via social media allows public figures to disseminate information with little or no gatekeeper intervention. This change in the communication process warrants continued updated research, as well as the testing of traditional theories in a new media environment. Such studies are particularly noteworthy as some observers predict user-generated content (UGC) such as YouTube videos, websites, blogs and other forms of mass media may eventually displace traditional broadcast media as the main outlet for news and entertainment.

Demonstrating the dual nature of the Web, on one hand the cases in this book used statements released on TV shows, online publications and social media to explain and minimize actions. Conversely, viewers utilized the Web to as a feedback loop to respond to the case. It is hoped that studies such as this one will serve as a springboard to support and encourage imperative discussions on the tenets of IRT.

These studies foreshadow the promise that social media offer for celebrities who use them to attempt to repair their image. However, it is important for scholars to continue to research the topic. As the various types of social media continue to transform as well as how people use them, it is for scholars to continue to study their effectiveness.

VISUAL IMAGES AND IRT

In our visual-obsessed culture, future studies must also address the role one's physical appearance may play in the success of a person's image restoration tactics. In the present digital era, celebrities and the public communicate to key audiences in a way that can build a brand or destroy it. A study that examines comparison in a person's looks in the success of his or her image repair might also be noteworthy. Part of that communication may be visual images that portray the perpetrator as victim as part of the image repair strategy; vulnerable or immature.

Future studies might use empirical research, such as a survey approach, to quantify these phenomena in the realm of an image repair study. Qualitative methods, such as focus groups, may also be utilized to gain insight on the visual elements of the subject researched to determine what, if any, role does visual imagery play in audience perception, forgiveness or redemption that may lead to the opportunity of image repair.

CASE STUDY LIMITATIONS

There are several limitations involved in our analyses of image repair. First, because little research has been conducted involving social and new media, we had very little framework to build upon. Fortunately, the studies in this text may be replicated. We set the initial parameters for researching and gathering information on IRT, CRT and social media platforms. Analyzing tweets, Facebook posts and other forms of social media presents a very broad scope of opinions, preventing our ability to generalize study findings.

The rise in popularity of certain forms of social media has an impact on the number of posts we use to form our findings. Previous studies address the successful and unsuccessful approaches to image restoration. Findings are in line with previous studies that indicate celebrities who used mortification and apology as a tactic of image repair are more successful than those who continued denial throughout their entire image repair campaign.

Secondly, we did not have access to publicists or public relations teams. In many cases, they remain anonymous—leaving us to question if image restoration tactics are executed by individuals or teams. Due to this limitation, we are unable to determine whether social media posts are simply publicity stunts to draw attention or whether they are genuine attempts to repair one's image. Collectively it looks as though most of the celebrities featured in our case studies are taking steps to repairing their tarnished image.

Many of them—such as Bieber and Brown—are young and are able to use the "young and dumb" plea. However, considering celebrities are under a microscope for being in the public eye and representing themselves and the people they report to. Fame has its price. Because sports and entertainment have such a powerful presence in American society, the high-profile individuals do not live up to the high standards that the public sets for them and often involve themselves in scandals that hurt their image.

In addition, most cases in this book only looked at a series of social media content in a small date range. This proved limiting for individuals that had ongoing or multiple scandals or developing cases to consider. Audience response was also hard to gauge using secondary sources. In many instances, media coverage and public opinion polls were so polarized, it was hard to get an accurate understanding of individuals under analysis. Empirical research that assesses audience response to image restoration tactics is also import to the development of IRT literature.

Lastly, since many of the cases in this text are ongoing, including conclusions and recommendations are difficult to develop. Public relations practitioners have various strategies for handling crisis situation arises among high-profile people. The effectiveness of the campaign is proved by the result of the perception of the audience. Because many of the celebrities featured in this book continue to remain in the public eye, they still have potential to cause more damage and generate media coverage.

Also worth noting is many of the cases in this text produced positive results. For instance, after West's outburst at the charity show for Hurricane Katrina victims, media changed the way they portrayed Katrina victims. Yahoo removed pictures of black men who were allegedly looting. West's fate was different in 2009 after the Swift incident. The media climate had changed and social media was in full swing. Twitter and Facebook comments reflected negativity associated with the incident.

However, unfortunately, scandals are not always guaranteed a successful image repair—as was the case for West. Celebrities must be careful when sharing content about upcoming creative projects, such as a movie, when they have not apologized or attempted to repair a tarnished image. Findings have implications for other organizations, celebrities, business owners and high-profile individuals that may have to use similar strategies to repair, change or overhaul an image following a race-related crisis/scandal.

The authors encourage scholars to use this study as a springboard for future studies that explore constitutional opposites of free speech and hate speech, crisis strategy and IRT. Based on our findings, we identified successful applications of online image repair strategies through the new media outlets of professional athletes who find themselves in crises in the future. When using Twitter specifically, celebrities should make sure to find the balance in their tweets between being friendly and oversharing with their followers. They must interact with their followers in a genuine way while being careful to not give too much personal information that might have the potential to harm their image repair progress. By playing an active role in the distribution of the most easily accessible information concerning their careers that exists today, future professional athletes have the potential to fix a problem before it ever happens.

The potential benefits available through the appropriate use of new media outlets as image repair strategies are virtually limitless. When using Twitter specifically, celebrities should make sure to find the balance in their tweets between being friendly and oversharing with their followers. Public figures must interact with their followers in a genuine way while being careful to not give too much personal information that might have the potential to harm their image repair progress.

Future texts should continue to look at cases under different circumstances. Studies that build on this research might also focus on how audiences respond online to messages they receive. Such a project may utilize a focus group format in which participants discuss uses and gratifications for responding to Twitter and Facebook posts about crises.

Studies that build on this research might also focus on how individuals respond online to race-related messages. Such studies may utilize focus groups in which participants discuss their responses to blog entries and Facebook posts about such shows. Findings are important as perceptions and stereotypes often become the dominant viewpoint whether they are accurate or not.

Another area of interest is how individuals personally identify with celebrities who use image restoration tactics. An analysis may help scholars offer suggestions on to model positive and negative characteristics about the people of color and women. It is our hope that the case studies provided in this text help PR practitioners develop solutions and measurable objectives that have an impact in addressing shortcomings related to image restoration following race and gender-related crises. Public relations specialists must become more knowledgeable and better able to help clients navigate and avoid such cases.

Ongoing analyses of IRT, race and gender in varying settings may help consumers become more aware of the dynamics at play in such cases. Chapter findings are useful for social media and celebrity crisis/scandal management and provide insight into the best strategies for improving a scarred public image in today's rapidly changing media climate. The exploration of the various types of racially charged cases is important, as they illustrate the importance of image restoration using cases that explore gender and race.

Appendix A

HARVEY WEINSTEIN TIMELINE[1]

October 5: *The New York Times* publishes a story of sexual harassment against Harvey Weinstein. Actresses Rose McGowan and Ashley Judd are among the women who come forward.

October 6: The Weinstein Company says it takes the allegations "extremely seriously" and is launching an inquiry.

October 7: Weinstein's lawyer Lisa Bloom announces her resignation, saying she understands that "Mr. Weinstein and his board are moving toward an agreement."

October 8: It is announced that Harvey Weinstein has been sacked by the board of his company, with immediate effect. They say the decision was made "in light of new information about misconduct."

October 10: Allegations from 13 more women are published in the *New Yorker* magazine, including three accusations of rape, which Weinstein strongly denies.

Weinstein's wife Georgina Chapman announces she is leaving him and that her priority is her young children.

October 11: Bafta says it is suspending Weinstein's membership, with immediate effect. A number of senior Labor MPs call for Weinstein's honorary CBE to be taken away.

October 14: The organization behind the Oscars votes to expel Weinstein following the allegations. In a statement, the Academy of Motion Picture Arts and Sciences says: "What's at issue here is a deeply troubling problem that has no place in our society."

October 16: The board of the Producers Guild of America vote to terminate Weinstein's membership. In a statement, the guild says he will be given the opportunity to respond before it makes its final decision on 6 November.

October 17: Harvey Weinstein resigns from the board of the company that bears his name, according to multiple reports. According to Variety, Weinstein still owns 22 percent of his company's stock.

October 18: Harvard University announces it is stripping Weinstein of the Du Bois medal it gave him in 2014 for his contributions to African American culture.

October 19: A group of Weinstein Company employees write an open letter asking their employer to release them from the non-disclosure agreements (NDAs) that stop them speaking publicly about what they have experienced and witnessed.

October 27: Weinstein takes legal action against his former company after his lawyer alleges The Weinstein Company has denied requests for documents to defend him from allegations.

The Sopranos actress Annabella Sciorra accuses Weinstein of forcing himself into her apartment and raping her in 1992.

October 28: *The New York Times* reports on new allegations made against Weinstein dating from the 1970s when he was a concert promoter in Buffalo, New York.

October 30: The Producers Guild of America bans Weinstein for life. It says the "unprecedented" step reflects the seriousness with which it regards reports of his "reprehensible" conduct".

November 3: Police in New York say they have "an actual case" against Weinstein, citing the "credible and detailed narrative" an unidentified woman—believed to be Paz de laHuerta—has given them.

November 7: The Television Academy expels Weinstein from its organization.

November 8: Weinstein's representatives say they "do not believe" an indictment is imminent from the New York Police Department. "We strongly believe we will demonstrate that no criminal charges are warranted," the statement continues.

November 16: Warner Bros severed ties to Weinstein by buying the rights to the film *Paddington 2*.

February 2: Bafta announces it has formally terminated Harvey Weinstein's membership.

February 11: After a four-month investigation, New York state prosecutors announce they have filed a lawsuit against the Weinstein Company on the basis the studio failed to protect employees from his alleged harassment and abuse.

May 25, 2018: Harvey Weinstein may finally be ready to face the music. NBC News, ABC News, CNN and *The New York Times* report that the disgraced studio boss is planning to turn himself in to the New York Police Department and Manhattan District Attorney's office on Friday. *New York Daily News* was the first outlet to report the story.

NOTE

1. Adapted from "How the Harvey Weinstein Scandal Unfolded." *BBC News*, February 12, 2018, sec. Entertainment & Arts. http://www.bbc.com/news/entertainment-arts-41594672.

References

A life less ordinary with Lisa Bonet. Retrieved March 11, 2018 from https://www.net-a-porter.com/us/en/porter/article-33a55e73f6c7ac7b?cm_sp=Homepage-_-ED1-_-CS-_-09-03-18.

Abdul-Jabbar, K. (2015). Let Rachel Dolezal be as black as she wants to be. *Time Magazine*, 185(24), 25–26. Retrieved from http://ezproxy.baylor.edu/login?url=http://search.ebscohost.com/login.aspx?direct=true&db=a9h.

Addley, E. (2013). Disgraced fashion designer John Galliano makes a comeback. *The Guardian*. Guardian News and Media.

Alaniz, A. (2013). Rape culture' needs to stop. *The Eastern Echo*. Retrieved from http://www.easternecho.com/article/2013/09/rape-culture-needs-to-stop.

Allan, K. (2015). When is a slur not a slur? The use of nigger in "Pulp Fiction." *Language Sciences*, 52, 187–199. doi:10.1016/j.langsci.2015.03.001.

Allen, C., & Schouten, F. (2016). Trump apologizes for video bragging about groping women. Retrieved from https://www.usatoday.com/story/news/politics/onpolitics/2016/10/07/trump-washington-post-women-billy-bush-video/91743992/.

Allen, P. (2011). Your forefathers would all have been gassed: John Galliano questioned by French police as tape of second anti-Semitic rant emerges. *Daily Mail Online*. Retrieved from http://www.dailymail.co.uk/news/article-1361462/Your-forefathers-gassed-John-Galliano-questioned-French-police-tape-second-anti-semitic-rant-emerges.html.

Anderson, B. (2014). V. Stiviano gets confrontational in new interview. Etonline.com. *CBS News*, 21 May 2014. Web. 15 Nov. 2014.

Anderson, L., & Lepore, E. (n.d.). Slurring words 1. *Noûs*, 47(1), 25–48. doi:10.1111/j.1468–0068.2010.00820.x.

Anderson, M., & Hitlin, P. (2016). Social media conversations about race: How social media users see, share and discuss race and the rise of hashtags like #BlackLivesMatter. Pew Research Center.

Ardener, S. (1975). *Perceiving women*. London, England: Malaby Press.

Armfield, G. A., & McGuire, J. (2017). Peddling the truth or coasting downhill? Lance Armstrong and the use of image repair strategies. *Sport Journal*, 1.

Associated Press. (April 7, 2007). After apology, critics still calling for Imus to be fired. Accessed from http://www.espn.com/ncw/news/story?id=2829410.

Bachman, G. F., & Guerrero, L. K. (2006). Forgiveness, apology, and communicative responses to hurtful events. *Communication Reports*, 19(1), 45–56. doi:10.1080/08934210600586357.

Banwart, M. (2010). Gender and candidate communication: Effects of stereotypes in the 2008 election. *American Behavioral Scientist*, 54(3), 265–283. doi:10.1177/0002764210381702.

Barksdale, A. (November 24, 2015). Black Twitter hilariously nails thanksgiving with black families. *Huffington Post*. Retrieved from https://www.huffingtonpost.com/entry/black-twitter-hilariously-nails-thanksgiving-with-black-families_us_565475a7e4b0879a5b0c5cc1.

Bartolomeo, J. (2010). Boy wonder. PEOPLE.com. Retrieved March 24, 2018 from http://people.com/archive/cover-story-boy-wonder-vol-73-no-15/.

Bastos, M., Raimundo, R., & Travitzki, R. (2013). Gatekeeping Twitter: Message diffusion in political hashtags. *Media, Culture & Society*, 35(2), 260–270. doi:10.1177/0163443712467594.

Bauer, Susan Wise. (2008). Chapter 9: Clinton and the three public confessions. *Art of Public Grovel* (pp. 152–182). Princeton University Press.

Begley, S. (September 30, 2015). 3 more women accuse Bill Cosby of sexual assault. Accessed from http://time.com/4056054/bill-cosby-sexual-assault-rape-accusers/.

Benoit, W. L. (2014). *Accounts, excuses, and apologies, second edition: Image repair theory*. Albany: State University of New York Press.

Benoit, W. L. (1995). *Accounts, excuses and apologies: A theory of image restoration strategies*. Albany: State University of New York Press.

Benoit, W. L. (1997). Hugh Grant's image restoration discourse: An actor apologizes. *Communication Quarterly*, 45(3), 251–267.

Benoit, W. L. (1997). Image repair discourse and crisis communication. *Public Relations Review*, 23(2), 177–186.

Benoit, W. L. (2006). Image repair in President Bush's April 2004 news conference. *Public Relations Review*, 32, 137–143.

Benoit, W. L. (2006). President Bush's image repair effort on meet the press : The complexities of defeasibility. *Journal of Applied Communication Research*, 34(3), 285–306.

Benoit, W. L. (2011). NPR's image repair discourse on firing Juan Williams. *Journal of Radio & Audio Media*, 18(1), 84–91. doi:10.1080/19376529.2011.562818.

Benoit, W. L. (2014). Preparing crisis response plans, future research on image repair accounts, excuses, and apologies: Image repair theory and research (2nd Edition). Albany, NY: SUNY Press.

Benoit, W. L. (2014). President Barack Obama's image repair on HealthCare.gov. *Public Relations Review*, 40, 733–738. doi:10.1016/j.pubrev.2014.07.003.

Benoit, W. L. (2016). Barack Obama's 2008 speech on Reverend Wright: Defending self and others. *Public Relations Review*, 42(5), 843–848. doi:10.1016/j.pubrev.2016.09.003.

Benoit, W. L. (2017). Image repair on the Donald Trump "Access Hollywood" Video: "Grab them by the p*ssy". *Communication Studies*, 68(3), 243–259. doi:10.1080/10510974.2017.1331250.

Benoit, W. L., & McHale, John P. (1999). Kenneth Starr's image repair discourse viewed in 20/20. *Communication Quarterly*, 47(3), 265–280.

Bentley, J. M. (2012). Not the best: What Rush Limbaugh's apology to Sandra Fluke reveals about image restoration strategies on commercial radio. *Journal of Radio & Audio Media*, 19(2), 221–238. doi:10.1080/19376529.2012.722474.

Bernstein, B. (2012). Crisis management and sports in the age of social media: A case study analysis of the Tiger Woods scandal. *The Elon Journal of Undergraduate Research in Communications*, 3(2), 1–3.

Blaney, J. (2015). *Putting image repair to the test quantitative applications of image restoration theory*. Rowman Littlefield: Lanham.

Blaney, J., & Benoit W. (2001). *The Clinton scandals and the politics of image restoration*. Westport: Praeger.

Blaney, J. R., Lippert, L., & Smith, S. J. (Eds.). (2012). *Repairing the athlete's image: Studies in sports image restoration* (First Edition). Lanham, MD: Lexington Books.

Bontemps, T. (April 27, 2014). Michael Jordan 'outraged, disgusted' by Donald Sterling. *New York Post* (blog). https://nypost.com/2014/04/27/michael-jordan-outraged-disgusted-by-donald-sterling/.

Boone, M. (September 2, 2017). Hulk Hogan polls fans on wrestling future: "should i come back or stay away?" Retrieved June 12, 2018 from http://www.24wrestling.com/hulk-hogan-polls-fans-on-wrestling-future-should-i-come-back-or-stay-away/.

Bowie, D. (July 8, 2015). Where do they stand now? 11 stars who defended Bill Cosby. Retrieved December 1, 2016 from https://madamenoire.com/545289/in-defense-of-cosby-10-celebs-who-have-his-back/.

Brazeal, L. M. (2007). The image repair rhetoric of Terrell Owens. Conference Papers National Communication Association, 1.

Brazeal, L. M. (2008). The image repair strategies of Terrell Owens. *Public Relations Review*, 34, 145–150.

Brewer, P. (2006). National interest frames and public opinion about world affairs. *Harvard International Journal of Press/Politics*, 11(4), 89–102.

Brinson, S. L., & Benoit, W. L. (1999). The tarnished star. *Management Communication Quarterly*, 12(4), 483.

Brock, A. (2012). From the blackhand side: Twitter as a cultural conversation. *Journal of Broadcasting & Electronic Media*, 56(4), 529–549.

Brown, R. A., Anderson, R., & Thompson, J. (2012). New news, hegemony and representations of black male athletes. In Campbell, C. P., LeDuff, K. M., Jenkins, C. D., & Brown, R. A. (Eds.), *Race and news: Critical perspectives* (pp. 64–87). New York: Routledge.

Buchwald, E., Fletcher, P., & Roth, M. (2005). *Transforming a rape culture*. Minneapolis, NM: Milkweed Editions.

Burke, K. (1973). *The philosophy of literary form*. Berkeley: University of California Press.

Burns, J., & Bruner, M. (2000). Revisiting the theory of image restoration strategies. *Communication Quarterly*, 48(1), 27–39.

Caldiero, C. T., Taylor, M., & Ungureanu, L. (2009). Image repair tactics and information subsidies during fraud crises. *Journal of Public Relations Research*, 21(2), 218. doi:10.1080/10627260802557589.

Caliendo, S. M., & McIlwain, C. D. (2006). Minority candidates, media framing, and racial cues in the 2004 election. *Harvard International Journal of Press/Politics*, 11(4), 45–69.

Carlin, D. B., & Winfrey, K. L. (2009). Have you come a long way, baby? Hillary Clinton, Sarah Palin, and Sexism in 2008 Campaign Coverage. *Communication Studies*, 60(4), 326–343.

Carter, C., & Steiner, L. (2003). *Critical readings: Media and gender*. Maidenhead: Open University Press.

Carvajal, Doreen. (September 8, 2011). Court convicts Galliano in anti-semitism case. *The New York Times*, sec. Europe. https://www.nytimes.com/2011/09/09/world/europe/09galliano.html.

Center, E. (2009). Another American race riot: A differential racialization/image restoration analysis. Conference Papers—International Communication Association, 1–28.

Ceulemans, M., & Fauconnier, G. (1979). *Mass media: The image, role, and social conditions of women: A collective and analysis of research materials*. Paris: UNESCO.

Chaudhary, A. (1980). Press portrayals of black officials. *Journalism Quarterly*, 57, 636–641.

Cheever, Susan. (2011). Is Anthony Weiner an addict or just an ass? The fix: Addiction and recovery, straight up. http://www.thefix.com/content/tweet-heard-round-world?page=all.

Cho, S. H., & Gower, K. K. (2006). Framing effect on the public's response to crisis: Human interest frame and crisis type influencing responsibility and blame. *Public Relations Review*, 32(4), 420–422.

Clinton's speech in oak bluffs. (1998). *WashingtonPost.com*. http://www.washingtonpost.com/wp-srv/politics/special/clinton/stories/clintontex   t082898.htm#forgive.

Collins, P. H. (1990). *Black feminist thought: Knowledge, consciousness, and the politics of empowerment*. New York: Routledge.

Collins, P. H. (2004). *Black sexual politics: African Americans, gender and the new racism*. New York: Routledge.

Colmes, A., & Hannity, S. (Hosts). (2008, February 22). FOX Hannity & Colmes [Television Transcript] Hillary Clinton makes questionable remark at end of debate. *FOX News*. Retrieved from Lexis Nexis.

Compton, J. J., & Compton, J. L. (2018). The athlete's image, visual representation, and image repair/image prepare: Tom Brady, Jane Rosenberg, and the courtroom sketches. *International Journal of the Image,* 9(2), 73–88.

Compton, J., & Miller, B. (2011). Image repair in late night comedy: Letterman and the Palin joke controversy. *Public Relations Review*, 37, 415–421. doi:10.1016/j.pubrev.2011.08.002.

Conway, M., Grabe, M., & Grieves, K. (2007). Villains, victims and the virtuous in Bill O'Reilly's no spin zone. *Journalism Studies*, 8, 2, 197–223.

Coombs, T., & Holladay, S. J. (Eds.). (2010). *The handbook of crisis communication* (pp. 335–358). West Sussex, UK: Wiley-Blackwell.

Coombs, T., & Schmidt, L. (2000). An empirical analysis of image restoration: Texaco's racism crisis. *Journal of Public Relations Research*, 12(2), 163–178.

Coombs, W. T. (1999). *Ongoing crisis communication*. Thousand Oaks, CA: Sage.

Cooper, A. (Host). (April 21, 2008). Anderson Cooper 360 degrees [Television Transcript] Countdown to Pennsylvania showdown; single women and the presidential campaign. *Cable News Network CNN*. Retrieved from Lexis Nexis.

Cottle, M. (Host). (December 23, 2008). CNN reliable sources [Television Transcript] the drudge factor; how are media treating Hillary? *Cable News Network CNN*. Retrieved from Lexis Nexis.

Crenshaw, K. (1988). Race, reform and retrenchment: Transformation and legitimation in anti-discrimination law. *Harvard Law Review*, 101(7), 1331–1387.

Crenshaw, K. (1991). Mapping the margins: Intersectionality, identity politics, and violence against women of color. *Stanford Law Review*, 43(6), 1241–1299.

Creswell, J. (2004). *Qualitative inquiry and research design: Choosing among five approaches* (2nd Edition). Thousand Oaks, CA: Sage Publication.

Crowley, C. (Host). (2008, February 25). The situation room [Television Transcript] Obama Photo Firestorm; Interview with Arizona Governor Janet Napolitano; McCain Iraq's Fear. *Cable News Network (CNN)*. Retrieved from Lexis Nexis.

Cunningham, G. B., Ferreira, M., & Fink, J. S. (2009). Reactions to prejudicial statements: The influence of statement content and characteristics of the commenter. *Group Dynamics: Theory, Research, and Practice*, 13(1), 59–73.

Curnutt, H. (2012). Flashing your phone: Sexting and the remediation of teen sexuality. *Communication Quarterly*, 60(3), 353–369. doi:10.1080/01463373.2012.688 728.

Dates, J., & Moody-Ramirez, M. (2018). *From blackface to black Twitter: Reflections on black humor, race, politics & gender*. Bern: Peter Lang.

Dates, J. L., & Barlow, W. (1993). *Split image: African-Americans in the mass media* (Second Edition). Washington, DC: Howard University Press.

Dates, J. L., & Pease, E. C. (1994). Warping the world: Media's mangled images of race. *The Freedom Forum Media Studies Center Media Studies Journal*, 8(3), 81–88.

Davis, C. B. (2013). An inconvenient vote: Hillary Clinton's Iraq war image repair debate strategies and their implications for representative democracy. *Public Relations Review*, 39(4), 315–319. doi:10.1016/j.pubrev.2013.07.008.

Dawkins, R. (1989). *The selfish gene*. Oxford: Oxford University Press.

Deetz, S. (2005). Critical theory. In May, Steve & Mumby, Dennis K. (Eds.), *Engaging organizational communication theory and research: Multiple* perspectives (pp. 85–112). Thousand Oaks: Sage.

Delgado, R., & Stefancic, J. (1993). Critical race theory: An annotated bibliography. *Virginia Law Review*, 79(2), 461–516.

Delgado, R., & Stefancic, J. (2012). *Critical race theory: An introduction* (2nd ed, pp. 7–10). New York: New York University Press.

Denton, R. E., & Holloway, R. L. (2003). *Images, scandal, and communication strategies of the Clinton presidency.* Praeger: Santa Barbara.

Devere, H., & Davies, S. (April, 2006). The Don and Helen New Zealand election 2005: A media a-gender? *Pacific Journalism Review,* 12(1), 65–85.

Dolezal, R. (2017). *In full color: Finding my place in a black and white world.* Dallas: BenBella Books Inc.

Domke, D., Garland, P., Billeaudeaux, A., & Hutcheson, J. (2003). Insights into U.S. racial hierarchy: Racial profiling, news sources, and September 11. *Journal of Communication,* 53(4), 606–623.

Douglas, D. (2018). Black women say #MeToo: The #MeToo movement gives women of color a space to share struggle. *Crisis,* 125(1), 5–6. Retrieved from http://ezproxy.baylor.edu/login?url=http://search.ebscohost.com/login.aspx?direct=true&db=a9h&AN=128897899&site=ehost-live&scope=site.

Drummond, W. J. (1990). About face: From alliance to alienation blacks in the news media. *American Enterprise,* 1(4), 24–29.

Durham, M. G. (2013). Vicious assault shakes Texas town. *Journalism Studies,* 14(1), 1–12. doi:10.1080/1461670X.2012.657907.

Dwyer, Devin. (2011). Rep. Anthony Weiner: A timeline of deceit. *ABC News.* Retrieved from http://abcnews.go.com/Politics/anthony-weiner-scandal-timeline-deceit/story?id=13781381#.T6gNpRwvgRg.

Camp, E. (2013). Slurring perspectives. *Analytic Philosophy,* 54(3), 330–349.

Eastman, T., & Billings, A. C. (2001). Biased voices of sports: Racial and gender stereotyping in college basketball announcing. *Howard Journal of Communications,* 12, 183–201.

Ebesu, H., Hendrickson, B., Fehrenbach, K., & Sur, J. (2013). Effects of timing and sincerity of an apology on satisfaction and changes in negative feelings during conflicts. *Western Journal of Communication,* 77(3), 305–322.

Edge, A. (2018). The #MeToo moment: Sexual misconduct charges force industry to confront itself. *Quill,* 106(1), 22–26. Retrieved from http://ezproxy.baylor.edu/login?url=http://search.ebscohost.com/login.aspx?direct=true&db=ufh&AN=128448996&site=ehost-live&scope=site.

Einwiller, S. A., & Steilen, S. (2015). Handling complaints on social network sites—an analysis of complaints and complaint responses on Facebook and Twitter pages of large US companies. *Public Relations Review,* 41(2), 195–204. doi:10.1016/j.pubrev.2014.11.012.

Elsbach, K. D. (1997). Accounts, excuses, and apologies: A theory of image restoration strategies. *Administrative Science Quarterly,* 42(3), 584–586.

Enriques, E. (2001). *Feminism and feminist criticism: An overview of various feminist strategies for reconstructing knowledge.* Manila: Isis International.

Entman, R. (1991). Framing U.S. coverage of international news: Contrasts in narratives of the KAL and Iran air incidents. *Journal of Communication,* 41(4), 6–27.

Entman, R. M. (1992). African-Americans in the news: Television, modern racism and cultural change. *Journalism Quarterly,* 69(2), 341–361.

Entman, R. M. (2000). *The black image in the white mind: Media and race in America.* Chicago: University of Chicago Press.

Estrada, I., & Shoichet, C. (2014). Donald Sterling tells Anderson Cooper: I was 'baited' into 'a terrible mistake.' *CNN.com.*

Evans, G., & Patten, D. (2017). Harvey Weinstein hints at legal action against Uma Thurman|Deadline. Retrieved May 22, 2018 from http://deadline.com/2018/02/harvey-weinstein-response-uma-thurman-photos-1202277657/.

Farrow, R. (October 10, 2017). From aggressive overtures to sexual assault: Harvey Weinstein's accusers tell their stories. *The New Yorker.* Retrieved from https://www.newyorker.com/news/news-desk/from-aggressive-overtures-to-sexual-assault-harvey-weinsteins-accusers-tell-their-stories.

Fearn-Banks, K. (2010). Crisis communications: A casebook approach/edition 4. Retrieved November 1, 2017 from https://www.barnesandnoble.com/w/crisis-communications-kathleen-fearn-banks/1101588883.

Ferber, A. L. (February, 2007). The construction of black masculinity white supremacy now and then. *Journal of Sport & Social Issues,* 31(1), 11–24.

Finance, Y. (January 5, 2017). We deleted an earlier tweet due to a spelling error. We apologize for the mistake. [Tweet]. Retrieved from https://twitter.com/YahooFinance/status/817234871018024961.

Folkenflik, D. (2014). In NPR and AP Cosby interviews, a 'no comment' that said everything. Retrieved October 30, 2017 from http://www.npr.org/2014/11/22/365828829/in-npr-and-ap-cosby-interviews-a-no-comment-that-said-everything.

Ford, D., & Botello, G. (2015). Who is Rachel Dolezal?-CNN.com. Retrieved July 8, 2015 from http://www.cnn.com/2015/06/16/us/rachel-dolezal/index.html.

Francese, A. (2008). Charlie Sheen's nasty voicemails to ex-wife Denise Richards fuel the media once again. Yahoo Contributor Network. *Yahoo Voices,* 21 June 2008. Web. 05 Dec. 2013. Retrieved from http://voices.yahoo.com/charlie-sheens-nasty-voicemails-ex-wife-denise-1589163.html.

Frankovic, K. (2018). Americans think Weinstein is a harasser|YouGov. Retrieved May 24, 2018, from https://today.yougov.com/topics/politics/articles-reports/2017/10/20/americans-think-weinstein-harasser.

Freedman, E., & Fico, F. (2005). Male and female sources in newspaper coverage of male and female candidates in open races for governor in 2002. *Mass Communication & Society,* 8(3), 257–272.

Friedman, E., Morison, K., & Griffin, J. (2011). Timeline: Edwards affair through the years. *ABC News.* Retrieved from http://abcnews.go.com/Politics/edwards-scandal-timeline-john-edwards-rielle-hunter-affair/story?id=9621755#.T6h3GBwvgRg.

Gajanan, M. (May 16, 2017). Bill cosby says racism could have played a part in sexual assault allegations. *TIME.* Retrieved March 8, 2018 from http://time.com/4780353/bill-cosby-racism-sexual-assault-allegations/.

Gallagher, M. (1981). *Unequal opportunities: The case of women and the media.* Paris: Unesco Press.

Gans, H. (1979). *Deciding what's news.* New York: Vintage Books.

Garcia, C. (2011). Sex scandals: A cross-cultural analysis of image repair strategies in the cases of Bill Clinton and Silvio Berlusconi. *Public Relations Review*, 37(3), 292–296.

Gayle, D. (June 13, 2015). Rachel Dolezal accused of "blackface" by adopted brother-Local NAACP chapter president told Ezra Dolezal not to "blow my cover" when she began calling herself black after moving to Spokane. *Guardian, The*: Web Edition Articles (London, England). Retrieved from http://infoweb.newsbank.com/resources/doc/nb/news/155F2F48C872E720?p=AWNB.

Gibson, J. (Host). (January 8, 2008). The big story with John Gibson [Television Transcript] Obama vs. Clinton Out West? Will Oscars be held this year? *FOX News*. Retrieved from Lexis Nexis.

Glenn Beck: Associated Press "raped" Bill Cosby. (n.d.). Retrieved December 14, 2016, from https://www.rt.com/usa/207811-beck-ap-raped-cosby/.

Goffman, Erving. (1974). *Frame analysis: An essay on the organization of experience*. London: Harper and Row.

Goldwert, L. (2011). John Galliano anti-semitic rant caught on video; slurs on camera 'I love Hitler' – *NY Daily News*. Retrieved from http://www.nydailynews.com/news/world/john-galliano-anti-semitic-rant-caught-video-slurs-camera-love-hitler-article-1.122548.

Golliver, B. (2014). Donald Sterling calls the NBA "a band of hypocrites and bullies" in angry statement. Retrieved November 26, 2014 from http://www.si.com/nba/point-forward/2014/06/10/donald-sterling-statement-nba-lawsuit-rant.

Goode, L. (2009). Social news, citizen journalism and democracy. *New Media & Society*, 11(8), 1287–1305. doi:10.1177/1461444809341393.

Goodman, J. (November 14, 2014). Bill Cosby's "late show with David letterman" appearance canceled. *Huffington Post*. Retrieved from http://www.huffingtonpost.com/2014/11/14/bill-cosby-letterman-cancel_n_6160866.html.

Gordon, J. (2007). Voters prefer men, political study finds; Election 2007-Australia Decides. The Age 1.

Goyette, B. (April 26, 2014). LA clippers owner Donald Sterling's racist rant caught on tape: Report (UPDATES). Retrieved October 26, 2014 from http://www.huffingtonpost.com/2014/04/26/donald-sterling-racist_n_5218572.html?

Graham, R. G. J. (2015). Rachel Dolezal's deception inflicts pain on black women. *The Boston Globe*. Retrieved July 30, 2015 from https://www.bostonglobe.com/opinion/2015/06/16/rachel-dolezal-deception-inflicts-pain-black-women/AsZo3zi-PA3dCvErhhzBJ3L/story.html.

Grebe, S. (2011). Re-building a damaged corporate reputation: How the Australian wheat board (AWB) overcame the damage of the UN "Oil For Food" scandal to successfully reintegrate into the Australian wheat marketing regulatory regime. *Corporate Reputation Review*, 16(2), 118–130. doi:10.1057/crr.2013.5.

Greene, L. S. (1995). Racial discourse, hate speech, and political correctness. *National Forum*, 75(2), 32–35.

Greenwood, C. (November 11, 2013). Charlie Sheen apology to two and a half men creator three years from his very public meltdown. *mirror*.

griffin, t. (n.d.). Black Twitter roasted Yahoo Finance after the "Nigger Navy" Typo Tweet. Retrieved April 11, 2018 from https://www.buzzfeed.com/tamerragriffin/yahoo-finance-nigger-navy-typo.

Grossberger, L. (1995). Plea me a grant. *Media Week*, 5(28), 30. Retrieved April 17, 2010 from http://search.ebscohost.com.

Gruber, J. (December 11, 2014). Poll: Where do you stand with Bill Cosby? *MSNBC*. Retrieved from http://www.msnbc.com/msnbc/poll-where-do-you-stand-bill-cosby.

Guimarães, T. (2018). Pinterest's demographics mean it could become the next monster social advertising platform. *Business Insider*. Retrieved June 15, 2018 from http://www.businessinsider.com/pinterest-as-a-brand-platform-2014-11.

Hall, S. (1980). Cultural studies: Two paradigms. *Media, Culture, and Society*, 2, 57–72.

Hall, S. (1986). Gramsci's relevance for the study of race and ethnicity. *Journal of Communication Inquiry*, 10(5), 5–27. doi:10.1177/019685998601000202.

Hall, S. (2003). Marx's notes on method: A 'reading' of the '1857 Introduction'. *Cultural Studies*, 17(2), 113–149.

Hanna, J. (2014). Donald sterling purportedly says jealousy behind racist comments. *CNN*. Retrieved from https://www.cnn.com/2014/05/09/us/nba-donald-sterling-audio-recording/index.html.

Harlow, S. (2013). It was a "Facebook revolution": Exploring the meme-like spread of narratives during the Egyptian protests. Fue Una "Revolución de Facebook": Explorando La Narrativa de Los Meme Difundidos Durante Las Protestas Egipcias., 12, 59–82. Retrieved from http://ezproxy.baylor.edu/login?url=http://search.ebscohost.com/login.aspx?direct=true&db=ufh&AN=92630500&site=ehost-live&scope=site.

Harris, C., Rowbotham, J., & Stevenson, K. (2009). Truth, law and hate in the virtual marketplace of ideas: Perspectives on the regulation of Internet content. *Information & Communications Technology Law*, 18(2), 155–184.

Hartmann, H. (1981). The unhappy marriage of Marxism and feminism: Towards a more progressive union. In Sargent, L. (Ed.), *Women and revolutions: A discussion of the unhappy marriage of Marxism and feminism* (pp. 1–41). Boston: South End Press.

Heider, D. (2000). *White news: Why local news programs don't cover people of color*. New Jersey: Lawrence Erlbaum Associates.

Heldman, C., Carroll, S. J., & Olson, S. (2005). She brought only a skirt: Print media coverage of Elizabeth Dole's bid for the Republican presidential nomination. *Political Communication*, 22(3), 315–335.

Hemant, S., & Thornton, M. C. (1994). Racial ideology in the U.S. mainstream news magazine coverage of Black-Latino interaction, 1980–1992. *Critical Studies in Mass Communication*, 11(2), 141–161.

Hernandez, L., North, J., Mir, N., Holguin, R., & Miller, L. (2011). Schwarzenegger fathered child with staffer. *ABC7 Los Angeles*. Retrieved from http://abc7.com/archive/8134962/.

Herrnson, P., Lay, J., & Stokes, A. (2003). Women running "as women": Candidate gender, campaign issues, and Voter–Targeting strategies. *Journal of Politics*, 65(1), 244–255.

Hertog, J. K., & McLeod, D. M. (1999). Social control, social change and the mass media's role in the regulation of protest groups. In Demers, David & Viswanath, K. (Eds.), *Mass media, social control, and social change: A macrosocial perspective* (p. 179). Ames, IA: Iowa State University Press.

Hines, R. (October 13, 2015). Keshia Knight Pulliam on Cosby scandal: That wasn't "my experience with him." Retrieved December 14, 2016 from http://www.today.com/popculture/keshia-knight-pulliam-bill-cosby-scandal-was-never-my-experience-t49781.

Holt, L. (2008). That's enough "Nigger": An argument for regulating hate speech. Conference Papers—International Communication Association, 1–24. Retrieved from http://ezproxy.baylor.edu/login?url=http://search.ebscohost.com/login.aspx?direct=true&db=ufh&AN=36956377&site=ehost-live&scope=site.

Holtzhausen, D., & Roberts, G. (2009). An investigation into the role of image repair theory in strategic conflict management. *Journal of Public Relations Research*, 21(2), 165–186. doi:10.1080/10627260802557431.

hooks, B. (1992). *Black Looks: Race and Representation*. Boston: South End Press.

Horkheimer, M., & Adorno, T. (1972). *Dialectic of enlightenment* (J. Cumming, Trans.). New York: Herder and Herder.

Howard, A. (2016). Judd Apatow defends criticism of Cosby: 'I have two daughters'. Retrieved December 1, 2016 from http://www.msnbc.com/msnbc/judd-apatow-defends-criticism-cosby-i-have-two-daughters.

Hristova, S. (2014). Visual memes as neutralizers of political dissent. TripleC (Cognition, Communication, Co-Operation) *Journal for a Global Sustainable Information Society*, 12(1), 265–276. Retrieved from http://ezproxy.baylor.edu/login?url=http://search.ebscohost.com/login.aspx?direct=true&db=ufh&AN=103378636&site=ehost-live&scope=site.

Huddy, L., & Terkildsen, N. (1993). Gender stereotypes and the perception of male and female candidates. *American Journal of Political Science*, 37(1), 119.

Hume, B. (Host). (January 23, 2008). FOX Special Report with Brit Hume [Television Transcript] FOX News all-stars. *FOX News*. Retrieved from Lexis Nexis.

Husselbee, L. P., & Stein, K. A. (2012). Tiger Woods' apology and newspaper's responses: A study of journalistic antapologia. *Journal of Sports Media*, 7(1), 59–87.

Hutchins, A., & Tindall, N. (2016). *Public relations and participatory culture fandom, social media and community engagement*. Taylor and Francis.

Isaac, M. (2015). Pinterest crosses user milestone of 100 million. *The New York Times*.

Jaffe, S. (2018). The collective power of #MeToo. *Dissent*, 65(2), 80–87. Retrieved from http://ezproxy.baylor.edu/login?url=http://search.ebscohost.com/login.aspx?direct=true&db=a9h&AN=129106015&site=ehost-live&scope=site.

Jamieson, A., Shin, H., & Day, J. (2002). *Voting and registration in the election of November 2000*. U.S. Bureau of the Census, Current Population Reports, P20 (542).

Justin Bieber "crying a lot." (2014). *People magazine*. Retrieved from http://www.peoplemagazine.co.za/article.aspx?id=58634&h=Justin-Bieber-%E2%80%98crying-a-lot%E2%80%99.

Justin Bieber—I'm sorry for my racist joke. (2014). Retrieved November 25, 2014 from http://www.tmz.com/2014/06/01/justin-bieber-racist-joke-apology/.

Justin Bieber: Biography. (1981). Hellomagazine.com. Retrieved March 24, 2018 from https://us.hellomagazine.com/profiles/justin-bieber/.

Kanter, R. (1977). *Men and women of the corporation*. New York: Basic Books.

Kantor, J., & Twohey, M. (2017). Harvey Weinstein paid off sexual harassment accusers for decades. *The New York Times*. Retrieved May 24, 2018 from https://www.nytimes.com/2017/10/05/us/harvey-weinstein-harassment-allegations.html.

Kasich, J. (Host). (November 2, 2007). The O'Reilly factor [Television Transcript] political assault against Hillary Clinton. *FOX News*. Retrieved from Lexis Nexis.

Kauffman, J. (2012). Hooray for Hollywood? The 2011 golden globes and Ricky Gervais' image repair strategies. *Public Relations Review* 38(1), 46–50. doi:10.1016/j.pubrev.2011.09.003.

Kauffman, J. (2008). When sorry is not enough: Archbishop cardinal Bernard Law's image restoration strategies in the statement on sexual abuse of minors by clergy. *Public Relations Review*, 34(3), 258–262.

Kaufman, J. (1988). The fall of Jimmy Swaggart. *People Magazine*, 29(9). Retrieved from http://www.people.com/people/archive/article/0,,20098413,00.html.

Kennedy, K., & Benoit, W. (1997). The Newt Gingrich book deal controversy: Self-defense rhetoric. *Southern Communication Journal*, 62(3). Retrieved April 12, 2012 from doi:10.1080/10417949709373055.

Kevito. (2018). Rachel Dolezal's son drags mom in trailer for new Netflix doc "The Rachel Divide". *OkayPlayer*. Retrieved from http://www.okayplayer.com/culture/rachel-dolezals-rachel-divide-netflix-trailer-video.html.

Kiambi, D. M., & Shafer, A. (2016). Corporate crisis communication: Examining the interplay of reputation and crisis response strategies. *Mass Communication and Society*, 19(2), 127–148. doi:10.1080/15205436.2015.1066013.

Kim, S., Scheufele, D., & Shanahan, J. (2002). Think about it this way: Attribute agenda-setting function of the press and the public's evaluation of a local issue. *Journalism & Mass Communication Quarterly*, 79(7), 25.

Kimble, L. (July 24, 2015). Hulk Hogan apologizes for 'unacceptable' racist rant as he is scrubbed from WWE hall of fame. Retrieved May 22, 2018 from http://people.com/tv/hulk-hogan-statement-on-racist-rant/.

Kowalczyk, C. (2016). Transforming celebrities through social media: The role of authenticity and emotional attachment. *Journal of Product & Brand Management*, 25(4). Retrieved May 17, 2018 from https://www.emeraldinsight.com/doi/full/10.1108/JPBM-09-2015-0969.

Kramer, M. R. (2014). Image repair rhetoric and shock radio: Don Imus, Al Sharpton, and the Rutgers women's basketball team controversy. *Journal of Radio & Audio Media*, 21(2), 247–257. doi:10.1080/19376529.2014.950148.

Krolokke, C., & Sorensen, A. C. (2006). *Gender communication theories and analyses: From silence to performance.* Thousand Oaks, CA: Sage.

Kroon, Å., & Ekstrom, M. (2007). Vulnerable woman, raging bull, or mannish maniac? gender differences in the visualization of political scandals. Conference Papers—International Communication Association, 1. Retrieved April 20, 2010, from Communication & Mass Media Complete database.

Lafayette, J. (2017). Weinstein scandal roils TV business, too. *Broadcasting & Cable*, 147(22), 4–4. Retrieved from http://ezproxy.baylor.edu/login?url=http://search.ebscohost.com/login.aspx?direct=true&db=ufh&AN=125701423&site=ehost-live&scope=site.

Lancaster, K., & Boyd, J. (2015). Redefinition, differentiation, and the farm animal welfare debate. *Journal of Applied Communication Research*, 43(2), 185–202. doi: 10.1080/00909882.2015.1019541.

Lara, M. M. (2015). Rachel Dolezal maintains that she identifies as black: "I'm not confused about that any longer". Retrieved July 29, 2015 from http://www.people.com/article/rachel-dolezal-vanity-fair-interview.

Lassiter, J. (1979). *Meta-anthropology, normative culture and the anthropology of development.* A paper read at the 1979 Annual Meeting of the Northwest Anthropological Conference, Eugene, Oregon, March 23.

Lau, R., & Pomper, G. (2002). 143 U.S. Senate Elections, 1988–1998 effectiveness of negative campaigning in U.S. Senate elections. *American Journal of Political Science*, 46(1), 47–66.

Lee, E. (2016). Piers Morgan rips Phylicia Rashad for defending Bill Cosby: "Reprehensible." Retrieved December 1, 2016 from http://www.usmagazine.com/celebrity-news/news/piers-morgan-rips-phylicia-rashad-for-bill-cosby-defense-201581.

Lee, E., & Peros, J. (July 24, 2015). Hulk Hogan admits he made racist remarks, asks for forgiveness. Retrieved May 22, 2018 from https://www.usmagazine.com/celebrity-news/news/hulk-hogan-admits-he-made-racist-remarks-asks-for-forgiveness-2015247/.

Len-Rios, M., Finneman, T., Han, K. J., Bhandari, M., & Perry, E. L. (2015). Image repair campaign strategies addressing race: Paula Deen, social media, and defiance [Electronic version]. *International Journal of Strategic Communication*, 9(2), 148–165. doi:10.1080/1553118X.2015.1008637.

Levy, L., & Karst, K. (2000). *Encyclopedia of the American Constitution Vol. 3* (2nd Edition). Detroit: Macmillan Reference USA.

Lippmann, W. (1922). *Public opinion.* New York: Macmillan.

Lipshutz, J. (June 2, 2014). Justin Bieber's racist joke: Understandable or unforgivable? (Poll) [Text]. Retrieved November 26, 2014, from http://www.billboard.com/articles/columns/pop-shop/6106405/justin-bieber-racist-joke-video-poll.

Liu, B. F. (2008). From aspiring presidential candidate to accidental racist? An analysis of Senator George Allen's image repair during his 2006 reelection campaign. *Public Relations Review*, 34(4), 331–336. doi:10.1016/j.pubrev.2008.06.002.

Lydiate, H. (2018). Reputation. *Art Monthly*, 416, 45–45. Retrieved from http://ezproxy.baylor.edu/login?url=http://search.ebscohost.com/login.aspx?direct=true&db=a9h&AN=129270981&site=ehost-live&scope=site.

Manfred, T. (2015). Hulk Hogan fired by WWE amid racist audiotape reports. *Business Insider*. Retrieved April 11, 2018 from http://www.businessinsider.com/hulk-hogan-removed-from-wwe-website-2015-7.

Marati, M. W., Bobier, D. M., & Baron, R. S. (2000). Right before our eyes: The failure to recognize non-prototypical forms of prejudice. *Group Processes & Intergroup Relations*, 3, 403–418.

Marin, C. (February 20, 2009). Michelle Obama standing by her man. *Chicago Sun-Times*. Retrieved from LexisNexis.

Martindale, C. (1990). Changes in newspaper images of Africans Americans. *Newspaper Research Journal*, 11(1), 46–48.

Mastro, D. E., & Behm-Morazwitz, E. (2005). Latino representation on primetime television. *Journalism & Mass Communication Quarterly*, 82(1), 110–130. Retrieved from EBSCOhost.

Mataconis, D. (2015). *The strange case of Rachel Dolezal*. Retrieved October 4, 2015 from http://www.outsidethebeltway.com/the-strange-case-of-rachel-dolezal/.

Mayer, J. (2004). The contemporary presidency: The presidency and image management: Discipline in pursuit of illusion. *Presidential Studies Quarterly*, 43(3). Retrieved on April 12, 2012 from http://www.jstor.org/stable/27552616.

McAlone, N. (2016, March 20). Everything you need to know about the Hulk Hogan sex-tape lawsuit that could cost Gawker over $115 million. Retrieved May 22, 2018 from http://www.businessinsider.com/hulk-hogan-versus-gawker-lawsuit-explained-2016-3.

McDonald, S. N. (2014, January 20). *Black Twitter: A virtual community ready to hashtag out a response to cultural issues*. Retrieved June 8, 2018 from https://www.washingtonpost.com/lifestyle/style/black-twitter-a-virtual-community-ready-to-hashtag-out-a-response-to-cultural-issues/2014/01/20/41ddacf6-7ec5-11e3-9556-4a4bf7bcbd84_story.html?utm_term=.6fdbd16e3800.

McLuhan, M., & Fiore, Q. (1967). *The medium is the message*. New York: Bantam Books.

Media Insight Project, P. 03/17/14 3:00. (March 17, 2014). *The personal news cycle: How Americans choose to get news*. Retrieved February 15, 2016 from https://www.americanpressinstitute.org/publications/reports/survey-research/personal-news-cycle/.

Media Matters. (February 27, 2008). Media diagnose Hillary "Sybil" Clinton with "mood swings," depression, and "multiple personality disorder. *Media Matters for America*. Retrieved from http://mediamatters.org/items/200802270010.

Meyrowitz, J. (1985). *No sense of place: The impact of electronic media on social behavior*. New York: Oxford University Press.

Mezzofiore, G. (2017). *Yahoo accidentally tweeted a racist slur and Twitter is dragging them*. Retrieved December 17, 2017 from http://mashable.com/2017/01/06/yahoo-finance-racial-slur-twitter/.

Miller, J. (2015). *Hillary Clinton announces 2016 White House bid*. Retrieved December 9, 2016 from http://www.cbsnews.com/news/hillary-clinton-announces-2016-white-house-bid/.

Mitchell, A. (2014). *Justin Bieber's friends standing by him & deny that he's racist.* Accessed from https://hollywoodlife.com/2014/06/05/justin-bieber-friends-defend-racist-one-less-lonely-n-word-video-lil-za/.

Momoc, A. (2011). The blog—political PR tool in the 2009 presidential electoral campaign. *PCTS Proceedings (Professional Communication & Translation Studies)* 4(1/2), 11–20.

Moody-Ramirez, M., & Cole, H. (2018). Victim blaming in Twitter users' framing of Eric Garner and Michael Brown. *Journal of Black Studies*, 49(1), 21934718754312. doi:10.1177/0021934718754312.

Moody, M. (2011). Jon and Kate Plus 8: A case study of social media and image repair tactics. *Public Relations Review*, 37(4), 405–414. doi:10.1016/j.pubrev.2011.06.004. Retrieved from www.sciencedirect.com/science/article/abs/pii/S036381111000749

Moran, M. (2012). Image restoration in political sex scandals: What to do (And what not to do) when you're caught with your pants down. *Elon Journal of Undergraduate Research in Communications*, 3(2), 43–62.

Moraski, L. (March 7, 2012). Bill Maher: Accept Rush Limbaugh's apology. *CBS News*. Retrieved from http://www.cbsnews.com/8301-31749_162-57392383-10391698/bill-maheraccept-rush-limbaughs-apology/Net-A-Porter, March 9, 2018.

Most Black voters don't think Rachel Dolezal should have resigned from NAACP – Rasmussen Reports®. (2015). Retrieved from http://www.rasmussenreports.com/public_content/politics/general_politics/june_2015/most_black_voters_don_t_think_rachel_dolezal_should_have_resigned_from_naacp.

Mrosko, G. (2012, May 30). Hulk Hogan is he most popular pro wrestler of all time. Retrieved June 3, 2018 from https://www.cagesideseats.com/2012/5/30/3052011/poll-results-hulk-hogan-is-the-most popular-pro-wrestler-of-all-time.

Mullin, G., & Marsh, J. (2018). Harvey Weinstein settles mega-million divorce with British ex Georgina Chapman. Retrieved May 22, 2018 from https://www.thesun.co.uk/news/5314587/harvey-weinstein-divorce-georgina-chapman/.

Nahmias, L. (March 28, 2018). @NYGovCuomo responds to @politico report on Trump's handling of Hurricane Mariapic.twitter.com/s7HbPlH7y6 [Tweet]. Retrieved from https://twitter.com/nahmias/status/979025147150655488.

Nelson, L. (2015). Your White opinion on Dolezal is probably irrelevant. Retrieved from http://rethinktherant.com/2015/06/17/your-white-opinion-on-dolezal-is-probably-irrelevant/.

News, A. B. C. (n.d.). "Scandal" for real: Judy Smith's famous clients. Retrieved October 11, 2017 from http://abcnews.go.com/US/slideshow/scandal-real-judy-smiths-real-life-scandals-20833182.

O'Connell, J. (2015). Jennifer O'Connell: Bill Cosby story highlights troubling societal attitudes to consent. Retrieved November 1, 2017 from https://www.irishtimes.com/life-and-style/people/jennifer-o-connell-bill-cosby-story-highlights-troubling-societal-attitudes-to-consent-1.2010334.

O'Connor, M. (2010). All the terrible things Mel Gibson has said on the record. *Gawker*. Retrieved from http://gawker.com/5582644/all-the-terrible-things-mel-gibson-has-said-on-the-record.

O'Dea, C. J., Miller, S. S., Andres, E. B., Ray, M. H., Till, D. F., & Saucier, D. A. (2015). Out of bounds: Factors affecting the perceived offensiveness of racial slurs. *Language Sciences*, 52, 155–164. doi:10.1016/j.langsci.2014.09.005.

O'Kelly, M. W. (June 11, 2014). Usher's defense of Justin Bieber is indefensible. Retrieved November 26, 2014 from http://www.huffingtonpost.com/morris-w-okelly/ushers-defense-of-justin-_b_5482147.html.

Oles-Acevedo, D. (2012). Fixing the Hillary factor: Examining the trajectory of Hillary Clinton's image repair from political bumbler to political powerhouse. *American Communication Journal*, 14(1), 33–46.

Oles, D. (2010). Deny, delay, apologize: The Oprah Winfrey image-defense playbook. *Northwest Journal of Communication*, 39, 37–63.

Omi, M., & Winant, H. (1994). *Racial formation in the United States: From the 1960s to the 1990s*. New York: Routledge.

Orbe, M. (1998). The relationship between communication and power. In Martin, J. N. & Nakayama, T. K. (Eds.), *Intercultural communication in contexts*. New York: McGraw-Hill.

Page, C. (2015). A fake black woman's "passing" fancy. *Caribbean Business*, 43(24), 19–19. Retrieved from http://ezproxy.baylor.edu/login?url=http://search.ebscohost.com/login.aspx?direct=true&db=bth&AN=103541049&site=ehost-live&scope=site.

Parker, L., & Lynn, M. (2002). What's race got to do with it? Critical race theory's conflicts and connections to qualitative research methodology and epistemology. *Qualitative Inquiry*, 8, 7–22.

Parks, G., & Rachlinski, J. (2008). Unconscious Bias and the 2008 presidential election. *Cornell Legal Studies* Research Paper No. 08–007. Retrieved from SSRN http://ssrn.com/abstract=1102704.

Patton, S. (2015). Rachel Dolezal case leaves a campus bewildered and some scholars disgusted. *Chronicle of Higher Education*, 61(39), 21–21.

Paul, M. (November 26, 2006). Michael "Kramer" Richards' reputation in crisis: Racist or ignorant and angry? *The Reputation Doctor*. Retrieved from http://reputationdoctor.com/2006/11/michael-"kramer"-richards-reputation-in-crisis-racist-or-ignorant-and-angry/.

Pearce, M. (2018). Weinstein stories that sparked #MeToo win Pulitzer Prize. Retrieved May 24, 2018 from http://www.latimes.com/local/la-me-pulitzer-prize-awards-20180416-story.html.

Pew Survey. (2004). Attitudes toward the news: News audiences increasingly politicized. Retrieved from http://people-press.org/reports/.

Phillips, B. J., Miller, J., & McQuarrie, E. (January 1, 2014). Dreaming out loud on Pinterest. *International Journal of Advertising*, 33(4), 633–655. doi:10.2501/IJA-33-4-633-655.

Pickert, K. (November 18, 2014). A timeline guide to guide to the Bill Cosby rape allegations. *Time*. Retrieved from http://time.com/3592547/bill-cosby-rape-allegations-timeline/.

Poindexter, P., Smith, L., & Heider, D. (2003). Race and ethnicity in local television news: Framing, story assignments, and source selections. *Journal of Broadcast Electronic Media*, 47(4), 524–540.

Poll: Where do you stand with Bill Cosby? *MSNBC*, December 11, 2014. http://www. msnbc.com/msnbc/poll-where-do-you-stand-bill-cosby.

Potok, M. (2010). The year in hate & extremism. *Intelligence Report Journal*, 141. Retrieved from http://www.splcenter.org/get-informed/intelligence-report/ browse-all-issues/2011/spring/the-year-in-hate-extremism-2010.

PWTorch Pro Wrestling News. (May 6, 2018). POLL: How you would feel about WWE bringing Hulk Hogan back as a regular featured legend on TV after what he said on two occasions about black people? Retrieved June 12, 2018 from https:// www.pwtorch.com/site/2018/05/06/poll-pick-which-of-the-options-below-most-applies-to-how-you-would-feel-about-wwe-bringing-hulk-hogan-back-as-a-reg-ular-featured-legend-on-tv-after-what-he-said-on-two-occasions-about-black-people/.

Randall, K. (2008). *Nigger: The strange career of a troublesome word*. New York: Random House.

Rasmussen, L. (2015). Planned Parenthood takes on live action: An analysis of media interplay and image restoration strategies in strategic conflict management. *Public Relations Review*, 41(3), 354–356. doi:10.1016/j.pubrev.2015.01.004.

Real, E. (May 2, 2016). Hulk Hogan is suing Gawker again, this time for allegedly leaking his racist remarks. Retrieved May 18, 2018 from https://www.usmagazine.com/celebrity-news/news/hulk-hogan-suing-gawker-for-allegedly-leaking-racist-remarks-w204856/.

Respers France, L., & Selter, B. (2018). Harvey Weinstein's wife announces she is leaving him. Retrieved May 22, 2018 from https://www.cnn.com/2017/10/10/ entertainment/georgina-chapman-leaves-harvey-weinstein/index.html.

Rhodan, M. (November 19, 2014). Bill Cosby on rape allegation: 'I don't talk about it.' *TIME.com*. Retrieved December 1, 2016 from http://time.com/3596545/ cosby-responds-rape-allegations-ap-video/.

Rice, L. (2014). Bill Cosby's lawyer speaks out: The media vilification has to stop. *PEOPLE.com*. http://people.com/celebrity/bill-cosby-lawyer-statement-martin-singer-speaks-out/.

Ricker, D. (2018). #MeToo movement sparks national legal response. *ABA Journal*, 104(3), 1–1.

Roig-Franzia, M., Higham, S., Farhi, P., & Flaherty, M. (November 22, 2014). Bill Cosby's legacy, recast: Accusers speak in detail about sexual-assault allegations. Retrieved December 1, 2016 from https://www.washingtonpost.com/ lifestyle/style/bill-cosbys-legacy-recast-accusers-speak-in-detail-about-sexual-assault-allegations/2014/11/22/d7074938–718e-11e4–8808-afaa1e3a33ef_story. html?utm_term=.3018e74b4427.

Rosenblatt, C. (2014). Telltale signs of Donald Sterling's dementia. Retrieved from https://www.forbes.com/sites/carolynrosenblatt/2014/07/30/telltale-signs-of-donald-sterlings-dementia/#28267b4ecf2d.

Rosenfield, L. W. (1968). A case study in speech criticism: The Nixon-Truman analog. *Speech Monographs*, 35, 435–450.

Ross, K. (2002). *Women, politics, media. Uneasy relations in comparative perspective*. Creskill: Hampton Press.

Ross, M. (June 5, 2014). Lil Za: Justin Bieber's friend defends his racist rant on Instagram. Retrieved from http://hollywoodlife.com/2014/06/05/lil-za-justin-bieber-racist-rant-defend-instagram/.

Rottenberg, Josh, Olsen, M., & Whipp, G. (2017). Harvey Weinstein is finding that few in Hollywood want to be on his side. Retrieved from http://www.latimes.com/entertainment/movies/la-et-mn-harvey-weinstein-rise-fall-20171008-story.html.

Round, B. F. O. H. A. Y. (January 5, 2017). #NiggerNavy gonna be two years late to the war. [Tweet]. Retrieved from https://twitter.com/TerrellChuggs/status/817226 565767544835?ref_src=twsrc%5Etfw&ref_url=https%3A%2F%2Fwww.buzzfeed.com%2Ftamerragriffin%2Fyahoo-finance-nigger-navy-typo&tfw_creator=tamerra_nikol&tfw_site=buzzfeednews.

Rowland, R. (1988). The fall and fall of Gary Hart. *e-book*. Retrieved December 30, 2010 from ERIC, Ipswich, MA.

Rowley, K. (2003). Separate and still unequal: A comparative study of blacks in business magazines. *Journal of Communications*, 14(4), 245.

Rozee, P. D., & Koss, M. (n.d.). Rape: A century of resistance. *Psychology of Women Quarterly*, 25(4), 295–311. doi:10.1111/1471–6402.00030.

Ryschka, A. M., Domke-Damonte, D. J., Keels, J. K., & Nagel, R. (2016). The effect of social media on reputation during a crisis event in the cruise line industry. *International Journal of Hospitality & Tourism Administration,* 17(2), 198–221. doi:10 .1080/15256480.2015.1130671.

Sager, J. (2018). Harvey Weinstein Was 'paternal' to Jennifer Lawrence. *Page Six*. Retrieved from https://pagesix.com/2017/12/06/harvey-weinstein-was-paternal-to-jennifer-lawrence/.

Sailes, G. A. (1996). An investigation of campus stereotypes: The myth of black athletic superiority and the dumb jock stereotype. In Lapchick, R. E. (Ed.), *Sport in society: Equal opportunity or business as usual* (pp. 193–202). Thousand Oaks: Sage.

Sanderson, J., & Hambrick, M. (July 24, 2016). Riding along with Lance Armstrong: Exploring Antapologia in response to athlete adversity. *Journal of Sports Media*, 11(1), 1–24. doi:10.1353/jsm.2016.0002.

Schrobsdorff, S. (2018). When the court of public opinion begins to favor women. *Time*, 191(7/8), 17–18. Retrieved from http://ezproxy.baylor.edu/login?url=http://search.ebscohost.com/login.aspx?direct=true&db=a9h&AN=128020248&site=ehost-live&scope=site.

Sci, S. A., & Dare, A. (2014). The pleasure and play of pepper spray cop photoshop memes. *The Northwest Journal of Communication*, 42 (1), 7–34. Retrieved May 17, 2018 from https://www.academia.edu/26813008/Sci_S._A._and_Dare_A._M._2014_._The_pleasure_and_play_of_Pepper_Spray_Cop_Photoshop_memes._The_Northwest_Journal_of_Communication_42_1_7–34.

Scott, E. (2014). Regulating 'Nigger': Racial offense, African American activists, and the MPPDA, 1928–1961. *Film History*, 26(4), 1–31. doi:10.2979/filmhistory.26.4.1.

Scrill Murray on Twitter: "#NiggerNavy the boat would stay leaning." (n.d.). Retrieved April 11, 2018 from https://twitter.com/Im_VelvetJones/status/

817224472457379840?ref_src=twsrc%5Etfw&ref_url=https%3A%2F%2Fwww.buzzfeed.com%2Ftamerragriffin%2Fyahoo-finance-nigger-navy-typo&tfw_creator=tamerra_nikol&tfw_site=buzzfeednews.

Seeger, M. W., Sellnow, T. L., & Ulmer, R. R. (1998). Communication, organization, and crisis. In Roloff, M. E. (Ed.), *Communication Yearbook*, 21 (pp. 231–276). Thousand Oaks, CA: Sage.

Selepak, A. G. (2004). *AIM report: New evidence of liberal media bias.* Retrieved from http://www.aim.org.

Semetko, H., & Boomgaarden, H. (2007). Reporting Germany's 2005 Bundestag election campaign: Was gender an issue? *Harvard International Journal of Press/Politics*, 12(4), 154–171.

Shabad, R., & Perry, S. (2018). *Poll: Majority says #MeToo movement has helped address gender inequality.* Retrieved May 24, 2018 from https://www.nbcnews.com/politics/politics-news/poll-majority-says-metoo-movement-has-helped-address-gender-inequality-n854576.

Shah, H., & Thornton, M. C. (1994). Racial ideology in U.S. mainstream news magazine coverage of Black-Latino interaction, 1980–1992. *Critical Studies in Mass Communication*, 11, 141–161.

Shea, Danny. (March 28, 2008). Limbaugh: 'Does our looks-obsessed culture want to stare at an aging woman?' *Huffington Post*, sec. Media. https://www.huffingtonpost.com/2007/12/17/limbaugh-does-our-looksob_n_77199.html.

Sheldon, C. A., & Sallot, L. M. (2009). Image repair in politics: Testing effects of communication strategy and performance history in a faux pas. *Journal of Public Relations Research*, 21(1), 25–50. doi:10.1080/10627260802520496.

Shifman, L. (2013). Memes in a digital world: Reconciling with a conceptual troublemaker. *Journal of Computer-Mediated Communication*, 18(3), 362–377. doi:10.1111/jcc4.12013.

Shoemaker, P., & Reese, S. (1996). *Mediating the message: Theories of influence on mass media content.* New York: Longman.

Shome, R. (2001). White femininity and the discourse of the nation: Re/membering Princess Diana. *Feminist Media Studies*, 1(3), 323–342.

Smith, A., & Anderson, M. (March 1, 2018). Social media use in 2018. *Pew Research Center: Internet, Science & Tech* (blog). Retrieved from http://www.pewinternet.org/2018/03/01/social-media-use-in-2018/.

Smith, D. (2009). Intersex history. Caster Semenya Row. The Observer.

Smith, E. (July 8, 2016). Bill Cosby is 'completely blind' and homebound. Retrieved December 1, 2016 from http://pagesix.com/2016/07/18/bill-cosby-is-completely-blind-and-trapped-in-his-home/.

Smith, W., Yosso, T., & Solórzano, D. (December, 2007). Racial primes and black misandry on historically white campuses: Toward critical race accountability in educational administration. *Educational Administration Quarterly*, 43(5), 559–585. Retrieved from http://ejournals.ebsco.com.ezproxy.baylor.edu/direct.asp?ArticleID=467D9CCABA42040768CB.

Snider, P. B. (1967). "Mr. Gates" revisited: A 1966 version of the 1949 case study. *Journalism Quarterly*, 3, 419–427.

Solove, D. (2007). *The future of reputation: Gossip, rumor, and privacy on the Internet.* Yale University Press: New Haven and London.

Solove, D. J., & Schwartz, P. M. (2009). *Information privacy law* (3rd Edition). New York: Aspen Law & Business.

Spitzberg, B. H. (2014). Toward a model of meme diffusion (M3D). *Communication Theory*, 24(3), 311–339. doi:10.1111/comt.12042.

Statista.com. (2018). Statistics on active Twitter Users. Retrieved from https://www.statista.com/statistics/274564/monthly-active-twitter-users-in-the-united-states/.

Stebbens, S., Comen, E., Sauter, M., & Stockdale, C. (2018). America's most hated companies – 24/7 wall st. Retrieved from https://247wallst.com/special-report/2018/01/22/americas-most-hated-companies-5/.

Stein, K. A. (2008). Apologia, antapologia, and the 1960 Soviet U-2 Incident. *Communication Studies*, 59(1), 19. Retrieved from https://www.questia.com/library/journal/1G1-177552966/apologia-antapologia-and-the-1960-soviet-u-2-incident.

Stein, K. A. (2010). Jewish antapologia in response to Mel Gibson's multiple attempts at absolution. *Relevant Rhetoric: A New Journal of Rhetorical Studies*, 1–14. Retrieved from http://ezproxy.baylor.edu/login?url=http://search.ebscohost.com/login.aspx?direct=true&db=ufh&AN=59522583&site=ehost-live&scope=site.

Steinem, G. (January 7, 2008). Women are never front-runners. *The New York Times*. Retrieved from Lexis Nexis.

Tardio, A. (2014). Justin Bieber racist comments unearthed, singer uses n-word; rappers respond. Retrieved November 25, 2014 from http://hiphopdx.com/index/news/id.29033/title.justin-bieber-racist-comments-unearthed-singer-uses-n-word-rappers-respond.

Tatko-Peterson, A. (2017). Yahoo Finance under fire for offensive "spelling error" in tweet. Retrieved April 11, 2018 from https://www.mercurynews.com/2017/01/05/yahoo-finance-under-fire-for-offensive-typo-in-tweet/.

Taylor, M., & Kent, M. (2010). Anticipatory socialization in the use of social media in public relations: A content analysis of PRSA's Public Relations Tactics. *Public Relations Review*, 36, 207–214. doi:10.1016/j.pubrev.2010.04.012.

TED2015. (2015). The price of shame. Retrieved from https://www.ted.com/talks/monica_lewinsky_the_price_of_shame.

Topic: Twitter. (2017). Retrieved March 1, 2017 from https://www.statista.com/topics/737/twitter/.

Tripathi, S. (2003). In the footsteps of Colin Powell. *New Statesman*, 132(4660), 15–16.

Trotter, J. K. (2015). Hulk Hogan refers to "fucking niggers" in leaked transcript. Retrieved April 11, 2018 from http://gawker.com/hulk-hogan-refers-to-fucking-niggers-in-leaked-transc-1719933145.

Tuchman, G. (1978). *Making news: A study in the construction of reality*. New York: The Free Press.

Van Zoonen, L. (1994). *Feminist media studies*. London: Sage Publications.

Vavrus, M. (2009). What is this post- in postracial, postfeminist. *Journal of Communication Inquiry*, 34, 210–253.

Verser, R., & Wicks, R. (2006). Managing voter impressions: The use of images on presidential candidate web sites during the 2000 campaign. *Journal of Communication*, 56(1), 178–197.

Wagner, K. (2014). Exclusive: The extended Donald Sterling tape. Retrieved November 26, 2014 from http://www.viddler.com/embed/9a7cf786/?f=1&autoplay=false&

player=mini&disablebranding=0;offset=0&autoplay=015-Year-Old   Justin Bieber Tells Racist Joke [VIDEO]. (2014). Retrieved November 25, 2014, from http://www.tmz.com/2014/06/01/justin-bieber-racist-joke-video-n-word/.

Walsh, J., & McAllister-Spooner, S. M. (2011). Analysis of the image repair discourse in the Michael Phelps controversy. *Public Relations Review*, 37(2), 157–162. doi:10.1016/j.pubrev.2011.01.001.

Wang, J., & Wang, H. (2015). From a marketplace to a cultural space: Online meme as an operational unit of cultural transmission. *Journal of Technical Writing & Communication*, 45(3), 261–274. doi:10.1177/0047281615578847.

Ware, B. L., & Linkugel, W. A. (1973). They spoke in defense of themselves: On the generic criticism of apologia. *Quarterly Journal of Speech*, 59, 273–283.

Warner, B. R., Carlin, D., Winfrey, K., Schnoebelen, J., & Trosanovski, M. (2011). Will the 'real' candidates for president and vice president please stand up? 2008 pre- and post-debate viewer perceptions of candidate image. *American Behavioral Scientist*, 55, 232–252.

Warner, J. (1993). *Hillary Clinton: The inside story*. New York: New American Library/Signet Books.

Washington Post. (1998). Clinton: 'There is no improper relationship.' *Federal News Service*, A13.

Weatherly, Jeffrey N., Petros, Thomas V., Christopherson, Kimberly M., & Haugen, Erin N. (2007). Perceptions of political bias in the headlines of two major news organizations. *Harvard International Journal of Press/Politics*, 12(2), 91–104.

West, C. (2001). *Race matters*. Boston: Beacon Press.

What's a "Clapback"? (n.d.). Retrieved December 28, 2017 from https://www.merriam-webster.com/words-at-play/clapback-meaning-origin.

Wheatstone, R., & Baker, N. (2018). Here's a list of the women making allegations against Harvey Weinstein. Retrieved May 22, 2018 from https://www.thesun.co.uk/news/4658251/harvey-weinstein-sex-allegations-accusers-full-list/.

White, D. M. (1950). The "gatekeeper": A case study in the selection of news. *Journalism Quarterly*, 27(4), 383–390.

White, J. (2018). Harvey Weinstein responds to sexual harassment allegations with bizarre statement. *The Independent*. Retrieved May 22, 2018 from https://www.independent.co.uk/arts-entertainment/films/harvey-weinstein-statement-sexual-harassment-claims-allegations-response-lisa-bloom-jay-zlatest-a7985631.html.

Why anti-trump protests matter. (2017). *Rolling Stone*. Retrieved February 23, 2017.

Wiggins, B. E., & Bowers, G. B. (2014). Memes as genre: A structural analysis of the memescape. *New Media & Society*, 17(11), 1886–1906.

Wilcox, D. L., & Cameron, G. T. (2006). Public relations strategies and tactics (8th Edition). Boston, MA: Pearson.

Williams, B, Sawyer, S., & Wahlstrom, C. (2013). Marriages, families, and intimate relationships. Retrieved from https://www.pearson.com/us/higher-education/product/Williams-Marriages-Families-and-Intimate-Relationships-3rd-Edition/9780205717804.html.

Williams, S. (July 6, 2015). The power of black Twitter. *The Daily Beast*.

Willis, J. (2014). Bill Cosby asks reporter to edit out his response to rape allegations. *Entertainment Tonight*. Retrieved from https://www.etonline.com/news/154167_bill_cosby_asked_about_rape_allegations_avoids_questions.

Wood, J. T. (1994). *Gendered lives: Communication, gender, and culture*. Belmont, CA: Wadsworth, Inc.

Workneh, L. (2016). How Twitter has helped amplify black voices around the world|HuffPost. Retrieved July 11, 2017 from http://www.huffingtonpost.com/entry/black-twitter_us_56ef1198e4b09bf44a9d9d60?ncid=engmodush pmg00000004.

Worthington, N. (2013). Explaining gang rape in a "rough town": Diverse voices in gender violence news online. *Communication, Culture & Critique*, 6(1), 103–120. doi:10.1111/j.1753–9137.2012.01145.x.

Wright, D., & Hinson, M. (2008). How blogs and social media are changing public relations and the way it is practiced. *Public Relations Journal*, 2(2), 1–21.

Xifra, J. (2012). Sex, lies, and post-trial publicity: The reputation repair strategies of Dominique Strauss-Kahn. *Public Relations Review*, 38(3), 477–483. doi:10.1016/j.pubrev.2012.03.002.

Yioutas, J., & Segvic, I. (2003). Revisiting the Clinton/Lewinsky scandal: The convergence of agenda setting and framing. *Journalism & Mass Communication Quarterly*, 80(3), 567–582.

Zilber, J., & Niven, D. (2000). Stereotypes in the news: Media coverage of African-Americans in Congress. *Harvard International Journal of Press/Politics*, 5(1), 32–49.

Index

About the Editors

Hazel James Cole, PhD, is the Concentration Head and Associate Professor of Public Relations at the University of West Georgia (UWG). She is the faculty advisor of *bluestone*: Student-run Public Relations Firm at UWG and the Public Relations Student Society of America. Cole is a public relations professional and critical scholar conducting research in the areas of public relations, crisis, and race, gender and media.

Mia Moody-Ramirez, PhD, is Graduate Program Director and Professor of Journalism, Public Relations and New Media at Baylor University. Moody-Ramirez has conducted research on the portrayals of minorities and women in reality television, print, rap music and social media.

About the Contributors

Elizabeth Fassih is a law student at the University of Pennsylvania Law School. She attended Bowling Green State University for her undergraduate degree in Social Studies Education, and then completed a master's degree American Studies at Baylor University.

Macarena Hernández is a U.S. academic and journalist from La Joya, Texas, who has written about Latino issues such as immigration and education. She is a Fred Hartman Distinguished Professor of Journalism at Baylor University.

Tina Libhart works for Waco ISD as a high school English teacher at Wiley Opportunity Center.

Mayra Monroy is a Digital Content Producer at Central Texas News Now. She holds a master's degree in Journalism, PR & New Media from Baylor University and a bachelor's degree from Aquinas College.

Endia Turney is a marketing professional in Austin, Texas. She graduated from Baylor University in 2015 with a bachelor's degree in Journalism, PR & New Media.